THE KATY RAILROAD
AND THE LAST FRONTIER

D0861394

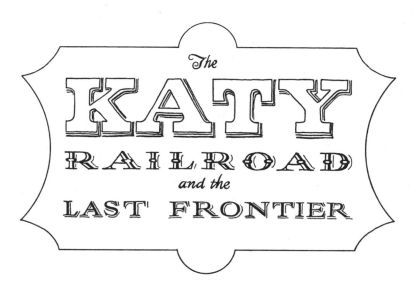

The KATY RAILROAD and the LAST FRONTIER

BY

V. V. MASTERSON

FOREWORD BY
DONOVAN L. HOFSOMMER

UNIVERSITY OF OKLAHOMA PRESS
NORMAN

To the memory of

ROBERT S. STEVENS

Indian Territory pioneer

and

JOHN SCULLIN

"the great American tracklayer"

Few railroads of comparable mileage or corporate strength have been more readily identifiable in the mind's eye of shippers and travelers, Wall Street observers, transportation historians, railroad buffs, and the public at large than the Katy—the Missouri-Kansas-Texas Company. The Katy is linked closely with the heroic era of western railroad construction, the machinations of well-known plungers during the Gilded Age, fine passenger trains during the road's salad days, and the opening of the "Great Southwest."

The enterprise was begun in 1865 when the Union Pacific Rail Way Company, Southern Branch was incorporated under the laws of Kansas. In the months following, its boosters oriented their priorities, reorganized the company as the Missouri, Kansas & Texas Railway, won an exciting race to the frontier of Indian Territory, and in 1872 saw Katy rail penetrate Texas and thus forge a new north-south route to the Gulf.

Euphoria passed to pessimism, however, when the company suddenly succumbed during the Panic of 1873. Thereafter followed what the author calls "The Dark Years"—hard times coupled with the passage of corporate control to the redoubtable Jay Gould. These twin burdens were lifted simultaneously; the company enjoyed financial recovery in 1891 and weathered the Panic of 1893. It approached the twentieth century with confidence and with plans for continued growth. To this end the Katy extended its own lines into new service areas, secured new traffic gateways, and purchased connecting roads such as the Texas Central and the Wichita Falls & Northwestern. Overexpansion was the result, and the Katy went into receivership in 1915, to emerge eight years later as the Missouri-Kansas-Texas Railroad. Prosperity attended the "new" Katy for the remainder of the 1920's, but the company suffered along with the rest of the country during the Great Depression. World War II brought renewed prosperity for the railroad and new hopes and plans for the future.

Such was the mood in 1952 when Vincent Victor Masterson finished this story of the Katy. As an insider—Masterson was a Katy official—he had access to corporate records and used them skillfully.

Moreover, he adeptly placed the Katy experience in proper local, regional, and even national perspective. In his foreword to the first printing, Grant Foreman said that "Writing the history of the Missouri-Kansas-Texas Railroad inevitably involves writing the history of Oklahoma and the Southwest, which is impossible to conceive without" at the same time comprehending the subject of transportation." The impact of the railroad as a device of transportation was so great, as both Foreman and Masterson clearly understood, that to write a history of a certain line or certain company means also to write a history of its service area.

Shortly after Masterson's book first appeared, the Katy suffered declining fortunes complicated by controversial management. A new and vigorous management was summoned and took immediate and frequently drastic action. All passenger service was terminated, many miles of trackage were abandoned, and additional financing was arranged, but the M-K-T survived as a railroad transportation firm, although now as a part of the newly created Katy Industries, a diversified holding company.

The mood at Katy remains optimistic. Substantial improvements in the property have been made, and the road has succeeded in making its service attractive to shippers. To be sure, the M-K-T's main line from Kansas City to Dallas-Fort Worth and on the Gulf seems especially well situated to serve that burgeoning and lengthy corridor leading from the North to the Sun Belt area of the Southwest. Its present management views the future with expectant confidence, forecasts sustained growth, and believes that Katy can go it alone as an independent carrier. To remain independent will be no mean feat, for all indications are that there will be fewer, if larger, railroad companies in the future. Yet the Katy has a long history of successfully weathering storms and meeting challenges.

The Katy Railroad and the Last Frontier makes a particular contribution in relating and interpreting the history of the road and its service area from the inception of the Union Pacific Rail Way, Southern Branch in 1865 to the passage of the MK&T to the Gould Empire in 1874. This is an especially happy development since the book documents the story of one of the country's most colorful lines during the period of great railroad development.

DONOVAN L. HOFSOMMER

Plainview, Texas
June 27, 1977

vi

Contents

Illustrations

Maps

Introduction

This is the story of the first railroad to enter the Indian Territory, a development that opened up the legendary Southwest to settlement and modern progress. Historically, this record of the building of the Missouri-Kansas-Texas Lines adds a long-missing chapter to the chronicles of the westward surge of empire which followed the close of the Civil War.

With the coming of the railways upon the pastoral American scene in the 1830's this book is little concerned. Able writers have already recorded the amazing tale of how the steam locomotive, in the three short decades before the Civil War, transformed the whole face of America east of the Mississippi River. This story deals only with the part played by one railroad in bringing civilization in its best connotation to a vast, primitive, and nearly empty land.

Lost in awe over the epic meeting of the Union Pacific and Central Pacific railroads at Promontory Point on May 10, 1869, the world little noted the fact that only forty-three months after the first transcontinental railroad became a reality, the North and South were united all along the churning frontier when the Missouri-Kansas-Texas Lines, on Christmas Day, 1872, spanned the storied Red River at Denison, Texas, and linked up with the Houston and Texas Central to give America a "new route to the Gulf."

It takes nothing from the glory of the first transcontinental builders to point out that if they had Indians they had few "Indians with vested rights" to contend with, and built through little territory which was not under the immediate jurisdiction of the "Great White Father." On the other hand, the line which was driven south through hundreds of miles of Indian country and notorious bad-lands had literally to batter its way along in the face of almost every conceivable

xiii

human obstacle, even though its engineering problems were not extraordinary. White man's law did not reach Indian Territory until 1889, nearly twenty years after the railroad went through—and tribal law frequently was blood brother to jungle law.

The prize which lured the builders of the Katy ever on was, naturally enough at the time, the golden promise of millions of acres of wonderfully fertile land to be awarded them by a grateful government in acknowledgment of their contribution to colonization. The fact that the railroad was destined to be denied the coveted land-grant acres never occurred to these pioneering railroaders—which is perhaps just as well, for without this incentive the extraordinary development of the Southwest of today would have been long retarded.

But the railroad went through from Kansas to the Gulf despite every obstacle, and today its builders have a lasting monument to their labors, their foresight, and their intrepidity. The monument exists not so much in the 3,200 miles of first-class railroad which they brought into being, but in the magnificently developing Southwestern territory their shoestring railway first made productive. Hitherto unhonored and unsung, this achievement entitles them to a niche alongside their more famous contemporaries, who by their achievements in opening up the West justly came to be known as "America's Empire Builders."

This, then, is the story of the little-known builders of the great Southwest.

V. V. MASTERSON

St. Louis, Missouri

THE KATY RAILROAD
AND THE LAST FRONTIER

ONE

The Awakening West

The story of the Missouri-Kansas-Texas Railroad, better known as the "Katy," is also the story of the modern development of the four great states it serves—Missouri, Kansas, Oklahoma, and Texas. Their histories and vicissitudes are parallel in time and importance. The idea of a railroad to span the frontier from north to south was first proposed in Kansas Territory during the bloody travail of that historic state, whose birth was attended by fratricidal war. The actual surveying of its route gave assurance both to Missouri and to Kansas that the lion's share of southwestern trade would flow through their great gateways and lay open to them the vast potential markets of the Indian country and far Texas.

The railroad's story is also the story of settlement along its right of way, of the growth of communities, the building of cities, the taming of the land—and its occupants—and the expansion of industry and trade.

The Katy Railroad, originally incorporated as the Union Pacific Railway Southern Branch, came into legal being on September 20, 1865, less than three months after the famous Indian Confederate general, Stand Watie, surrendered the battered and broken Indian Territory to the Federals.[1] One or two of the "corporators" were pro-slavery in the earliest beginnings but most were dyed-in-the-wool Free Staters. Young and truculent as they undoubtedly were, most of the Katy's originators took up arms "in the '61" and went loyally off to fight—generally with fat commissions in famous Kansas regiments.

Because this is a story of railroad development, however, and not of war, it seems advisable first to examine the picture puzzle of a

[1] June 23, 1865.

slowly westering civilization before the Missouri-Kansas-Texas Railroad came upon the scene to add impetus to the movement. To evaluate it is also important, else the achievement of the Katy's builders might easily be underestimated.

All the world knows that rivers were the West's first highways; but after people began settling in small communities west of the Mississippi, not much more than a hundred years ago, they wanted to move produce to places inaccessible by water. So they took to the Indian paths and buffalo trails, much as they had done earlier in the East. The first east-west highway across Missouri was the romantic Boon's Lick Trail, which started at St. Louis and meandered along the banks of the Missouri River to the far-west boat-landing at storied old Franklin in mid-state; in 1819 this "trace" had reached Fort Osage and was called the Osage Trace; in 1825 it was extended to Santa Fé. It is interesting to note that for hundreds of miles west from St. Louis the Katy Railroad follows Boon's Lick Trail and the Osage Trace, and, south through Eastern Oklahoma, it follows for additional hundreds of miles the famous Texas Road.

A generation after the establishment of wagon trails, came the West's first railroads. The Hannibal and St. Joseph Railroad, now a part of the Burlington System, was incorporated in 1847. The Pacific Railroad of Missouri was chartered in 1849, and two years later the North Missouri Railroad, now a part of the Wabash System, was incorporated.

The first railroad construction was begun in St. Louis by the Pacific Railroad on July 4, 1851. Although begun later, the Hannibal and St. Jo, completed in 1859, was the first to reach the western border of Missouri. During the same year a junction was effected between this line and the North Missouri Railroad at Macon, providing through rail service from St. Louis to St. Joseph. Meanwhile, south of the Missouri River, the Pacific had pushed construction to Jefferson City by 1855, and to Sedalia by January, 1861.

The Missouri River, forming the northeastern border of Kansas, was a regular trade route in the 1850's and 60's, but was comparatively unimportant to Kansas as a transportation route, since it touched only a small portion of the territory. It did, however, permit the extension of steamboat service west along the Kaw (Kansas) River.

But the steamboat came too late to Kansas. In 1855 the territorial legislature was already granting railroad charters with magnificent —and munificent—abandon, and the railroad fever quickly burned the idea of Kaw River development cleanly and permanently out of mind. Among the several railroads incorporated at that time was one, the Elwood and Marysville Railroad, conceived as an extension of the fast-building Hannibal and St. Joseph. This little line ultimately had the honor of becoming Kansas' first railroad. It was organized in January, 1857, but had not laid a single length of rail by the time the Hannibal and St. Jo was celebrating its arrival at St. Joseph, Missouri, just across the river from Elwood, on February 23, 1859. Obviously, the E. & M. R.R. was awaiting the shipment of its iron by rail from the East. Immediately, however, there was a spurt of building on the west bank of the Missouri, and on March 20, 1860, the first rail was laid. By April 23, they had five miles of iron wandering unsteadily down to Wathena. On that day the "Albany," a locomotive "which had been used from Boston to Missouri as railroads successfully stretched their length toward the setting sun," was ferried across the Missouri and triumphantly placed upon the tracks—the first Iron Horse that ever touched Kansas soil.[2]

In the late fifties it was more than apparent that railroads were fast reaching the vanguard of civilization, for development along the frontier had not kept pace with progress in the nation as a whole. The passage of the Kansas-Nebraska Act and the organization of Kansas as a territory on May 30, 1854, had exactly the reverse of the effect intended. As historians have amply documented, this step brought into headlong collision all the basic principles and early forces of the "irrepressible conflict," and from that moment until the issues between the North and the South were bloodily resolved there was scarcely a moment of peace—and few of constructive development—anywhere along the frontier line.

Kansas was torn by internecine strife. Pitiful little frontier settlements, struggling for permanency against a vast wilderness that threatened to extinguish them by natural means, were raided and raped time and again, either by the proslavery banditti of western Missouri or by night-riding Jayhawkers in retaliatory strikes. Never was human life more precariously or more cheaply held than along this fatal frontier. Yet there were men in Kansas at that moment who were visioning a great frontier railroad!

Down in the Indian country, too, the tribes were at each other's throats all through the decade preceding the Civil War. The principal chief of the Cherokee Nation, the enlightened and powerful John Ross, had never entirely succeeded in welding his riven tribe into an effective body politic. As head of the Eastern Cherokees, who

[2] *The Elwood Free Press*, April 28, 1860.

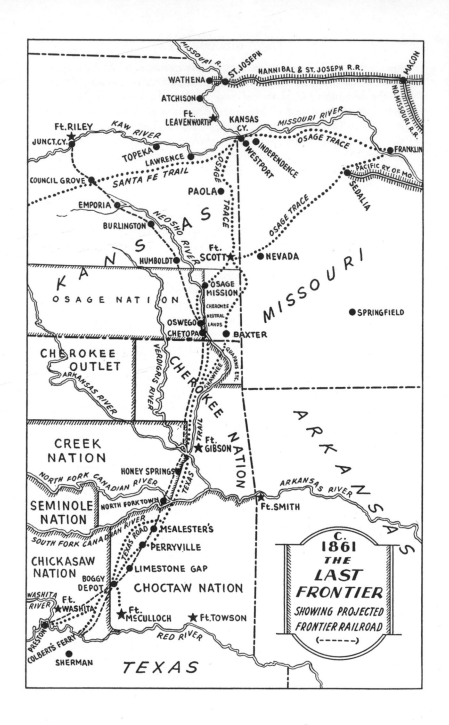

C.
1861
THE
LAST
FRONTIER
SHOWING PROJECTED
FRONTIER RAILROAD
(------)

were dominant in numbers, he had efficiently extinguished and absorbed the enterprising but smaller tribes of Western Cherokees, whose title to the Indian Territory was undisputed until he and his hordes of obedient and fanatical full-bloods arrived. But he hadn't made the early settlers like it. Another disturbing faction in the "Nation" was composed of the survivors of the famous Treaty Party, headed by Stand Watie and his brilliant nephew, Elias C. Boudinot. The early leaders of this group had been slain in tribal strife, and their adherents were feuding with the forces of Chief Ross. As a consequence the entire Indian Territory was in turmoil.

In Texas in the fifties, civilization had a respectable foothold only in the southern areas; to the west the Mexican War cession had created a huge vacuum and there was nothing to fill it. Galveston and Houston were showing great promise; the Alamo city of San Antonio was thriving by reason of its strategic location on the highway to Mexico and California; Austin, a well-chosen state capital, was still "on the fringes," but north thereof settlements were few, small, and very much self-contained. The rest of the Southwest, rumor had it, was a vast rancho where wild long-horned cattle, known as "Texans," roamed the limitless prairie in competition with great herds of buffalo which annually filtered down from the northern plains.

On January 29, 1861, barely three months before the North and the South joined battle, the state of Kansas was admitted into the Union. The outbreak of war stopped further western railway development, but it speeded up federal aid as a war measure. On July 1, 1862, President Abraham Lincoln signed the Pacific Railway Act (later amended by the Act of July 2, 1864) to "aid in the construction of a Railway and Telegraph from the Missouri River to the Pacific Ocean." This legislation granted to the projectors of the first transcontinental railroad a land bonus of ten sections (ten square miles) for each mile of road built, and a loan varying from $16,000 to $48,000 a mile. The act incorporated the Union Pacific (the Central Pacific was already incorporated) and, as amended to appease St. Louis interests, provided for not one but two points of beginning on the Missouri. The Union Pacific of Nebraska, therefore, was chartered to build west from Omaha, and the Leavenworth, Pawnee and Western Railroad[3] authorized to build west from Kansas City.

[3] Chartered 1855. Its line was located to Pawnee (Fort Riley) and grading commenced May, 1857. The name of the road was changed to Union Pacific Eastern Division June 6, 1863, and to Kansas Pacific May 31, 1868. In 1880 this line was merged with the present Union Pacific.

Financial and other difficulties delayed construction during the war years but amended legislation, which increased the land grant to double the original figure, soon gave new impetus to building. War's teachings, too, are evident in the later acts, which were designed to bring outlying military posts into closer connection, as well as to promote the development of the West. All this legislation vitally affected several embryo frontier railroads and out of it grew the present-day Katy.

By 1865 and war's end the transcontinental railroad was under way, with the Central Pacific working east over the Sierras, the Union Pacific of Nebraska creeping west to meet it, and the Union Pacific Eastern Division (the old Leavenworth, Pawnee and Western) slowly feeling its way west from the mouth of the Kansas River towards Junction City (Pawnee).

The Union Pacific Southern Branch, which shortly was to become the Katy, shared all the hardships of the transcontinental line, but by extraordinary interpretations of the Congressional acts did not receive the compensating reward of millions of acres of government lands. In the case of the Katy the federal government actually "gave the country back to the Indians!" But more of that later.

In the fall of 1865, with the Union once again at peace, it appeared to the Katy railroad's progenitors that Kansas was rich and ripe for an era of rapid railroad development.

TWO

A Railroad Is Born

It was September 20, 1865, and the sweltering little hamlet of Emporia, Kansas, which lay panting in the nearly dry forks of the Cottonwood and Neosho rivers, was almost lost in the swirling dust kicked up by countless riders "hightailing it" into that Indian frontier town. The hitching rails all along the main street already were full, and the livery stables and horse lots were jammed with saddled horseflesh of every size, shade, and breed. Wagons and liveries of every description littered the town. Boisterous cowhands and wild-looking frontiersmen good-naturedly rubbed elbows with sedate and substantial townspeople on the crowded plank sidewalks. A sprinkling of soldiers, over from Fort Riley, and unusual numbers of hangdog but colorful Indians from the Sac and Fox, the Kaw, and the Osage reservations indicated something important was in the wind.

Stimulating sounds of honky dance issued in pulsating waves from every swinging door along Main, which was understandable. It had been authoritatively reported that the Osage Indians had finally been persuaded to relinquish title to their immense reservation, which had barred all settlement to the south, and move with all their goods and chattels into the Indian Territory south of the Cherokee Strip. This rumor of the opening up of the great tract, some fifteen hundred square miles of the finest agricultural land in Kansas, to pre-emption and settlement, had stirred the cupidity of the frontier. Every footloose cowpuncher and displaced settler, every investor, promoter, projector—every out-and-out adventurer—who had heard the rumor began converging on southeastern Kansas.

At this time, too, the Neosho Valley settlers were discussing with mounting excitement the hectic race of the Union Pacific Eastern Division to outbuild the Union Pacific of Nebraska to the one-hun-

9

dredth meridian. This in order to secure all the endowments of the main transcontinental line and the added privilege of participating in the race to a junction with the east-building Central Pacific.

The first rail of the Union Pacific Eastern Division[1] had been laid in Wyandotte (Kansas City) on April 14, 1864, and by the fall of 1865 the line had been completed through Lawrence and was fast approaching Topeka, the state capital. Grading had been finished on the line between Topeka and Fort Riley, and surveyors were far out on the wild western prairies.

The wide-gauge Pacific Railroad of Missouri,[2] with its 5 foot, 6 inch track as compared with the Union Pacific's 4 foot, 8½ inch, was making preparations to celebrate the completion of its line into Wyandotte (Kansas City) from the east, scheduled for October 3, 1865. Colonel Cyrus K. Holliday's Atchison & Topeka line, incorporated in 1859 but dormant during the war years, had been reorganized as the Atchison, Topeka and Santa Fé, and the fiery Topeka booster with a luscious land grant in his pocket was spell-binding the crowds with tales of another great transcontinental line to serve his favorite city.

Small wonder, then, that in the fertile valley of the Neosho, which runs southeasterly from the area of Fort Riley to the Indian Territory, excitement ran particularly high in September, 1865. Emporia, unofficial capital of this wonderfully promising agricultural region, was alarmed over the fate which might soon befall it. Council Grove, common meeting point of the "councilling" Indians and trading white men for decades, foresaw its early demise. The drying up of the highly profitable prairie-schooner traffic that rowdily but steadily plied the Santa Fé trail, and the diversion of all trade and commerce to the areas to be served by the westering railroads, was shaking the confidence of many a frontiersman turned settler.

This, then, was the situation on the afternoon of September 20, 1865, in Emporia, Kansas. Popular conversation no longer centered around the "reservation Injun" and how to hornswoggle him out of his lands and possessions. That problem was practically settled! Now the burning questions were pre-emption and railroads—how to get a railroad down through the Neosho Valley, a railroad guaranteed to turn these vast but nearly useless acres into valuable farm lands, invaluable townsites, or speculative property.

[1] Control of the Leavenworth, Pawnee and Western Railroad passed into the hands of General John C. Frémont and other New York interests in 1863, and the corporate name was changed to Union Pacific Railway Company, Eastern Division, on June 6, 1863.

[2] Now the Missouri Pacific.

A Railroad Is Born

In the stuffy little law offices of Ruggles and Plumb that afternoon, things were fast coming to a head. Judge Ruggles had gathered together two dozen of the Valley's most influential citizens to take some effective action.

Prominent at the meeting but taking no active part in it was popular former Senator Robert S. Stevens, the stormy petrel of the 1862 session of the "impeaching legislature." Young, handsome, and devil-may-care, Stevens with his dark flashing eyes and meticulous style of dress was a striking personality. He it was whose testimony had led to the impeachment of the governor, secretary of state, and state auditor of Kansas on June 3, 1862. The trial, it will be remembered, concerned fraudulent disposition of state bonds. Stevens, with character unblemished and with a neat profit on the transaction, soon resigned to accept a commission in the Bourbon County Battalion of the Kansas State Militia. He was at the meeting "merely to look the situation over." This fragment of history is given because Stevens looms large in the early picture of the Katy's development.

With all the life and color of newspaper reporting of those days, Bob McBratney, one-time editor of the *Squatter Sovereign*, in telling phrases, retailed the latest railroad news from Topeka, and Colonel Goss harangued the meeting about the railroad activity up around Junction and Fort Riley. But there was little need for oratory; everyone knew what was going on around them; it was common knowledge that the "Injuns" were soon to be moved out of their "diminished" and diminishing reserves, clear out of Kansas and into the Indian Territory. And hadn't the government actually offered thousands of these fertile acres to anyone who would undertake to build a railroad through the area?

Talk finally died down, and at the proper moment Senator Maxson revealed that he had been studying recent railroad legislation and had drawn up a rough draft of a charter for a railroad to serve not only the Neosho Valley but the entire frontier line. Copies of the draft were passed around. There was much discussion of the proposed route of the line and its ultimate destination. All were agreed it should begin at or near Fort Riley in order to fill the military requirement and afford a good connection with the Union Pacific Eastern Division; then it should follow the Valley of the Neosho down through Emporia to Indian Territory. But there agreement ended. Some urged that Fort Gibson be made the end of the line, others favored Fort Smith. The more enthusiastic naturally suggested Mexico City, the Rio Grande, Galveston, even New Orleans.

Here is the charter they finally drew up that hot September night in 1865:

> We ... do hereby associate ourselves together as a Railroad Company under the Act of Legislature of the State of Kansas, entitled "An Act to Provide for the Incorporation of Railroad Companies," approved February 13th, A.D. 1865, to be known as the

Union Pacific Railway Company
Southern Branch

The object of this Association shall be the construction of a railway, commencing at or near Fort Riley, or the junction of the Republican and Smoky Hill forks of the Kansas River, and on the line of the Union Pacific Railway, E. D., running thence, via Clarke's Creek and the Neosho River, to a point at or near where the southern boundary-line of the State of Kansas crosses the said Neosho River.

The ultimate object of this Association being to secure the construction of a continuous line of railway from the points

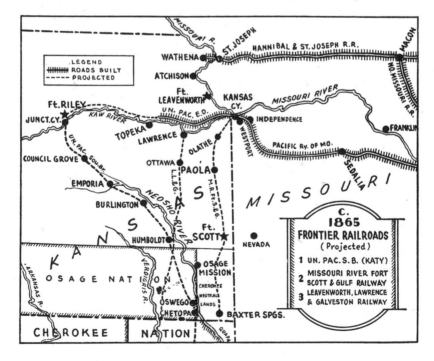

above named, via the Arkansas and Red Rivers, to the City of New Orleans in the State of Louisiana.

The capital stock of this Association shall be One Million of Dollars, divided into shares of one hundred dollars each.

This charter, signed by all present except Bob Stevens, was filed in the office of the secretary of state for Kansas, in Topeka, on September 25, 1865, and the Katy's "corporators" were in the railroad business for better or for worse.

Nine days later, on September 29, 1865, the rumors of the Indian exodus were substantiated. At Canville's trading post on the reservation that day, a crestfallen but still dignified group of chiefs of the Great and Little Osage Indian bands set their "X" marks to a treaty which removed them forever from Kansas.[3] The redoubtable White Hair, better known as Paw-hus-ka, principal chief of the mighty Osage, bowed his head in shame.

[3] Treaty between the United States of America and the Great and Little Osage Indians: amended September 21, 1866; proclaimed January 21, 1867.

THREE

A Railroad Is Organized

The first stockholders' meeting of the embryo Katy was held in the offices of Ruggles and Plumb in Emporia on February 13, 1866.

At this meeting, the matter of the division of the Indian lands was very much to the fore, as might be expected. The committee reported, "There are 140,000 acres of the Trust Lands and 75,000 acres of the Diminished Reserve, the fair value of the whole 215,000 acres to be 60 cents per acre." Already there appeared to be a question in the minds of the stockholders as to whether any grants of land from state or nation would apply to the Indian lands when vacated, pointing to an awareness of possible defects in land-grant legislation.

On March 2, the first meeting of the regularly constituted board of directors was held in the Masonic Hall in Council Grove. N. S. Goss was elected vice president and made president pro tempore. Business was rather dull at this time, for the treasurer's report showed a balance on hand of only $343.55, and from the frenzied activity thereafter it is apparent someone must have sourly observed that such a sum was scarcely sufficient to build and equip a railroad for good running order.

At this time President Goss reported that, through the good offices of the Honorable Andrew Akin, he and his colleagues had been successful in having the Union Pacific Southern Branch named a participating beneficiary in a bill passed on February 23, entitled "An Act Providing for the Sale of Public Lands, to Aid in the Construction of Certain Railroads." This bill provided for the sale of half a million acres of public lands[1] "at no less than $1.25 an acre" and the

---

[1] It is mortifying to recall that in the treaty concluded at Canville Trading Post on September 29, 1865 (just nine days after the birth of the railroad), the chiefs of the Great and Little Osage tribes were beguiled into agreeing that

proceeds donated and prorated between the Northern Kansas Railroad Company, the Leavenworth, Lawrence and Fort Gibson Railroad, the Kansas and Neosho Valley Railroad Company (which has a brief and inglorious part later in this story), and the Union Pacific Southern Branch.

It was obvious that, with his special talents, Akin's sphere of activities should be in the East rather than in penny-pinching Kansas, and off to Washington he was sent. He must have been a fast worker, for on July 26 Congress passed a bill entitled "An Act Granting Lands to the State of Kansas, to Aid in the Construction of a Southern Branch of the Union Pacific Railway and Telegraph, from Fort Riley, Kansas, to Fort Smith, Arkansas."

This Act granted the Katy "every alternate section of land . . . to the extent of five alternate sections per mile on each side of said road" and authorized construction also "from the southern boundary of Kansas, south through the Indian Territory, with the consent of the Indians, and not otherwise, along the Valley of Grand and Arkansas Rivers, to Fort Smith, in the State of Arkansas; and the right-of-way through said Indian Territory is hereby granted to said company . . ." The Katy land grant, then, was similar to that originally awarded to the first transcontinental line, ten square miles for each mile of road built. It did not, however, include a bond subsidy.

Because of his immediate and complete success in the halls of Congress, there seemed to be the shadow of someone bigger, much more influential, behind Akin. Perhaps it was Colonel R. S. Stevens, former senator, former bond salesman, and politico par excellence. Bob Stevens was a native of Attica, New York, and in the East his people were well connected and influential. Northern New York interests were soon to provide the millions that built the Katy; hence it is probable that Stevens at this time was laying the groundwork for a big railroad drive. Moreover, this gay and guileless gentleman personally owned a 51,689 acre tract of fine Indian land he had somehow bought from the government for a record-low 71 cents an acre[2] and he was not one to neglect improving a property like that if a little political skulduggery would help.

"having now more lands than are necessary for their occupation, and all payments from the government to them under former treaties having ceased, leaving them greatly impoverished," they were "desirous of improving their condition by disposing of their surplus lands. . . ." See John Joseph Mathews, *Wah'Kon-Tah:The Osage and the White Man's Road*, 356.

[2] Daniel W. Wilder, *The Annals of Kansas*, 483.

At the next board meeting, on August 8, a committee consisting of President Goss and Secretary Maxson was named to secure the "consent of the Cherokee Indians, and not otherwise" to enter and cross their domain with a line of shiny new rail. By October the deed was done. The committee reported:

> Set out on mission October 4, 1866—spent 22 days in attendance on the Council, negotiating with said Nation, which resulted in securing a pledge of $500,000 of funds, and a bonus of the proceeds of the sales of 250,000 acres of land and outlet lands and some privileges in addition to those secured by Congressional Treaty, approved by a unanimous vote of both branches of the Council.

This juicy contract was completed October 31, approved November 27, and ordered filed with the U. S. secretary of the interior on December 5, 1866. It is sad to relate that the Katy Railroad committee was a little too optimistic in its report and neglected to record the great difficulties in the way of final fulfillment. True it was that Chief Ross had appointed a committee under Assistant Principal Chief Downing to conclude such an agreement, and had approved their findings. The latter, however, contemplated the sale of Cherokee lands "west of ninety-six," in that part of the territory already beginning to be called Oklahoma,[3] in order to raise the necessary funds—but the government had other plans in mind for this area. All agreements with the tribes, moreover, required the approval of the commissioner of Indian affairs, and the enemies of Chief Ross were finally successful in blocking the contract.

It is difficult in the twentieth century to visualize conditions along the frontier in the 1860's, for the border lands were undergoing the metamorphosis preliminary to final settlement. Railroads were still lacking; there were no highways as such, merely trails between settlements. Creaking wagons drawn by mules or oxen still freighted such heavy goods as were moving, bull-whacked at a mile-an-hour pace, and passenger travel was by stage coach or on horseback. From the drought year of 1860, when "the bed of the Neosho was dry and regularly used as a public road to Humboldt," the settlers contended successively against short crops, no crops, Indian thieves and all-devouring grasshoppers. Whole areas of settlement had often win-

---

[3] Allen Wright, a Choctaw chief, is credited with suggesting the name Oklahoma in 1866. It is a Choctaw word meaning "red people."—Muriel H. Wright, *A Guide to the Indian Tribes of Oklahoma*, 4.

tered on poor buffalo meat and dressed almost entirely in the skins of these beasts—but the people were land rich![4]

Not far west, a trek of just a day or two from the route of the Katy Railroad, great herds of buffalo still roamed the Kansas plains, and reservation Indians still were living largely from the proceeds of the chase. They traded skins and meat for smuggled whiskey, with results well known to history. In the southeastern towns the standard "likkers" were not the mild concoctions we know today, but fiery brands identified as "stone-fence," "forty-rod," and "tarantula juice," and they played no small part in making the frontier an uncertain area for large investment. Adding to the confusion, hordes of squatters were pouring into the Cherokee Neutral Lands in the southeastern corner of Kansas, and they were also settling, in spite of all warnings, on the edge of the Cherokee Strip which still extended all along the border and served as a buffer between Kansas and the Indian Territory.

As a final nightmarish touch, great herds of longhorn Texan cattle were being driven aimlessly about the border during 1865-1866, their drivers and cowboys unable to bribe or force their way through to northern railheads and markets. The local herdsmen, desperately afraid of "Spanish fever" in their own shorthorn cattle by reason of importation of the "Texas tick" which infested most Texas herds, wouldn't stop short of gun play to turn the drives aside. And gangs of border ruffians naturally took advantage of the situation to rob and pillage the herds and herders alike.[5]

Treatment such as this stifled the cattle trade up the Texas Road, and thereafter the drives were made farther west, up what came to be known as the Chisholm Trail. Upon Abilene and other inland Kansas tent towns were booming, cattle rich—and southeastern Kansas thereafter stayed more or less respectably poor.

This, then, was the trade territory of the new-born Katy—a not too inviting locale for the building of a great railroad empire as envisioned by the founding fathers. But they went right ahead with their plans.

The year 1866 passed with few regrets, but 1867 opened auspiciously. Four counties lying along the route of the projected railroad —Davis, Morris, Lyon and Coffee—were prevailed upon to subscribe to the cause a total of $730,000 in thirty-year bonds.[6] This, plus the

---

[4] J. H. Beadle, *The Undeveloped West*, 209.
[5] J. G. McCoy, *Cattle Trade of the West and Southwest*, 21-24.
[6] *Kansas Historical Collections*, Vol. xi, p. 104.

fact that the Union Pacific Eastern Division had reached Junction City with its first passenger train on November 10, 1866, spurred officials to start actual work on the road. The line had been "located" all the way to the border during the summer; tangents were long, grades were easy, and river crossings presented no unusual problems. George W. Walker was appointed chief engineer and by the fall of 1867 he was ready to begin construction.

Now was the time for publicity, for the grand gesture. On September 5 Major General John Pope presided at "the erection of the initial stone" which was to be the cornerstone of the Katy, at Junction City; his presence with a detail of soldiers from Fort Riley lent the desired military aspect to the venture. Fulsome addresses were made by President Goss and others, and the project was formally launched.

A. F. Beach and Company got the contract for building the line. At four in the afternoon of October 15, following appropriate ceremonies at the Hale House in Junction City, President Goss turned the first spadeful of earth to give substance to the dreams of all who lived along the fertile Valley of the Neosho.

FOUR

The Derail

While the directors of the practically stillborn Katy were putting on a fine show of activity by ordering the grading of a few miles of track, they also were trying desperately to dig up sufficient capital to keep going, chiefly by peddling stock subscriptions in driblets all through the wild winter of 1867-68.

Subsequent developments, it is important to indicate here, make it evident that the affable and capable Bob Stevens was then hard at work promoting the venture among eastern interests and was meeting with considerable success. He, however, was not one to tip his hand too soon or let another reap the benefit of his efforts.

A sound reason for the drying up of the railroad money market at this time may have been the meteoric rise of James F. Joy, of Detroit, who then was having the nation's first important dreams of a western railroad empire. Joy was presiding over the destinies of the Chicago, Burlington and Quincy and the Michigan Central and also had an interest in the New York Central. During this period he secured control of the Hannibal and St. Jo and merged it with the Burlington. Completion of the building of the Kansas City, St. Joseph and Council Bluffs line gave him a through road from New York City via Chicago, Council Bluffs, or Kansas City to the entire frontier—hence his prospects for dominating the traffic of the virgin West were very good, and attracted much of the East's investment funds.

Besides his western connections, Joy was known to be interested in a route south from Kansas City to the Gulf, and he had the backing to see things through. Soon he had control of the Kansas and Neosho Valley and the Leavenworth, Lawrence and Fort Gibson lines, both in about the same stage of construction as was the Katy. There was the scent of trouble, heavy trouble, in the air.

With the annual meeting of the stockholders, held in the offices of Sam Prouty in Burlington, Kansas, on June 24, 1868, it was evident that the disgruntled investors were out for somebody's scalp. Led by Stevens' old friend Hiram F. Hale, proprietor of the Hale House in Junction City and a man of some wealth and influence, the group voted Akin off the directorate and clear out of the company, with scarcely a word of thanks for all his efforts. The new directorate then elected Hale vice president to fill his victim's shoes, and pointedly chastised Colonel Goss by leaving the presidency vacant.

Assuredly the fine hand of Bob Stevens was behind all this maneuvering, for interest in the East picked up almost at once. Throughout the summer there were strange comings and goings in the Valley, and on October 7, 1868, "a distinguished group of eastern financiers" staged into Emporia, in top hats and frock coats, to give the natives, Indian and white, something to talk about for months to come. The group consisted of Judge Levi Parsons, president of the Land Grant Railway and Trust Company of New York; A. P. Robinson, construction engineer; and Will Gaylord and O. P. Root, all names to conjure with in the railroad investment and building worlds.

The meeting of this delegation with the befuddled directors of the Union Pacific Southern Branch, was short and businesslike, as befits men of affairs. Said the properly bearded and dignified Judge Parsons, spokesman for the group: "Our object is to build your road and we come sufficiently endorsed to meet with no opposition." He gave no inkling of his plans, no word of how he proposed to go about building the road; the promise was all-inclusive—and it left the board speechless. Then he demanded, and received, a resolution empowering him to name the president and the secretary of the company.[1]

Parsons then named for the presidency J. B. Dickinson, president of the Tenth National Bank of New York, and for secretary George C. Clark, partner in Clark, Dodge and Company, the big New York investment house. Parsons, Dickinson, and Thad Walker, a Kansas director, were constituted an executive committee with power to act for the entire board, and thereafter the business of the railroad was transacted largely in the offices of the Land Grant Railway and Trust Company, 19 Broad Street, New York City.

Judge Levi Parsons was a man of fine family and background. Retired, wealthy, and looking for good opportunities for investment, he was confident the frontier was in for an era of fast development, and

[1] Union Pacific Railway, Southern Branch, Minute Book No. 1.

he was prepared to back his judgment with what the section needed most—money. Born July 1, 1822, at Kingsboro, New York, he was scion of a long line of legislators and ministers and a direct descendant of Deacon Benjamin Parsons, famed early settler of Springfield, Massachusetts, who had emigrated from England in 1627. The pioneer strain apparently was strong in him, for after he had been admitted to the bar he practiced law in Little Falls, New York, for only two years before the urge came to head west.

By the end of 1848 the gold fever, which had spread rapidly eastward following the California discoveries, reached the Valley of the Mohawk, and Levi Parsons was one of the first to feel it. On March 4, 1849, the day of President Zachary Taylor's inauguration, he wound up his affairs in the East, took schooner at New York, and was off to his El Dorado.

In San Francisco, the young lawyer found more opportunities in his profession than in the gold fields and his rise to prominence was little short of meteoric. When the first California legislature in joint convention, March 30, 1850, elected the first district judges, Levi Parsons, at the age of 28, was chosen for the Fourth, or San Francisco, District. Thus he was the first to bring law—the majesty of a formal court—to this hitherto lawless community.

The Judge's fame was more fleeting than his fortune, however. In the early sixties Parsons' San Francisco friends turned on him and overnight his reputation was torn to shreds. He had sponsored the so-called "Parsons Bulkhead Bill" which proposed to give to the San Francisco Dock and Wharf Company (composed of Judge Parsons and half a dozen of his wealthy friends) the "right to build a bulkhead or seawall, with the necessary piers, wharves and docks, upon the water line of 1851, with the right to collect dockage, wharfage and tolls, also to construct wharves and piers projecting at right angles from the seawall to a length of 600 feet." This great scheme was of the Judge's own inspiration and his would have been the greater part of the wealth and political power which must have resulted from the enactment of the measure. The bill passed both branches of the legislature against the overwhelming protest of the city of San Francisco, but was vetoed by Governor Downey. The governor's veto message not only killed the bill, it killed Judge Parsons' interest in his adopted state.[2]

At the outbreak of the Civil War Levi Parsons, then only 39 years old, had amassed a fortune and was footloose, but not quite fancy

[2] Oscar T. Shuck, *History of the Bench and Bar of California,* 476.

free. On September 3, 1861, he married at Fort Plain, N. Y., the sweetheart of his youth, the beautiful and talented Mary Jane Cuyler. She was the niece of the learned Judge Yost, in whose offices Parsons had been taught his trade.

Although he maintained his headquarters on California Street in San Francisco until 1866, for several years after his marriage the Judge traveled the length and breadth of the country. He became thoroughly familiar with the great undeveloped areas of the West and Southwest. He saw at first hand the amazing changes that followed swift upon the western sweep of colonization, and here, he knew, were opportunities unlimited for organizers, for investors, for projectors, for financiers—for himself. Armed with the intimate knowledge gained from his travels, Judge Parsons in 1866 decided that Wall Street, New York, offered a better strategic site and greater facilities than California Street, San Francisco. There he finally settled down, to invest and to speculate as a wealthy capitalist should.

In the summer of '68, when Judge Parsons and his group first began taking an interest in the Kansas Railroad land grants, the business of making a fast million dollars was temporarily in the doldrums. The small investor was beginning to be wary, and for good cause. The fact that the evil-smelling Credit Mobilier Company had declared a first dividend of $2,500,000 in Union Pacific bonds and the same in stock, or 100 per cent on its capital, had shocked the nation, and voices were being raised for a Congressional investigation of western railroad financing. The Pacific Railroad of Missouri, hopelessly in debt to the state of Missouri, had managed to stay in operation only by persuading the state to release its lien, at a squawking loss to Missourians of about $10,000,000.

On May 31, 1868, the Union Pacific Eastern Division, which was then nearly four hundred miles west of Kansas City and headed for Denver, changed its name to Kansas Pacific Railway, thus neatly divorcing itself in name as in fact from the Nebraska line's odious Credit Mobilier scandals. The Union Pacific Southern Branch was soon to do likewise on Judge Parsons' order, but reluctantly, for the name had a certain magic then, even as today.

As 1868 drew to a close, Parsons had his reorganization well under way. He and President Dickinson had replaced General Mc-Millan and Representative Isaac Dow on the directorate; the redoubtable Colonel Bob Stevens, no longer an undercover man, had secured for himself a post that fitted him admirably, that of "Agent and Attorney for the Purchase of Lands." Senator Maxson was elected

Assistant Secretary to handle the legal and political work that could not be done in New York. Asa P. Robinson was appointed chief engineer, and work on the line, at a standstill when the Judge took over, was resumed December 15.

In January, 1869, Capital Stock was increased from the original modest $1,000,000 to $4,250,000, and a first mortgage was immediately placed on the "170 miles of railroad . . . and about 1,300,00 acres of land donated by Congress, to aid in building of said railroad." Naturally Parsons' Land Grant Railway and Trust Company handled the transaction and Russell Sage and N. A. Cowdray were named trustees. Now, with plenty of funds available and his own men in the key jobs, the Judge was ready for action.[3]

It is obvious from the record that the Judge thought he had found a good thing in the Union Pacific Southern Branch. It is evident in the way he proceeded to let in on the ground floor such men as his illustrious namesake Levi P. Morton, president of Morton, Bliss and Company and one day to become vice president of the United States; Joe Seligman of the great banking house of J. and W. Seligman; the rising young financier August Belmont; and George C. Clark, partner in the Clark, Dodge Investment Company.

From the inception of the railroad until the coming of Levi Parsons and his empire builders it had been three long years. But that is how railroads came into being during the winning of the West—tentative, faltering steps in the beginning, then an unholy rush to completion. The Atchison, Topeka and Santa Fe, chartered in February, 1859, had not yet laid a mile of track, but eventually it went on to Chicago. But hadn't the Union Pacific Southern Branch at least broken ground!

The year 1869 saw the actual beginning of the construction of the railroad. Colonel Stevens, now publicly acknowledged as the moving spirit of the company and Judge Parsons' right-hand man, together with Chief Engineer Robinson, set up operating headquarters in Junction City. One of his first acts was to terminate the construction contract with Beach and Company and bring in his own forces. Work on the line, however, "progressed slowly" according to Stevens' reports. By mid-August "grading was done to Council Grove, about 37 miles, and very little south of that point," and the Colonel's reports to his eastern superiors began to be charged with dissatisfaction.[4]

[3] Minute Book No. 1.
[4] Mrs. Elliott Yost Simpson, Sedalia, Mo., daughter of Richard S. Yost, reports that her father "ran the first center south of Smoky Hill River, June 6, 1869."

In September Stevens was furiously demanding action, and quickly he got it. He was given complete charge of the work as General Manager, urged to push ahead with all speed, and authorized to make whatever changes he thought necessary to accomplish that end. Almost immediately Director N. S. Goss, the former president who was now acting as land commissioner, was removed from his post of patronage and replaced by the able Professor Isaac T. Goodnow, former state superintendent of public instruction, who was not closely affiliated with local interests. This change closed the last door to opportunity—and personal profit—for landholding leaders who were still on the board. Stevens was indeed in a class by himself.

When Stevens took full charge that autumn, "only five miles of track had been laid from Junction City." By October 27 the road was open to Council Grove, that famous and lovely spot on the Santa Fé Trail which marked the end of the fertile hardwood belt and the beginning of the old "American Desert." Here the great wagon trains were properly organized, military style, for the dangerous journey through the "Injun Country" to Santa Fé. Here in 1825 the treaty was made with the Osage Indian tribes which permitted peaceful passage through their domain, hence the name, and here now was the iron horse to replace the fast-fading prairie-schooner traffic.

With much fanfare that October, Stevens ran a big excursion down from Junction City to the railhead. On the train were the state officials commissioned to inspect the line preparatory to awarding it the 125,000 land-grant acres set aside for it by the Act of February 23, 1866.[5] The trip was a huge success and settled Stevens firmly in the saddle as chief bull-whacker of the line. By December 7 he had track laid to Emporia, cradle of the railroad sixty-one miles out, and was headed straight for the border.

It is a pity that the minutes of the December meeting of the board of directors, held in the company's offices at Junction City, are so scant. Considering the personalities involved and the grievances waiting to be aired, the report is remarkably restrained. But assuredly there were fireworks! And the results are significant. Thad Walker, the only Kansan on the executive committee, resigned in frustration, and Bob Stevens there and then replaced him on the board. Immediately, in open rebellion against Parsons' policies,

[5] The commission consisted of Governor Harvey, Secretary of State Thomas Moonlight, Treasurer Graham, Auditor Thoman, and Dr. J. W. Scott. They agreed that "there was no better constructed road in the State and that its rolling stock was the best in the State." Stevens apparently had the wheels well lubricated.

Colonel Plumb, Senator Maxson, P. Z. Taylor, Colonel Goss, and T.
S. Huffaker laid their resignations on the table and marched out of
the meeting.

With the mutinous faction out of the way, the remaining directors
voted to increase the board membership to thirteen, and at the request of Judge Parsons placed on the directorate his good friend and
investment partner, August Belmont. They also added to the board
Francis Skiddy, operating head of the Judge's Land Grant Railway
and Trust Company, and David Crawford, Jr., and George Denison,
both representing substantial eastern investment groups. From that
moment, local control of the railroad was a thing of the past, gone
with the buffalo, and no area to be served by the line would in the
future benefit more than another—excepting, perhaps, Bob Stevens'
quietly held acres.

At this time Chief Engineer Robinson's report that "65 miles of
railway are now completed and accepted" was met with something
less than enthusiasm, even though the line finally had reached the
heart of the lush Neosho Valley. The reconstituted board knew that
Bob Stevens, not Robinson, was the man who had given them action.

As the sixties drew to a close, Judge Parsons' predictions about
the development of the West were fast proving to be correct. Settlers
were pouring into southeastern Kansas by the thousands, buying,
pre-empting, squatting on the area's finest acres. The state, which
had a population of 107,000 in 1860, and had lost untold thousands
during the "Rebellion," boasted 362,307 inhabitants by 1870, according to the U. S. census. Although the Osages and Kiowas were still
hunting the buffalo on the western plains, results of the chase were
becoming poorer with each sally from the reservation. This not only
because the buffalo were being driven too far west, but also because
the wild plains Indians, chiefly the Comanches and Apaches, were
savagely pre-empting the hunting grounds. The *Osage Mission Journal* of January 18, 1870, in fact, reported, "The Osages and Apaches
met in battle a few days ago on the Little Caney River. The Osages
were defeated with the loss of 100 braves." It was about time for
them to leave Kansas forever.

Truly the southeastern counties were filling up and "civilizing"
fast. Here lay some of the most fertile acres in Kansas and some government land and much private land was for sale at three to five dollars an acre. The new era was at hand in Kansas if not in the Indian
Territory.

FIVE

Rebirth of the "Katy"

Looking down the long valley of the years to 1870 and beyond, one senses the hand of fate guiding the destinies of the men who built the Southwest. Parsons, Levi Morton, August Belmont and the other financial giants who first underwrote the projected Katy railroad had become vastly interested in western expansion, otherwise they might have become involved in much of the evil speculation of the times. Those were the days of Jay Gould's odoriferous manipulations of Erie stocks, and of the conspiracy to corner the gold market. The gold plot, involving bribery in the highest circles, was conceived by Gould and the notorious Jim Fisk, the revelation of which shocked the nation. The corner was broken on Black Friday, October 4, 1869, when the government stepped in and released its gold reserves, incidentally ruining hundreds of firms and thousands of individuals—but not the wily Gould.

Parsons and his colleagues, however, had a great deal of money tied up in legitimate construction work in the West and avoided the fate of the socially ostracized Gould, whose name became a synonym for organized greed and ruthless rapacity thereafter. Parsons at this period was giving his whole mind and devoting his boundless energies to the vision of a great railroad system, a railroad to serve the entire Southwest and bring the fruits of its wonderfully fertile acres to the populous North and East through Kansas City and St. Louis. The master design is apparent in his every move.

On January 10, 1870, Parsons called a special meeting of the board of directors in New York City and began to unfold his plans for building into the Indian Territory. Briefly he outlined the dangerous activities of the competing "Joy roads." The Kansas and Neosho Valley, reorganized by James F. Joy as the Missouri River, Fort

Scott and Gulf, and popularly known as the Border Tier Road, was, he said, already operating into Fort Scott from Kansas City. With one hundred miles of track down, they were only sixty miles from the border. Graders were already at work in the Cherokee Neutral Lands, the whole 800,000 acres of which Joy had purchased in the Summer of 1868 over the vociferous protests of settlers, squatters, and local politicians.

"The Border Tier Road is heading into serious trouble, I happen to know," the Judge reported, "and arrangements are now being made to make their difficulties more burdensome than ever. So I have little fear of the competition of the M.R.Ft.S.&G." Joy, however, was posing another and more serious threat, Parsons pointed out. The Leavenworth, Lawrence and Fort Gibson, which he also controlled, had been reorganized as the Leavenworth, Lawrence and Galveston Railroad. This line had been graded nearly to Garnett, fifty-two miles south from Lawrence, and was then about ninety miles from the border. "If it is upheld that only one line may enter Indian Territory," the Judge warned, "then it is up to us to win the race to the border. We are now about one hundred miles from the territory line, but I propose to be the first to cross it."

Parsons then went on to outline his plans for building east to a junction, probably at Sedalia, Missouri, with the Missouri Pacific. "The moment we reach Indian Territory," he told the board, "this line will require such a connection in order to handle effectively the potentially great traffic between that area and the markets of the North and East."[1]

The Judge's pronouncement did not surprise the directors members particularly, but Director Prouty, state printer for Kansas and now publisher of the *Topeka Leader* and the *Daily Commonwealth*, took it hard. This meant millions more in capitalization, eastern money of course. If the plan were carried out it also meant that the Junction City stretch of the road shortly would become little more than a branch line. Indignantly Prouty emphasized this to the board, and Parsons smoothly agreed with everything he said, at the same time pointing to the inevitability of it. Left with no alternative, Sam Prouty resigned from the board and the Kansas representation thereon was down to two, Hiram Hale and Rolla Norton.

On February 3, 1870, Judge Parsons called a special meeting of the stockholders in the offices of Ruggles and Plumb in Emporia in order to obtain formal authority for the drastic changes he proposed

[1] Company Minutes, Board of Directors.

to make, the bold steps he intended to take. The Santa Fé, he had been informed, was grading into Emporia, reached two months earlier by Bob Stevens' tracklayers. That line was beginning to pose a threat of competition for Neosho Valley traffic and something had to be done about it. Worse still, the question had been raised whether the Union Pacific Southern Branch had a separate right to build down through the Indian Territory. The implications of the question disturbed the Judge seriously. True it was that Congress by its Act of July 26, 1866, had clearly granted the right. The question arose from the fact that a day earlier Congress had given the same rights both to the Border Tier Road and to the Leavenworth, Lawrence and Galveston.

Now the Cherokee Nation was taking the position that by its Treaty of July 19, 1866, it gave permission for the building of only one railroad south through its domains, not three. An Indian delegation in Washington was already protesting to the secretary of the interior that, "The whole scheme of treaties and legislation looked to the construction of but a single trunk road through the territory . . ." If the Indians were upheld in their contention, then it meant a three-way race to the border.[2]

The Judge's mind dwelt for a moment on his competitors. The hostility of settlers notwithstanding, the Border Tier Road[3] had put on a spurt of building, and reports had it that "Cars on the M.R.Ft. S.&G. will on February 21, 1870, run into Girard, 25 miles south of Fort Scott. The iron and ties are ready to complete the road to the south line of the state, which will be reached before the first day of July."

The Leavenworth, Lawrence and Galveston[4] line, too, had come very much alive and was building directly south from Lawrence via Ottawa. Local papers were jubilantly reporting, "On February 23 the

[2] The Indians spoke true. The Congressional act read: "That should the Leavenworth, Lawrence and Fort Gibson Railroad Company, or the Union Pacific Railroad Company, Southern Branch, construct and complete its road to that point on the southern boundary of the State of Kansas, where the line of said Kansas and Neosho Valley Railroad shall cross the same, before the said Kansas and Neosho Valley Railroad Company shall have constructed and completed its said road to said point, then and in that event the company so first reaching in completion the said point on the southern boundary of the State of Kansas shall be authorized, upon obtaining the written approval of the President of the United States, to construct and operate its line of railroad from said point to a point at or near Preston [Denison], in the State of Texas, with grants of land according to the provisions of this act. . . ." Report of J. D. Cox, Secretary of the Interior, to President U. S. Grant, May 21, 1870.

[3] Now part of the Frisco Lines.

[4] Now part of the Santa Fé.

28

opening of the LL&G to Garnett will be celebrated. The graders are already strung out over the Ozark range and our neighbors on the Verdigris may look out for the engine by October next. Truly Kansas is making history at a rapid rate."[5]

Parsons knew, of course, that both of these roads were controlled by James F. Joy, a shrewd managing director and a thorn in the side of his own man, Colonel Bob Stevens. Joy, it seemed, was convinced that the Cherokee chiefs were going to be upheld in their claim that only one railroad was authorized to build through the territory, and was racing to be first to the border.

The Judge stalked into the stockholders' meeting that raw February morning with much of purpose in his stride. With him were Colonel Stevens and a tall, dark, saturnine man he introduced as George Denison, "one of the new directors of the company who represents a substantial group of eastern interests." They selected seats up front and maintained a dignified silence while the stockholders were electing Judge Ruggles as chairman of the meeting. R. W. Ruggles, of course, was in partnership with Preston B. Plumb, one of the recently resigned directors, and the stage seemed set for more fireworks.

When the time came, Bob Stevens, with commendable modesty, reported that since he had taken over as General Manager good progress had been made. Only five miles of track had been laid up to October, he pointed out, yet "in November a regular passenger and freight train commenced running to Council Grove, 37 miles from our starting point in Junction City. The line reached Emporia in December . . . the track has just reached Burlington and is now 90 miles long. Service is now in operation to Emporia and will be extended to Burlington within the month."[6]

Then Judge Parsons rose, and his very presence quieted the murmur that had greeted the General Manager's report. After a few complimentary phrases to soothe his listeners' pride, he dropped his bombshell. "This little branch line," he declared, "beginning nowhere and ending in the same manner as it does, makes necessary some extensions as soon as possible." Then he proceeded to outline the activities of the "Joy roads" and of the Santa Fé, emphasizing that unless extensive growth were achieved, and quickly, these lines with their superior outlets to the north and east eventually would throttle the U.P.S.B., by providing quicker and cheaper service to the great consuming centers.

[5] *Southern Kansas Advance*, March 2, 1870.
[6] Company Report to the Stockholders.

Then he further jarred his hearers with the news that a majority of the directors agreed with James F. Joy that the Indian treaties apparently provided for only one railroad to enter the Cherokee Nation from the north. It had been intimated by the Department of the Interior, he said, that the first railroad to build to the state line would be given the exclusive right to enter the Indian Territory—and Joy's Missouri River, Fort Scott and Gulf was at the moment ahead in the race. It was his intention, with the able assistance of Bob Stevens, to beat Joy to the border and secure for his railroad the proffered 3,-100,000-acre land-grant prize.

Finally, he revealed his plans not only for reaching the state line and building into the Indian Territory but also for building or buying roads which would provide outlets, through fast-growing Kansas City and already great St. Louis, to the tremendous markets of the North and East. "It is evident that our lines will be instrumental in largely developing eastern Kansas and western Missouri, which are justly considered the finest agricultural sections of the West," he said, "and will form a connecting link between the great cattle-raising regions of Texas and the cattle-consuming sections of the North, the value of which can scarcely be too highly estimated."[7]

With the Judge's dazzling vision of the future misting all eyes, opposition to Parsons' pleas quickly evaporated. Soon he was on his feet again to propose "That the name of Union Pacific Railway Company, Southern Branch, be, and the same is hereby changed to and made, MISSOURI, KANSAS AND TEXAS RAILWAY COMPANY." This resolution was adopted unanimously, filed with the secretary of state for Kansas on March 31, 1870, and thereafter the Union Pacific Southern Branch was no more.[8]

A great new railroad, not a "branch," was brought into being that day. By a familiar process of elision, it almost immediately became best known not by its official designation but by the shorter, more familiar soubriquet of K-T or "Katy." And this is its story.

[7] *First Annual Report,* Missouri, Kansas and Texas Railway.

[8] Why it was ever named Union Pacific Railway, Southern Branch, is a mystery known only to its incorporators. The Union Pacific had no interest in the line whatever, financial or other, hence we might be forgiven for speculating that the "corporators" had fair visions of selling a juicy franchise to the U. P. in Junction City at a price that would make the Valley more fertile than ever.

SIX

"Lined and Locked for the Main"

The extent and variety of Colonel Stevens' activities in the early months of 1870 were little short of amazing. Judge Parsons was the strategist, but the General Manager was the experienced field commander who took the Judge's most impractical ideas and advanced them to practicality.

Because the railroad still was not getting built fast enough to satisfy the Judge's impatience, Stevens at this time threw out his entire engineering and construction staff and re-formed it from the top down. Out went Asa P. Robinson and in came Major Otis B. Gunn as chief engineer. Gunn, famous even then, was a strongly motivated western character. He had come to Kansas Territory in its wildest days, with a government survey party back in '57. He had been chief engineer on the staff of the governor during the Civil War, and lately had completed the first thorough survey for the newly reborn Santa Fé. For his assistant Gunn retained lt. B. (Dick) Yost, who was a cousin of Judge Parsons and a graduate of Union College, Schnectady, New York. (Right here one begins to wonder whether Parsons fully trusted Bob Stevens.) Major George Walker rounded out the engineering staff and Stevens turned his attention to the construction gangs.

Here the colonel's urgent need for speedy construction turned out to be a blessing in disguise. His search for a man with as much drive as himself, someone who could quickly reorganize the graders and the bridge-building and tracklaying gangs for a record breaking race for the border, led him inevitably to the one man in the West best fitted for the job. That man was the rough and tough John Scullin[1] of Leavenworth, a brash Irishman with as much of the devil

[1] Founder of the great Scullin Steel Company of St. Louis.

31

in him as Stevens had himself. Only thirty-four, already Scullin was becoming a legend in the frontier railroad world. He had done an outstanding job on a contract to build forty miles of the Union Pacific and had just finished a fast construction job on the Chicago, Rock Island and Pacific out of Leavenworth when his achievements began to attract the colonel's attention. Scullin's qualifications for the job, apart from his building experience, were unique and exactly fitted Stevens' needs. Nobody in the West, it was said, could handle as well as he the wild, rollicking Irishmen who made up the railroad construction crews of the time. Moreover, he knew the Indians and their ways and could handle them, too, as will be shown later. He was known as "a rugged man, who reveled in the rough life of railroad camps."[2]

Stevens was impressed. Up to Leavenworth he went for a long talk with the man who was so much like himself. That visit was epochal in the annals of the Katy. It marked the end of an era of frustration and the beginning of a remarkable railroad drive that captured the imagination of the country at a time when many railroads were commonly performing feats of construction that today seem almost incredible. General Manager Stevens laid all his cards on the table that day, and big John Scullin liked what he saw. The very thought of a hundred-mile railroad building race to the Indian Territory line, with more than three million acres of wonderfully fertile Indian lands as the stake, made his eyes sparkle. And Judge Parsons' vision of a frontier railroad system stretching from Chicago, Kansas City, and St. Louis to the very waters of the Gulf, and probably to old Mexico, intrigued him almost as much as the leprechauns of his ancestral bogs. When the colonel, attempting the tracklayers' brogue, said with a twinkle, "this, me buoy, isn't a private foight, anybody kin get in it," Scullin grinned back and the deal was made. The contract they drew up that day provided, among other things, that "Graders will keep out of the way of the tracklayers, who must lay at least a mile of track per day." Incidentally, Scullin's crews were laying more than two miles of railroad each day when they "were coming down the home stretch." But we are getting ahead of the story. It is enough to say now that Stevens and Scullin went down to Emporia together and began the historic race for the border.

Although nothing could be proved against Bob Stevens that February of 1870, it was being whispered around that the wily Colonel

2 *Dictionary of American Biography*, Vol. XVI, p. 527.

Judge Levi Parsons of New York, chief executive of
the Missouri, Kansas & Texas Railway during its construction

John Scullin, "the great American tracklayer," in his
later years—the founder and president of the Scullin
Steel Company, St. Louis

was secretly directing the activities of the Cherokee Neutral Lands settlers' league in their fight to prevent Joy's line going through. The suddenly renewed raids on the Border Tier railhead, the frequent burnings of ties and trestles, the constant tearing up of rail by well organized and armed bands, all pointed to a new and determined leadership. Certainly it was more than coincidence that the severe setback given to Joy at this time by the renewal of squatter warfare put John Scullin's construction gangs back in the race, gave them the opportunity to come abreast of their competitors.

Reports had it that Bob Greenwell, lank and swarthy ex-guerrilla, ex-border fighter, ex-squawman, and one of the most mysterious figures on the border, was on Colonel Stevens' payroll. Signs pointed that way. He could always be found these days, either circulating quietly around Joy's construction camps or furtively visiting the squatter groups. Greenwell, it was rumored, was whispering threats of the settlers' vengeance among Joy's men, spreading terror and disaffection among the crews and causing wholesale desertions. On the other hand, he was said to be secretly financing and arming the squatters, and assuring them that if they kept up the good fight, redoubled their efforts to sabotage the Border Tier, Joy's land purchase would soon be abrogated.

Bearing out the rumors, many years later the following story was told by Greenwell of his activities during the Spring of 1870:

> Chief Engineer Octave Chanute of the Border Tier Road was out looking for markers designating the border line between Kansas and the Indian Territory. As he and his party were scouting around the southern edge of Cherokee County, who should appear but a band of Quapaws, including their chief. Following tribal custom, the chief was the spokesman, although he did not deign to speak English. Through an interpreter the engineer made known the object of his search, and the obliging chief took the party a short distance and showed them a pile of stones that marked the line. Chanute was pleased; reaching that point first would be easy; he could lay off most of the construction gangs, save money, and still come in ahead, just coasting! Fortunately no one in the engineer's party recognized in the Quapaw chief the person of Bob Greenwell, who had shed his white man's attire for the robes of his adopted tribe.
>
> Shortly thereafter Bob Greenwell was hiring many of Joy's

Katy Special Agent Bob Greenwell,
in the guise of a Quapaw chief, meeting the engineers
of the Border Tier (Frisco) Road

workers, who had been laid off when the need for hurry was not apparent, and sending them over to John Scullin, whose graders were then approaching Ladore.

What had actually happened, Greenwell gleefully related afterwards, was that he had shown Mr. Chanute the old Mc-Coy survey line, established in 1837, which, of course, had been changed by the Kansas-Nebraska Act of 1854 to the 37th parallel. The actual border in 1870 was several miles south of the McCoy line.

W. W. Graves, publisher of the *St. Paul, Kansas* (formerly Osage Mission) *Journal,* and an authority on southern Kansas history, relates this story as having been told him personally by Bob Greenwell, and having known him well, doesn't doubt its authenticity. It is a fact that the survey was corrected, as reported, and that the February, 1870, issue of the *Osage Mission Journal* carried the following item: "Many teams and men passed through Osage Mission on their way from the Border Tier Road to the Valley [Katy] Road near Ladore."

If Levi Parsons had visions of a great railroad which would transform the frontier country into a settlers' paradise practically overnight, he was by no means a daydreamer. Action was the word. In order to devote his entire energies to the project, he had already turned over the presidency of the Land Grant Railway and Trust Company to Francis Skiddy, the suave socialite who was his next in command (the Judge admired and respected Frank's ability to find the capital to underwrite new enterprises)

Immediately after the Emporia meeting, Parsons hurried back to New York. There Skiddy awaited him with news that a Congressional committee had just been appointed to "visit the Cherokee Neutral Lands and investigate the matter of sending troops there," following reports that "the Leaguers have again driven off Joy's engineers, also the hands at work grading on the Border Tier Railroad, and burned their tools." Parsons rubbed his hands in glee. "Good!"

Feeling better, both settled down to work. Skiddy brought out a mass of data concerning railroad land grants, charters, existing short lines, and projected roads in the Missouri territory. Parsons had discussed all this with the board in January. With characteristic impatience the Judge riffled through the assortment of maps and profiles on the desk. Then picking up a charcoal pencil; he walked quickly to a huge map which took up nearly the entire wall of Skiddy's office. With one stroke he drew a straight line. From a point where his railroad was expected to reach the Kansas border the line ran directly northeast to Chicago.

"Look, Frank," he said, his voice rising, "our railroad is surely destined to open up the whole of the Southwest. Not only Kansas, and Missouri, and the Indian Territory, but all Texas! It will bring even the products of Old Mexico and the far West direct to eastern markets. I must have a direct line into Chicago from the Territory, and here's how we'll do it. We'll build along this pencil line, to Sedalia first. There we'll connect with the Missouri Pacific to give us an outlet to St. Louis and the East. After that we'll continue straight northeast. Let's bridge the Missouri River right here, between Boonville and Franklin, and then go through Fayette to Moberly for a connection with the North Missouri Railroad. Later we'll push through to Hannibal and connect with the Toledo, Wabash and Western,[3] then up to Quincy to meet the C.B.&Q. Joy's L.L.&G. and his Border Tier Road, that he's hoping will go through to the Gulf, will be throttled the moment we reach Sedalia."[4]

Parsons' enthusiasm was contagious. Skiddy began digging into the pile of material on his desk for the facts the Judge needed. Here was a complete profile on the projected Tebo and Neosho Railroad, chartered January 16, 1860, to build from Sedalia "in a southerly or southwesterly direction, through Henry County; thence to some point on the State line." Nothing had been done with the charter during the war, but in 1866 the people of Fort Scott and of Sedalia revived it and tried to stimulate interest in building. Here was a valuable franchise, for, although it provided no grant of land other than the right-of-way, it was unusually liberal and flexible in its other provisions. Parsons seized on it immediately. "From Sedalia to a junction point on the Indian border, near Labette, let's say, is about 160 miles. This charter will take us 100 miles to the Missouri state line, and it allows us to extend from Sedalia as far as we want to go."

The Judge leaned back in his chair, patted his forehead carefully with a fine handkerchief, and resumed: "I'll have Bob Stevens get a Kansas charter to build east from Labette to the Missouri State line—we'll call that piece the Labette and Sedalia Railway and Bob can be president 'til he gets it built. Then I want you to go out and

---

[3] Both of these lines are now part of the Wabash system.
[4] Here Parsons was prophetic. Joy was throttled and was never able to build beyond the border. He lost control of both lines during the panic of 1873.

reorganize the Tebo and Neosho; do it personally. We'll start construction at both ends at the same time. In the new charter, by the way, don't forget to provide for our extension in a northeastern direction from Sedalia, by way of Boonville and Moberly, to Hannibal—and, of course, to the railroad bridge at Quincy. We'll take all the joy out of Mr. Joy."

Frank Skiddy nodded assent, and they both smoked in silence for a few moments. But Parsons began to fidget again. "I'm still not satisfied. The Santa Fé's building into Emporia will short haul us on Neosho Valley traffic. Can't we get a line—build it or buy it—that will bring us straight east from Emporia? There's plenty agitation for it out there, so they ought to vote lots of bonds for it."

The Judge rose, strode over to the big map again, and drew a nearly straight line from Emporia to Sedalia. The line touched Ottawa and Paola in Kansas and ran through Harrisonville and Holden in Missouri to a neat junction with the Missouri Pacific and the projected Tebo and Neosho at Sedalia.

Back to his maps and profiles went Skiddy, and in a matter of minutes produced a map of the ambitious but bankrupt St. Louis

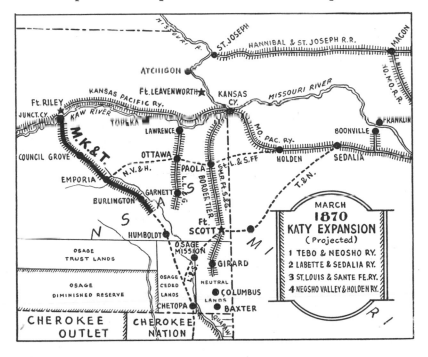

and Santa Fé Railroad, a short line which had attempted to build west from Holden, Missouri, to the Kansas state line. It was agreed to secure that charter and to organize a Kansas company to build from Emporia east to a junction with it at the state line. "We'll call that piece the Neosho Valley and Holden Railway," said Parsons expansively, "and when we get this system into operation there can be no competition."[5]

At that moment Judge Parsons was not a financier, he was an empire builder. He had delegated the sordid business of turning an honest—or reasonably honest—penny to his well-trained Land Grant Railway and Trust Company staff, in whom he had the greatest confidence. Buoyed up with enthusiasm over the splendid vision he was bringing to practicality, with benefit and profit to all, he was eager to return to Kansas, and to the battles he knew were ahead.

It is probably fortunate for all concerned that the Judge's vision didn't extend too far into the future.

[5] From official records, M.K.&T. files. Although no stenographic record was made of the New York conference described here, what transpired can be accurately reconstructed from the minutes of the executive committee and board of directors meetings, and from instructions issued and reports made after the conference. Much of the "conversation" is taken direct from these sources. Elsewhere in this history, it will be noted, similar "reconstructions" of important events in the history of the company have been made. All are factually accurate. See bibliographical essay at the close of text of this volume.

―――――――

SEVEN

Missouri "Lined and Locked"

With the tireless Parsons gone to secure the millions—and tens of millions—that would be required to bring his plans to fruition, Frank Skiddy settled down to study the assignment that was to keep him busy for a long time to come. The Tebo and Neosho Railway project, it soon became evident, was more advanced than at first appeared, although it was still a long way from being a railroad. The company's original charter, already ten years old, authorized it to build from "any point on the Pacific Railroad, between the west bank of the LaMine River and Muddy Creek, in Pettis County . . . to some point on the state line," with power to extend its line northeastwardly without limit.

That first charter is a revelation of the methods and activities of early railroad "projectors." On January 16, 1860, a full year before the Pacific road reached Pettis County, and almost a year before the city of Sedalia came into being, General George R. Smith, founder of Sedalia and one of the West's busiest projectors, persuaded the General Assembly of Missouri to award the Tebo and Neosho nearly every favor he could think of—and some that hadn't previously occurred to him! Land grants and subsidies were out of the question by 1860, of course, for the state's experience with the Pacific line made legislators shy of the voters' wrath in this direction, but they thought nothing of authorizing the company "to extend branch railroads into and through any counties the directors may deem advisable."

On October 16, 1860, General Smith, who was then actively promoting the building of the Pacific Railroad, filed a plat for a townsite on a piece of land which, by coincidence, he happened to own in Pettis County. As a further happy coincidence, Pettis County lay just about half way between Jefferson City and the railroad's proposed western terminus at Kansas City. So the General's townsite was ideally located to become an important division point on the projected route. He named the townsite "Sed-alia" in honor of his daughter "Sed," born Sarah.

With the railroad assured and grading parties already working in the area, town lots went like hot cakes that October, and by the time the railroad arrived in January, 1861, Sedalia was a bustling little community, the pride and joy of its projector. Then was the General's hand fully revealed. Provided the Tebo and Neosho Railway started at Sedalia, its lines could radiate in practically any direction its projectors pleased and still retain all the privileges of the franchise.

But war came in April and put an end to railroad construction there and then. Nevertheless, "it's an ill wind that blaws naebody guid," and new-born Sedalia grew lustily as the Union's southwestern railhead and a key military post. Its only setback during this period was the capture of this strategic outpost on October 15, 1864, by Colonel Jeff. Thompson, whose fifteen hundred half-starved Price Raiders sacked the town, killed a handful of the almost defenseless militia, and immediately departed with everything of value they could carry away.

With the end of the war and completion of the Pacific Railroad into Kansas City in the fall of 1865, the Tebo and Neosho project was revived. By March of the following year, so much enthusiasm had been stirred up along the route of the proposed line that General Smith had little difficulty in reorganizing the company. Thomas L. "Tebo" Wilson of Fort Scott was elected president of the corporation, for he more than any other had pushed the project during its darkest days.[1] By July of 1867, however, Asa C. Marvin, Sedalia's provost marshal during the war, had become board president, and Colonel A. D. Jaynes, the treasurer, was able to report subscriptions totalling $615,000 from the various counties and townships which hoped to be benefited by the coming railroad.

Work was actually begun on the road in July, 1867, at Fort Scott, Kansas. On September 18 "ground was broken" at Sedalia, Missouri,

[1] "Tebo" Wilson and his mule are legendary figures all along the Katy's Sedalia division. Tales of his plodding from hamlet to hamlet, promoting the project, locating the route, selling subscriptions, in fair weather and foul, make high romance today. Colorful and effective he undoubtedly was, for his home county of Henry alone contributed some $400,000 in bonds to help realize his dream.

and it appears that, as each county along the route was prevailed upon to make a substantial subscription, some grading work was done in that area as evidence of the projectors' good intentions. The net result was that, by the time Parsons and Skiddy became interested in the project, something like a hundred miles of line had been graded, in bits and pieces, and work was at a standstill for lack of capital. In short, the Tebo and Neosho road was in a situation similar to that of the Union Pacific Southern Branch prior to the advent of Judge Parsons—and a similar campaign of absorption seemed indicated.

March of 1870 arrived in Sedalia quite in character, bright but blustery. A cold sun sparkled the peculiar, off-center tracks of the Missouri Pacific Railroad[2] as Editor J. West Goodwin, publisher of the *Sedalia Bazoo*,[3] hobbled across them on his way to the Goat House, an odoriferously-named but super-clean inn, towards which most of the town's natives seemed to be drifting.

"What's going on, Captain?" several men asked eagerly as they respectfully made way for the editor of the *Bazoo*.

"That, gentlemen, is what I intend to find out," replied Goodwin as he passed inside and carefully closed the door after him.

Definitely there was something "going on," the editor decided, amused at his own deduction. His reportorial eye quickly picked out, in a far corner of the room, three imposing gentlemen whose attire indicated plainly they were from the East, probably New York. With them, in deep conversation, were Colonel Stevens and Major Otis B. Gunn. And seated at a long bench table at the opposite corner from the strangers, the editor noted an influential group of local "projectors" who already were coming to be looked upon as the City

---

[2] Sedalians were still marvelling over the efficiency of the track-laying crews who several months before had made an overnight change in the Missouri Pacific track gauge from the wide 5 feet, six inches to the new standard of 4 feet, nine inches. This change had become urgently necessary with the opening of the Missouri River railroad bridge at Kansas City on July 3, 1869, which greatly intensified competition between the Missouri Pacific and the Hannibal and St. Jo., by giving the latter a complete monopoly of the rich Texas cattle traffic delivered by the 4 feet, 8½ inch-gauge Kansas Pacific. On Saturday, July 25, 1869, section gangs strung the length of the line, began taking up and relaying one side of the rail, and the entire job was completed in sixteen hours. With through movement of cars then possible, the Missouri Pacific began to participate in the "longhorn haul" from such rowdy frontier shipping points as Abilene, which in 1869 alone shipped fully 150,000 head. J. Thomas Scharf, *History of St. Louis City and County*, Vol. II, pp. 1169–71.

[3] The slogan of this locally famous publication was "He who bloweth not his own Bazoo, the same shall not be blown."

Fathers. Mentally he checked them off: There was General Smith, of course; he was in, on, or behind, everything! And there was Colonel John F. Phillips, Major William Gentry, James A. Tesch, Colonel A. D. Jaynes, Cyrus Newkirk and Major Asa B. Marvin. There, too, was mule-driving Colonel "Tebo" Wilson, up from Fort Scott.

J. West Goodwin, long-time editor of the *Daily Bazoo*,
Sedalia, Missouri

As Goodwin made his painful way towards them, Colonel Stevens got up, came forward with outstretched hand.

"Hello, Captain Goodwin. How are you?" he asked. "I'm Bob Stevens of the M.K.&T. Remember me?"

"Indeed I do, Colonel," said Goodwin warmly. "You know how I've been following your railroad activities in Kansas. When you reach the territory line you'll need a Missouri connection. So—when are you going to start building into Sedalia?"

"Not so fast, Captain," said Stevens, grinning wryly. "Let me introduce a couple of people who might be able to tell you more about that than I can."

Stevens took Editor Goodwin by the arm, turned to his table companions and said, "Gentlemen, allow me to present Captain J.

West Goodwin, editor and owner of the Sedalia *Bazoo*—which blows a big horn in these parts."

Then slyly to the editor, "This is Frank Skiddy, who recently succeeded Levi Parsons as president of the Land Grant Railway and Trust Company of New York, and George C. Clark, secretary of the company. You know Major Gunn, of course, but you don't know George Denison, our new vice president and the man who is going to turn the land I build the railroad through into a land of opportunity for the millions that will follow us."

The group laughed lightly, but not Goodwin. Gravely he acknowledged the introductions, then turning to Skiddy he said dryly: "Quite a coincidence that the Tebo and Neosho Railway corporators are all in town today. Perhaps you'll have an opportunity to see them before you go?"

Skiddy laughed outright. "In about ten minutes, Captain. I hope you'll stick around to get the story."

Frank Skiddy's meeting with the perplexed directors of the Tebo and Neosho Railway that blustery March afternoon was essentially a repetition of Levi Parsons' session with the "corporators" of the Union Pacific Railway Southern Branch, back in October of '68. In return for an all-inclusive promise "to build your railroad," he demanded and received authority to name the president and the secretary of the company. Promptly he nominated George C. Clark for secretary and himself for the presidency. And that was that.

George Denison rose.

"We shall open up the whole Southwest," he told the startled group, which had had no previous inkling of the extent of Levi Parsons' plans. He then went on to outline the race for the Indian Territory, for enormous land grants, for the honor and glory and the material advantages that would accrue to the first railroad that reached Texas from the north—with the devil taking the hindmost.

As Bob Stevens and Chief Engineer Gunn unrolled and tacked up a huge map of the southwestern United States, Denison warmed to his subject.

They would start, he said, with two divisions, indicating with a ruler two converging red lines on the map. The first was the Neosho division, starting from Junction City hard by Fort Riley on the line of the Kansas Pacific and running down the Neosho Valley southeasterly. Colonel Stevens' gangs, he knew, were south of Burlington already and driving hard for the border.

The second was to be the Sedalia division. For it, Stevens and

Major Gunn had just completed a survey of the Tebo and Neosho route between the Kansas border and Sedalia. The line, Denison told the group, was well located for the purposes he had in mind. He proposed to rush construction and link this new line with the first, or Neosho, division as soon as the race to the Indian territory had been won.

Captain Goodwin, who meantime had been keeping notes of the meeting, in anticipation of a news story for the *Bazoo*, asked Frank Skiddy, "Just when and where do you expect to get construction started on this Sedalia division?"

Skiddy looked inquiringly at Stevens.

"I'll win that race to the territory line in ninety days," Stevens said confidently. "Then I intend to shift all the extra gangs over here and start construction at several places at once—here at Sedalia, and at Clinton and Fort Scott, and southwest through Kansas to a junction with the Neosho division. You'll get your railroad in a hurry."

Again Denison took up the ruler.

"We have completed a preliminary survey down through the Indian Territory, gentlemen, right to the Red River and the Texas line. Congress will go along with us—and best of all, we have contracts with all five of the Civilized Tribes for our passage through the nations. We have a lot of good Indians on our side."

Denison rubbed his hands together, a habit of his when excited, and looked at his colleagues for confirmation.

"Yes," said Stevens slowly, "Colonel Elias Boudinot has been our very good friend and has brought his great influence to bear on his people."

Major Asa C. Marvin, one of the shrewdest of the Sedalia corporators, said curiously, "We all know Boudinot is a man of some standing with his own people, but is the general opinion among the tribes favorable to the railroad?"

"Well, sir," cut in Skiddy, "we've got the Indians on the dotted line and that should be sufficient. What we're after now is to win the race—to get the right-of-way and land grant so we can channel trade and people in and out of Texas. The state legislature down there is ready to pass its own land grant to the first road which bridges Indian Territory and shoots its tracks down to Austin and then to the Rio Grande."[4]

As the meeting broke up to await further action by its new president, Editor Goodwin looked at Frank Skiddy with a new interest.

[4] From company records of the meeting. See Bibliography.

44

Here was the prospect of an era of colonization, of development, that challenged the imagination.

Skiddy took Goodwin by the arm and, as they left the room together, declared vehemently, "We'll open up a country which will be able to sustain a population almost equal to that of France. What do you think of that, Captain Goodwin?"

"A pretty broad statement," replied the editor, "but it is entirely possible, although we have passed our first youth, that we will both live to see a quarter of a population such as France boasts happily settled around your railroad."[5]

West Goodwin, his imagination fired by the picture of southwestern development drawn for him by Levi Parsons' eloquent emissaries, retired to his little cubbyhole of an office in a corner of the Sedalia *Bazoo's* printshop, wrote powerful editorials on the plans and ambitions of what the tracklayers of the new road were already calling, "The Katy." The effect was almost immediate. Eastern writers began to show renewed interest in the undeveloped Southwest. Glowing stories of the opportunities available in the southwestern section of the United States soon began appearing, in good and poor translations, in most of the press of European countries, and were pasted up in the steamship and sailing offices of the great transatlantic lines. Many a prosperous Texan, Oklahoman, Missourian, or Kansan has J. West Goodwin to thank for having made up his ancestor's mind to come to the great Southwest.

[5] Editor Goodwin lived to see it. In his later years he frequently recounted with relish the story of the Katy's beginnings.

EIGHT

The Race to the Indian Territory

The town which later was to achieve fame as the home of Editor William Allen White, the "Sage of Emporia," was scarcely recognizable to Stevens and his party when they pulled up before the offices of Ruggles and Plumb that March morning of 1870 following the Sedalia coup. The recent advent of the Iron Horse, a diamond-stacked locomotive,[1] "entirely new and built expressly for this road, with its splendid passenger car, the work of the Cummins Car Company of Jersey City," already had jolted the town into a frenzy of speculative growth.

Emporia town lots, homesteads, promising farm lands, and feeder lots adjacent to the heaven-sent railroad, were changing hands so fast at skyrocketing prices that the land office clerks couldn't keep up with the business. "Town lots that had gone begging at $500 were grabbed up at $1,000 each," and everybody was intoxicated as much with the town's magnificent prospects as with the "tangle-leg" that railroad money put easily within every new arrival's reach.

Already the entire frontier was asking what manner of man was this Stevens who was being hailed as the "Railroad King of Kansas." This much they quickly learned: He was born in Attica, New York, on March 27, 1824, the son of Assemblyman Alden S. and Achsa F. (Smith) Stevens, early settlers in the Tonawanda Valley. He was admitted to the bar in 1856, a fateful presidential year.

As was proper in the offspring of a deep-dyed Democrat who for years had successfully battled the majority in a rabidly Republican district, young Stevens had immediately followed his father on the hustings. Blessed with youthful verve, more than his share of per-

---

[1] The locomotive was a gaudy, high-wheeled Grant 4-4-0. It had 12-inch cylinders with a 22-inch stroke and had "ample strength to pull three to five cars."

sonality and patrician looks, plus a silvery tongue, he accomplished wonders for Buchanan and the Party—and won powerful friends. It was then he had met Wilson Shannon, recently ousted governor of Kansas Territory, whose hair-raising tales of the siege of Lawrence by Missouri border ruffians that summer, and of the territory's legal and illegal governments and legislatures, so appealed to his spirit of adventure that before the end of the year he had wound up his eastern affairs and was off for the frontier.

The crude, hand-painted shingle outside the clapboard shack that passed for his office in Lecompton, then capital of the Kansas Territory, had not been up three months when, in February, 1857, Stevens took it down and changed it to read: STEVENS & SHANNON, ATTORNEYS & COUNSELLORS AT LAW. REAL ESTATE AGENTS. Former Governor Shannon, it would seem, had left some unfinished business in Kansas and thought Bob Stevens might be the man to wind it up successfully.

Here Stevens really began to find himself. Self-described as a "resolute upholder and defender of the free-state theory," the versatile Bob somehow was able to remain alive and prosper in the midst of fratricidal war. By May, 1857, in fact, he was so trusted by all factions that the secretary of the interior appointed him special U. S. Indian commissioner to arrange the sales of vast tracts of Indian lands, an almost incredible appointment by a proslavery national administration. The Piankeshaws, Peorias, Kaskaskias, and Weas, those small Indian tribes whose domains were among the first to be engulfed by the onrush of "squatters," have Bob Stevens to thank for their successful, if penurious, relocation in the Indian Territory. At this time Stevens was displaying extraordinary resiliency of mind and political sagacity of a high order, as is evidenced by the fact that he served a term as mayor of Lecompton, the proslavery capital of Kansas Territory, and after statehood won election to the Kansas senate.[2]

Perhaps the most dramatic episode in Colonel Stevens' long career occurred in Lawrence on August 21, 1863. Before dawn that morning Quantrell's raiders came roaring into the still sleeping community. They sacked the town, slew indiscriminately, and put everything to the torch. The story of the attack and his reactions to it are best told in the Colonel's own words:

[2] Stevens family genealogical manuscript, unpublished.

Lawrence Kansas
August 23, 1863

Dear Friends:

This is the first moment that I could snatch from other duties in which to write. Of course you have heard by telegraph of our terrible calamity; but O God! no telegraph, no pen, no language, can fitly describe the awful scene. It was not a fight, not a murder, but the most terrible, cold-blooded, fiendish massacre ever heard of in this country, or any other where civilized people pretend to live.

Already we have the names of 123 killed, and more missing; over 100 were buried yesterday; the graveyard was the most busy place; many men were at work; long trenches were dug, two sets working, one digging, the other following and covering coffins. I can not yet give particulars, but will be brief. I arrived here on Thursday at night; retiring quietly. On Friday morning at daylight was awakened by firing and shouting; jumped to the window and saw a body of men riding in on Masse. Street, just opposite Frye's old livery stable, shouting: 'Kill every damned man!' In front of the building just south of Bank, the two Range boys, and two other Germans, lay asleep on the plank walk, under an awning. The horsemen rode up to them and shot all four dead; then fired the building. (The poor fellows I afterward found lay until ten o'clock and roasted to a crisp.)

I pulled on pants, shoes and coat (the only articles I saved) looked at watch; it was 15 minutes after five. The night watch then sounded the gong all over the house, while I went about and saw that all were up. A guard had been stationed at every door; two who tried to escape were killed. Soon four bandits came up and demanded watches, money, etc., which were generally given up; but mine I had handed to Mrs. Bancroft; so I had none to give; she was not asked. We all then went down to the first floor above the office, while trunks, etc., were rifled. Soon everything around was in flames; before long, Prentiss' drug store, right under us (some 65 in all, of us), was on fire.

For the first time, the thought flashed upon me, that we were to be burned in the hotel. At once I appealed to one of the guards (an old man whom I had 'made out'), and induced him to send for Quantrell, who soon came. I took him by the hand, led him aside, and finally got from him a promise of protection for the whole crowd.

We then moved out, and as we went downstairs, the chemicals in the drug store began to explode; marched down east to an open space on the grass, where drunken soldiers came up and began shooting at us. Again I sent for Quantrell, who took us to the Whitney House, and staid with us all the time. I was spokesman and surgeon, dressing the wounds of three men; was in the street, making acquaintances in the gang, one of whom was from Rochester. Quantrell staid till nearly ten, leaving with his column 450 strong.

In about ten minutes, four of his gang came back (stragglers), two of them drunk, swearing they would kill young Stone, Lydia Stone and Stevens. They did kill the old man Stone, and shot two others. None of the rest were hurt; young Stone and I jumped out of the window and got under the bank of the river. At eleven, all had gone, and we sallied out.

Such a sight! Scorched and burned bodies in the streets everywhere. We worked till night; then I went to Leavenworth in the night; got me some clothes, and bought a large lot of provisions, etc., for which the people of Leavenworth paid; loaded three two-horse wagons and six Government six-mule wagons, and got back here at 12 last night. This morning the provisions came. Shall remain here a while, to do all in my power to alleviate the sufferings and distress of the many who mourn.

Don't worry for me. God has saved me for minni. pui pupu und will protect me still.

ROBERT S. STEVENS

The Katy General Manager mused over the past as he waited for his chief engineer, Major Gunn, and construction boss, John Scullin, to unroll their maps and profiles and show what progress the railroad was making, or, more particularly, to show him the troubles they were having and the difficulties that confronted them. Scullin, the temperamental, table-pounding Irishman, did most of the talking. "Colonel, ye'll not find the likes of my boys between here and Donegal [he really meant Donnybrook]. They're strung out all the way between Burlington and the 'Strip,' but the half of them are loafing—and getting into all kinds of mischief—all for the want of materials and supplies. We need pilin's, masonry, iron, ties, rails, spikes—we're short of everything."

"That's right," added Gunn thoughtfully, "we are being held up at every river crossing for the lack of iron and timbers."[3]

"John," said Stevens slowly, "I want nothing, you hear, nothing to prevent the railroad from going forward. We can't wait for the work train to haul everything. Hire all the teams you need, all the men you want; buy anything you want, right on the spot. If you can't buy it, take it. Get the stuff ahead of the work crews. Tread on the heels of Gunn's locating parties with your iron, and your masonry and your timbers. For the next ninety days expense is no object."

After a long moment he said slowly: "We're still ninety miles from the border. I have given my word to President Parsons that I will cross into the Indian Territory in ninety days—and that's according to the terms of our contract, Scullin, isn't it?"

"Right, Colonel," agreed John Scullin.

The hint of frustration which had seemed to hover about the meeting lifted at once when Scullin added, "Get me the iron and the big stuff on time and I'll put your railroad down, if I have to lay it flat on the prairie. We'll go on extra shifts right away, with double gangs on the rough spots. With a free hand, now, I'll drive the men on, rain or shine, drunk or sober, so long as the material keeps coming. You'll get your mile a day and more—much more."[4]

March is a poor month for railroad building in southeastern Kansas, Colonel Stevens was ruefully forced to admit as he and Gunn and Scullin rode through the sloughs, ferried swollen creeks, and stumbled over location stakes as they inspected the route south to the border. High water was interfering with work on the nearly completed bridge over Big Turkey Creek, about ten miles south of Burlington, but grading was done as far as Neosho Falls, and the scrapers and haulers were moving away from the Neosho and into the long straight stretch to Humboldt. Poor, twice-tried Humboldt, chief sufferer of the wars, was soon to get its railroad, soon to forget its miseries in celebrating the arrival of the locomotive. In Humboldt, Stevens read reports of the arrival of the Leavenworth, Lawrence & Galveston Road in Garnett March 3, and saw Joy's location stakes crossing his own just west of town. It was galling to hear and to see, and the Colonel pushed hurriedly on.

[3] First bridges on the Katy's Neosho division, erected by L. T. Boomer, Chicago, were of Post's patent diagonal truss construction. This was one of the most useful styles of bridges ever devised for use in a new country. Constructed wholly of timber except for the tie rods, certain joint castings, etc., they could be built on the ground very cheaply by squads of bridge carpenters.

[4] Paraphrased from miscellaneous reports.

Entering the Osage lands, which began just south of Humboldt, the whole party sensed the change from comparative civilization to wilderness the moment they crossed the Indian line. Humboldt was the last stop. From here on settlements would be negligible and comforts few. From here on the railroad would create its own brand of civilization, build a settlement at the end of every ten-mile section, deposit the immigrants around these nuclei, and develop the country as it slowly snaked its way south. Stevens visioned the cities rising in his footsteps as he plodded doggedly through the rains.

To Ladore, an insignificant settlement at the crossing of Labette Creek, near the southern border of Neosho County, the General Manager paid particular attention. This was the site of the once famous Fort Roach, and here, all Kansas was sure, would be the junction point for the railroad's projected Sedalia–St. Louis division. Scullin and Gunn looked at him curiously, trying to divine his thoughts, but with an inscrutable smile Stevens motioned the party on.

Half a dozen miles south of Ladore, on the fertile delta-like plain that lay like a lazy wye between Labette and Little Labette creeks, he paused to look over the fair expanse of prairie. As the engineering crew plodded slowly on he motioned to Gunn and Scullin, wheeled and struck out over the prairie for a short distance. Then turning to his colleagues, he said abruptly, "Gentlemen, unless you know of some good reason to persuade me to the contrary, here on this spot I propose to place the junction of our Neosho and Sedalia divisions. Here we will build a city that will become the metropolis of this whole section of the country." With that he slowly turned and began to follow the main body of the party, now pretty far ahead.

When they had caught up with crew the Colonel said dryly, "Well, gentlemen, what do you think of the location?"

Gunn answered first. "It's ideal from an engineering viewpoint—as you know perfectly well. And there isn't a squatter within miles. We can plat the entire township and nobody the wiser."

"Mum's the word about this, of course," said Stevens unnecessarily. "Mr. Parsons chose this location personally, and I merely wanted to verify it. As soon as you can get the plats ready I'll file 'em."[5]

The City of Parsons, Kansas, home of the late and much beloved Senator Clyde Reed, had its conception that day.

---

[5] Paraphrased from official reports.

March 25, 1870, found Bob Stevens in New York. Levi Parsons needed only the approval of the board of directors to proceed with his empire building, and was careful to have the colorful Colonel on hand, not so much to have his vote as to fill the group with enthusiasm for the progress of the railroad and its rosy prospects.

The meeting was eminently successful from the would-be empire builder's point of view. J. B. Dickinson, the nominal president of the line who had never actually assumed office, declined the post of honor, pleading pressure of other duties ("Gold, Stocks, and Bonds Sold Strictly on Commission"), and Levi Parsons was formally made president in title as well as in fact. Moreover, all of his proposals were approved: the Tebo and Neosho Railway, the Labette and Sedalia, the St. Louis and Santa Fé, the Neosho Valley and Holden, all were his for the asking—and he left the meeting that day with "blanket authority to proceed with the plans." President Parsons then urged Stevens to get back to Kansas as quickly as possible: "We've a big job to do, Bob," he said expansively, "and there's only a couple of months to do it in. Think we can beat our friend Joy?"

Watching the Colonel's troubled face, Parsons, suddenly anxious, asked, "What's the matter, Bob? We've got the money; you've got the men and materials, haven't you? And you tell me you have the rail on the levee at St. Louis. Dammit, man, the weather will hold up Joy as much as it will you!"

Seemingly hunting for words, Stevens hesitated. Then—.

"Here's the trouble, chief. At the moment, Joy is working through better terrain than I am. Two months from now the situation will be reversed. I have my big bridges to build right now—the sloughs are full, rivers out of their banks. On the other hand, Joy has got pretty good going through his Neutral Lands, and if he keeps on down the center of his purchase and makes for Baxter Springs he'll beat us to the border easily. However . . ."

Parsons broke in. "But that's on the line of the Quapaw Reservation! You assured me Joy can't get right-of-way through their lands, and the Congressional grant restricts entry to the Indian Territory to a point in the Neosho Valley, so why worry if the damn fool hits the Quapaw line?"

"You didn't let me finish, Mr. Parsons," Stevens explained. "When the Border Tier Road reaches Columbus, a dozen miles north of Baxter, we all expect it to deflect to the right down the level valley of Fly Creek and strike the Cherokee line at Chetopa, where we're headed. He'll meet his bridges there, but the weather will be better then."

The Race to the Indian Territory

Parsons stroked the heavy black beard that was his most distinguishing characteristic. After a long pause: "I'm beginning to see your problem," he said, in a tone that matched the Colonel's expression. "You are in poor terrain now, when the weather is bad. You'll have easier going later, when the weather should be good. The Border Road is having an easy time now and will have the heavy going later, aided by better weather—that, of course, if they locate the route down Fly Creek to Chetopa."

"That's it exactly," said Stevens. "So now I have some friends—some powerful friends, I might say—who right now are proving to Joy and his colleagues that the Quapaw Reservation is in the Cherokee Nation, which of course it is, and assuring them that they'll be able to build on through—which they won't.[6] Mr. Joy should be easy to convince; he owns the Neutral Lands, and a line straight south to Baxter will kite the price of every inch of it!"

Parsons laughed uproariously. "Then why are you worrying, Bob? Your strategy is perfect. You'll win the race to the territory line hands down. Go to it—and good luck to you!"[7]

Stevens felt better as he hurried back to Kansas.

The Colonel's forecast was correct. S. W. Lee, principal assistant engineer on construction, and Irish John Scullin, the heavy-fisted boss of the track-laying gangs, were driving the line relentlessly south. They had passed LeRoy and reached Neosho Falls, home town of Colonel Goss of the Sixteenth Kansas Regiment, on March 10, and had shoveled their way over the sodden prairie in time to enter Humboldt with the construction train on the last day of the month.

By April 14 "the end of track" was perched precariously over Village Creek, ten miles south of Humboldt in the Osage Ceded Lands, where the unpredictable stream empties into the Neosho. The delirious citizens of Humboldt were making great preparations to celebrate the coming of the railroad, which they did on April 20, and the Colonel was finding each trip along the route something of a triumphal tour.

But that the battle had hardly begun, Stevens knew full well. His letters home at this time were charged with misgivings and reveal the strain of the race:

"I only wish you were with me," he wrote his wife, Mary. "Life is stirring, but very lonely, and whether you believe it or not, I so long

[6] The powerful friend was Senator S. C. Pomeroy.
[7] Conversation taken from Stevens' notes, M.K.&T. Archives, St. Louis.

for home and society of its loved ones. Tell Freddie I have a nice, new car all for my own use, fitted up nicely with beds, writing desk, kitchen, water closets, wash room &c. He must come out and have a ride in it. Possibly he might get a chance to sell papers &c on train . . ."

But sentiment had little place in the Colonel's life during these hectic days; there was no time for it. The board of directors had met in Junction City on April 15, and he had been required to provide detailed plans for the organization and building of the additional roads President Parsons required for his projected empire. On April 30, charters were filed for the Labette and Sedalia Railway, Robert S. Stevens, president; and for the Neosho Valley and Holden Railway, Robert S. Stevens, president. On May 7 both lines were merged with the parent Katy, and Chief Engineer Gunn and Surveyor George Walker were out in the field driving location stakes.

During this period the track-laying and bridge-building gangs were doing magnificent work in the face of atrocious weather. On April 14, for example, they were easing the construction train over the half-built, 130-foot truss that spanned Village Creek, 130 miles away from the starting point at Junction City which they had left a scant seven months before. Here was to rise the first of many permanent settlements that were to be created as the railroad split the wilderness. Incidentally, the town's "corporators" named the hamlet New Chicago, probably by way of forecasting its future, but today it is known as Chanute.[8]

By April 29, just two weeks after leaving the paper township of New Chicago, the end of track was at milepost 140, now Urbana. These extraordinary railroad builders had not only crossed Village Creek, they had thrown the iron across Big Turkey Creek, 160-feet, and Elk Creek, 130-feet, and had advanced the "end of track" eleven miles in just thirteen rain-soaked working days.

On May 10, 1870, the track reached Fort Roach, beginning to be known as Ladore, 150 miles from Junction City. This was the log-cabin, board-shanty, tent town that aspired to be the division point

[8] When Joy's Leavenworth, Lawrence and Galveston Railroad, now the Santa Fé, finally reached New Chicago, its builders declined to make the crossing at the Katy's thriving townsite, which by July, 1870, "boasted one hundred houses." Coming in at a long angle they by-passed the hamlet and made the crossing a mile away, where they established the townsite of Tioga. The two villages fought "until there was nothing left to quarrel about" and on January 1, 1873, united to form the town of Chanute. See Beadle, *The Undeveloped West*, 782.

for the Katy's projected Sedalia division. Here sprang up the kind of terminus town that plagued the Union Pacific throughout its building; the first of many created by the railroad as it labored south through the "Territory."

Immigrants, honest settlers, squatters, promoters, adventurers, all accompanied by the lowest riffraff of the frontier, were flooding into southern Kansas in the wake of the railroad. The removal of the Indians to new homes south of the Kansas line appeared imminent, and with most of the tribes out on the Spring buffalo hunt, squatters were swarming over the reservations in droves, pre-empting the best sections without a shadow of legal right. The Indians, and indeed the Indian agents with all the prestige and authority of the federal government, were powerless to prevent the influx of the hungry landseekers.

The day the track reached Ladore was probably one of the wildest in the history of the West. A report by L. A. Bowes, track foreman for John Scullin, portrays graphically the conditions under which pioneer railroads were pushed through to completion:

> Ladore was the toughest place I ever struck. Whiskey was sold in nearly every house in the town. Vice and immorality flourished like a green bay tree. At noon (May 10, 1870) seven hard-looking characters came into town. They commenced to fill up on Tangleleg. That evening about dusk they began operations by knocking men down and robbing them. As they were heavily armed, they soon had full possession of the town and had everything their own way during the night.
>
> An old man by the name of Roach kept a boarding house about a quarter of a mile south of town, close to the railroad. Twenty-five of our workmen were boarding with him. The house was a double log pen, with a stairway running up between, and the men slept upstairs. About seven o'clock that night the seven desperadoes went down to the Roach house, placed two men upstairs, while the other five took possession of the lower part of the house and captured the inmates.
>
> Roach and his two daughters and a hired girl were downstairs. They beat Roach over the head with their revolvers until they thought he was dead. They would have killed him but he played dead. They captured the three girls, carried them outside and kept them out all night. During the night they quarreled over them and the leader of the gang shot one

of his own men. The ball struck the man in the centre of the forehead and he fell dead on his face.

The man who shot him walked up to him, rolled him over on his back, and remarked: "What a fine shot that was!"

Along towards morning the citizens began to organize for the capture of those devils. We caught two of them before daylight in a drunken sleep in one of the saloons. We captured one in the timber with one of the girls shortly after daylight. The leader of the gang and two others had left for parts unknown. We started men out on every road in every direction, and captured them on the road to the Osage Mission.

We locked the men up in a log barber shop, put a guard over them, took them out one by one, led them down past the Roach house, had them identified by the girls, swung them up on a large projecting limb of a hackberry tree. By eleven o'clock five men hung lifeless on that one limb.[9]

Ladore, Kansas, May 11, 1870

One of the "leading men of the place" who accompanied track foreman Bowes was Jim Abell, who ran the Inn where the two desperadoes were captured. Shortly after midnight of that murderous Tuesday, while Abell was out rounding up a posse, the two men who were later found there broke into the Inn in search of more "tarantula juice." As the door began to give way, Abell's wife hurried her two young daughters, Elizabeth and Matilda, up a

[9] *Osage Mission Journal*, May 11, 1870. *Topeka Mail & Breeze*, September, 1902.

ladder into an unfinished attic. There was no trap door of any kind to bar entry, just a gaping hole in the floor, yet that pioneer woman who had come all the way from central Illinois to southern Kansas in a prairie schooner, successfully fended off her attackers. She wielded an axe to such purpose that the men got tired of the sport, gave their full attention to the "likker," and drank themselves into a stupor. Foreman Bowes and his posse took it from there.[10]

The days that succeeded the road's arrival at Ladore were both hell and high water for Bob Stevens. Scullin's Irish brigade just couldn't make its promised mile a day—and no wonder. It rained incessantly. The rivers were out of their banks and much of the bottom land inundated. Although the high trestle at New Chicago (Chanute) was nearly in, Boomer's men were still working on the 160-foot truss span over the Big Turkey. Worse still, the 130-foot bridge over Elk Creek was still perched precariously on falsework over the swollen stream and the big 160-foot double span which crossed the Labette at Ladore still rested on bents, the masonry not yet in for the 30-foot high piers.

Defeat hung its gloomy pall over the General Manager's office in Junction on that soggy Saturday morning of May 14. Unseeingly, Stevens passed through the outer office into his sanctum, but he came to with a start as his eye took in the delegation that sat around his desk apparently just waiting to pounce on him.

Chief Engineer Otis Gunn and construction boss John Scullin were there to report their progress, or lack of it, it could be assumed. But what was signified by the presence of Stevens' two Cherokee friends, General Stand Watie and Colonel Elias C. Boudinot? This part of the visitation must have something to do, apparently, with Bob Greenwell's undercover activities, for that elusive individual, one could have noted, was making himself as inconspicuous as possible behind the stately Indian chiefs.

Stevens expressed a pleasant "good morning" and asked what he could do for those present this fine spring day.

The General Manager held up a hand warningly as everyone started to talk at once. Turning to his Cherokee visitors he inquired about their mission.

[10] One shudders to think what might have been the outcome had Mrs. Abell been less resolute. Matilda grew up, a devout Catholic, to be married at the old Osage Mission. Her son, S. Adrian Hayden, General Purchasing Agent, Katy Lines, St. Louis, is authority for this story of his progenitor's maternal courage.

Colonel Boudinot, the able politician of the Cherokees and Stand Watie's chief interpreter and supporter, did the talking.[11]

"Bob," he said without preliminaries, "Joy has crossed the line!"

"The hell he has!" shouted Stevens. "When did that happen?"

"Just a few hours ago, I'd say," replied Boudinot.

Boudinot then went on to explain just what had happened.

On May 4 the Border Tier Road had reached Baxter Springs with its construction track, he said. Baxter, as many knew, considered itself on the Territory line, though it was not. So Boudinot, Stand Watie, and Greenwell had taken advantage of the ignorance of the Border Tier people. They had prompted Greenwell to promote a big celebration at Baxter Springs on May 12 to signal the supposed winning of the race to the Territory line. Boudinot and Greenwell, flush with Katy funds, provided the wherewithal for a wild orgy, and wild it was. The Honorable I. S. Kalloch was orator of the day and General Manager Joy and other officials of the M.R.Ft.S.&G. beamed happily on their delirious workers. As the day wore on, and the refreshments began to take effect, the cow town blew the lid right off, and in the blow Joy's railroad crews were scattered like straws before a Kansas cyclone. With them went Joy's hopes of reaching the line first, but he didn't know it then.

Apparently blinded by his eagerness to improve the value of his wholly owned Neutral Lands of nearly a million acres, and incredibly misinformed by his own agents, Joy had allowed himself to be hoodwinked into disaster like the veriest greenhorn.[12] These were the

[11] By the Spring of 1870 Cherokee lawyer Boudinot was hand in glove with Levi Parsons and Bob Stevens and with their aid was quietly promoting the interests of Stand Watie's Treaty Party at the expense of the other two factions in the Nation. Boudinot was then living on Russell Creek, just across the Territory line from Chetopa, and engaging in many activities designed to bring him good profits from the private use of tribal lands.

Colonel Horner of the *Southern Kansas Advance* took note of him in an item in his March 2, 1870, issue, which reported: "A company of Cherokee gentlemen intend to have a corral fenced in of about five miles square, or 16,000 acres, across the line from Chetopa. They expect this to be the great shipping centre and shipping point of the Texas and Indian cattle trade, and are preparing to receive stock, either for the purpose of recruiting and fattening up, wintering or holding till the drivers have time to sell and ship east. This enterprise will be a good thing for the dealers, the railroads, for the company having it in charge, and for Chetopa."

[12] On May 21, 1870, J. D. Cox, secretary of the interior, reported to President Grant that "Mr. Joy, one of the principal stockholders and directors of the Kansas & Neosho Valley Railroad Company [whose name had recently been changed to Missouri River, Fort Scott & Gulf and was commonly known as the Border Tier Road] in the year following the passage of the acts and the ratifica-

vital facts he overlooked in his race to the territory line: first, the
line was several miles south of Baxter; second, beyond Baxter lay
the reservations not of the Cherokees but of the Quapaws, the Peorias,
Ottawas, Shawnees, and other small tribes, where no right of entry
existed, and, third, the nearest legal point of crossing (which according to the Land Grant Act was "in the Valley of the Neosho")
was still some seventeen miles away to the west.

As Boudinot's story made clear the dilemma, not of the Katy, but
of the Border Tier, Stevens' anxiety slowly cleared and by the time
it ended he was wreathed in smiles. But Boudinot had to tell all while
he was at it. The Katy was not yet out of danger in the race for the
border. There was action needed at the end of track, he told Stevens.

Quickly the General Manager turned to Gunn and Scullin. In a
moment they, too, were going through hell and high water, explaining furiously why the railhead still was nearly thirty miles from the
territory line.

Boudinot let the inquisition run on for a few minutes, then broke
in to offer the counsel of Stand Watie, Greenwell, and himself: to
force the Katy gangs to go harder and faster than ever. Better still,
buy up Joy's men, whether they were needed or not, and then get
Levi Parsons to file the Katy claim the moment the rail head had
hit the Territory line.

He hesitated briefly, then looked at Gunn and Scullin. It would
take Joy a week or more to get his construction gangs and bridge
builders together again, Greenwell had assured him.[13] However, he

tion of the treaties which have been mentioned, procured the possession by
purchase of the land in part in Southeastern Kansas immediately north of the
boundary of the Indian Territory, known as 'the Cherokee Neutral Lands,' and
that soon after his purchase the line of said railway company was located due
north and south through the greater part of said Cherokee lands, and nearly,
if not exactly, upon the line dividing the land so purchased into two equal eastern and western parts; that the construction of the road upon this line, which I
believe to have been made for the purpose of giving, as nearly as possible,
equally increased values to the lands so purchased, in all their parts, has taken
this road off the line necessary to intersect the Indian boundary-line at the
Neosho River, or near the same; and that the road has, in fact, been constructed
to a point on the Indian boundary-line, about ten or more miles east of said
Neosho River, touching the reservation of the Quapaws, through which no
power to pass has been granted. . . . I would submit that it would be manifestly
unfair and inequitable if one company were allowed, at its own will, to change
the plan of route so as to shorten its own line to the common point, and lengthen
that of its competitors by a distance which might be twenty-five miles. . . ."
President U. S. Grant agreed.

[13] After the race was over, Bob Greenwell devoted the rest of his life to
blackmailing the company, asserting it, and R. S. Stevens as its agent, had

reminded Stevens, Joy already had a line run from his main track down the valley of Fly Creek to Chetopa. He, Boudinot, had already seen the location stakes. Now, if Joy could make a mile a day down that valley—and he could do it easily—he would be in Chetopa within three weeks!

Nobody, Stevens told them, was going to beat him to the line. He had about a week's vital work to do in Junction and in Emporia, where the Katy was holding its annual meeting of stockholders the following Wednesday. But by the week's end Stevens would be ready to go.

Fixing Gunn and Scullin with a hard stare, he said pointedly: "Gentlemen, you have one week in which to make up lost time. Next week I take command at the end of track, personally—and I'll see it through to the finish![14]

The annual meeting of Katy stockholders which was held in the offices of Ruggles & Plumb, Emporia, Kansas, May 18, 1870, is notable not only for the remarkable unanimity with which President Parsons' plans were approved but also for its remarkable lack of Kansas representation. Of a total of 38,180 voting shares represented, Bob Stevens held proxies for 34,510. To show the paucity of local capital and its distribution in the East, it may be of interest here to list the voting stock, its owners and proxies:

Morris County, Kansas	1,650 shares by G. M. Simcock
Lyon County, Kansas	2,000 shares by T. C. Hill

contracted with him to perform certain acts which were "illegal and void and contrary to public policy."

When the Katy's 3,100,000-acre land grant claim finally was denied by the U. S. Supreme Court in 1914, the company's legal staff then deemed it safe to put an end to the blackmailing by allowing Greenwell's claim to come to trial.

Alleging breach of contract, he sued for $100,000 due for services performed in misleading and disrupting the Missouri River, Fort Scott and Gulf (Joy's Border Tier) in the race to the Indian Territory. He testified that on orders from R. S. Stevens he not only misled the road's engineers, fomented strife and caused confusion, but also "trespassed upon the premises and property of said rival railroads and destroyed and took and misappropriated, without the knowledge and consent of said rival roads, ties, rails, bridge and other material of said rival roads and interfered with and obstructed progress of the work of said roads."

Twelve good men and true, sitting in Superior Court of Pottawatomie County, in Shawnee, Oklahoma, in 1916, listened to this incredible testimony—and promptly threw the case out of court. No more was heard of Greenwell. From Greenwell vs. M.K.&T. Ry. Docket No. 2723, October 25, 1916.

[14] Reconstructed from company records and personal correspondence of General Manager Stevens, the latter now being in possession of Mr. Frederick C. Stevens, Attica, N. Y.

J. B. Dickinson (erstwhile president)	1,501 shares by R. S. Stevens
Levi Parsons (president)	1,601 shares by R. S. Stevens
George Denison (vice president)	3,001 shares by R. S. Stevens
D. Crawford, Jr. (treasurer)	3,001 shares by R. S. Stevens
Francis Skiddy (president, Land Grant Railway)	1,749 shares by R. S. Stevens
August Belmont	1,501 shares by R. S. Stevens
H. A. Johnson	2,549 shares by R. S. Stevens
Levi P. Morton	1 share by R. S. Stevens
J. Seligman	1 share by R. S. Stevens
Shepard Gandy	1 share by R. S. Stevens
R. S. Stevens (general manager)	1 share by R. S. Stevens
Henry S. Warren	1,390 shares by R. S. Stevens
D. Crawford, Jr., trustee	1,504 shares by R. S. Stevens
D. Crawford and G. Denison, trustees	200 shares by R. S. Stevens
George C. Clark	200 shares by R. S. Stevens
L. C. Clark	124 shares by R. S. Stevens
F. R. Baby	200 shares by R. S. Stevens
John R. Parsons	120 shares by R. S. Stevens
Howard C. Dickinson	248 shares by R. S. Stevens
H. A. Johnson, in trust	600 shares by R. S. Stevens
James P. Robinson	700 shares by R. S. Stevens
George H. Morgan	800 shares by R. S. Stevens
Morton Bliss and Company	1,472 shares by R. S. Stevens
J. and W. Seligman and Company	1,000 shares by R. S. Stevens
Land Grant Railway and Trust Co.	10,135 shares by R. S. Stevens
Total shares voted	38,160

After the meeting, Bob Stevens took Chief Engineer Gunn aside and told him that more trouble seemed to be on the way, Indian trouble. He asked him to read a telegram he had just received:

Washington, D. C., May 18, 1870

Hon. R. S. Stevens—Emporia, Kansas

On May 13 a Cherokee delegation called on Secretary of the Interior Cox and complained about our working parties entering the Cherokee Country and grading the line. Secretary has ruled Indians need not recognize our right to intrude before land grant race is won and award made. We today appeared before him and moved for revocation of ruling but have little hope of success. Meanwhile get your men out of Indian Territory and rush completion track to border.

LEVI PARSONS

Gunn was able to account for the complaint. He had sent a handful of men into Indian Territory, he told Stevens: George Walker with a locating party doing a little survey work, and Dick Yost, his assistant on track, with a construction crew going over some of the bad spots just over the line. In fact, they were helping Boudinot lay out cattle yards and feeder lots at that very moment.

"Get 'em out of there—fast!" ordered Stevens, "and put them to work, any kind of work, north of the line." Then abruptly he asked: "Where's the railhead now?"

The end of track, Gunn told Stevens, was at that moment creeping slowly across the sodden prairie about five miles south of Ladore and just entering the projected townsite of Parsons.

This fact reminded the General Manager about the need for secrecy. Not a word was to be said about the Parsons division point plans to anyone. Better still, when Gunn had reached the end of the sixteenth section—Milepost 160 was a few miles south of the farthest Katy townsite—he was to throw up a shack that would look like a station and give that spot a big name. Stevens told him to print it in letters a yard high and make the place look like a real terminus town. That would put their townsite about halfway between Ladore, which was at Milepost 150, and their fake town. Gunn caught the significance of Stevens' scheme. People would never guess that the Katy would plat a town halfway between sections, Stevens assured the engineer. He urged him to make as big a smokescreen as he liked, so long as he kept everybody away from the Katy center of activities.

Gunn was soon on his way to pull the wool over the eyes of a number of smart squatters, claim jumpers and land speculators. The infinitesmal, God-forsaken town of Dayton was conceived that day, destined for illegitimate birth, and it died almost aborning.

NINE

The Katy Wins!

It was Friday, May 20, in Junction. The day was about done and the storekeepers and dram shop owners were getting ready for the morrow's trade. The "sojers" from Fort Riley, out-state settlers, railroad hands, frontiersmen, and the usual leavening of Indians of half a hundred tribes made Junction City a colorful if rowdy spectacle at week's end.

Bob Stevens was about to hie himself over to the Hale House for a spot of refreshment when Principal Assistant Engineer S. W. Lee laid a telegram on his desk, and stood expectantly waiting. The "flimsy" was briefly signed "Gunn & Scullin" and told a harrowing tale of frustration.

Work was at a standstill everywhere. High water and torrential rains had stopped work on bridges and culverts entirely. Grading was out of the question, and the track laying gangs were stymied for want of rail and "bedsticks" or ties. Moreover, the Osages and Delawares had just been paid their annuities and were demonstrating the effects, in typical reservation Indian fashion, of their temporary affluence. Scullin's devil-may-care Irishmen, with little or nothing to do to keep them out of mischief, were getting out of control again and "raising hell generally." Too, great herds of Texan and Indian cattle, in droves of many thousands, were streaming over the soaked prairie, ruining what little grading was already done and in places stomping the railroad clean out of existence.

Stevens looked at Lee wryly. "Why don't I get the hell out of the railroad and into the saloon business," he asked rhetorically. Then picking up a copy of the *Southern Kansas Advance* he handed it to Lee, pointing to an advertisement that read:

63

WHISKEY FOR CATTLE!
The undersigned are desirous of trading
KENTUCKY WHISKIES
for
INDIAN, TEXAN or NATIVE CATTLE
The same to be delivered within the
States of Kansas & Missouri
R. H. DRENNAN & COMPANY
406 Delaware Street, Kansas City, Mo.

As Lee looked questioningly at the general manager, Stevens hoisted himself out of his chair, stretched, and told Lee rather more lightly: "Oh, well—we shouldn't kick. Estimates are that a quarter of a million cattle will pass through Kansas this year on their way to market, and we'll haul a goodly portion of 'em."[1] That promised fine business for the new railroad. The thousands of cattle grazing along the Katy's right-of-way—three herds of something like two thousand head had been grazing on the Parsons townsite all winter—would soon mean money in the bank for the Katy.[2]

As he tried to figure out what the boss was driving at, Stevens suddenly became the railroad builder again.

"I want a work train made up, right away. Put the Prairie Queen on it, next the engine.[3] Load her with everything we've got for the end of track—and put her 'on the board' for midnight."

As Lee looked at him quizzically Stevens said: "We're off for the railhead tonight, and we'll stay 'til the job is finished."

"O. K., chief," said Lee resignedly.

On his arrival at the railhead just south of Ladore on the morning of May 21, Stevens found the situation worse, perhaps, than Gunn and Scullin had pictured it. Calling a council of war in the "Prairie Queen," the General Manager briefly stressed the urgent necessity for the immediate resumption of operations, regardless of "hell and high water." The success of the whole venture, he declared, depended upon reaching the border within two weeks. Millions of dollars, he told them impressively, were at stake. Millions of acres

[1] A drive of "fully 300,000 head of cattle from Texas to Western Kansas" alone was reported in 1870 by McCoy in his *Cattle Trade of the West and Southwest*. The Katy's Annual Report for 1870 announced "over 400,000 head of cattle were driven from Texas to Northern markets."

[2] *Westralia Vidette*, May, 1870.

[3] Stevens' brand-new "business" car, the "Prairie Queen," was a nine-day wonder in the wild Indian Territory all during the pioneer years.

Robert Smith Stevens, first general manager of the Missouri,
Kansas & Texas Railway, under whose direction
the railroad was built in the early seventies

Top: Chief Engineer Gunn's locating party. These men surveyed
the line during the railroad race to the Indian Territory

Bottom: "Chickasaw Ben" Colbert's ferry
across the Red River at Denison, Texas

of fertile lands, moreover, would be the reward of those who reached the border first.

The Colonel was eloquent when the need demanded, and this was his hour of need. When he terminated the conference by announcing his intention of staying with the men and personally supervising every operation, they were with him to a man. How he lived up to that promise is best illustrated by his own report:

> Thursday last our large bridge was resting on timbers or bents standing in creek. At noon it commenced raining, Kansas fashion, and continued till 4 P.M. When I went to bridge, finding men in tent, rain still falling, I called them out, told them we must not lose the bridge; that, with a continuous rain, the bents would wash out and down fall the bridge. Told them they must stand by me and work rain or shine—and 'twas $20 extra to every man who would work.
>
> 25 stepped right out onto the bridge; Chapman lit the lamps and lanterns, and there they worked till midnight, without a murmur. And from 7 till ten I never saw it rain harder, but not a man flinched.
>
> At 12 (midnight) all was safe. Before noon Friday water had run 12 feet, and a half our underbents gone. At 4 P.M. the train passed over.

The grading, bridge-building and track-laying effort during May was truly extraordinary. Day and night the work went on in a desperate fight against the elements, which seemed bent on destruction. Roadbed and track were washed out and replaced time and again. Trestling was built and rebuilt, fills tamped and retamped. And the road went forward at a rate of nearly three miles a day.[4] Rumors of John Scullin's remarkable progress in the face of almost insuperable difficulties evidently reached the ears of Border Tier men, for on the night of Saturday, May 28, 1870, they went Bob Greenwell "one better!" Warned by someone that Bob Stevens was stealing a march on them, Joy's construction gang raided Katy territory with a vengeance.

No record remains of the crude strategem that, legend has it, brought about the "Battle of Chetopa." No reporter "covered" it. Nothing survives but the stories of men and women whose fathers and grandfathers apparently took part in the fight.

[4] Under these adverse conditions, the record was four miles and one hundred feet of track laid in one day, an incredible performance.

On the night of May 28 a dozen horse-drawn wagons, accompanied by half a dozen men on horseback, arrived within half a mile of the border. One hundred of Scullin's toughest tracklayers descended from the wagons, proceeded to tear the lumber away from hidden dumps of railroad material—and to lay track in the direction of Indian Territory.

According to one Oklahoma oldster whose father was a member of this extraordinary nightshift, the plan of those in command was to show the Katy track firmly astride the border in the light of the early morning. In case of awkward questions, iron rails could be just thrown down on the prairie between the strip on the border and the track as completed, some twenty miles to the north.[5]

But someone, aroused by the noise of the hammers on the spikes, got up out of his Chetopa bed to find out what was going on down in Russell Creek. It may have been someone who held stock in Mr. Joy's road. In any event, whoever it was, he was "agin" such lawlessness. He got his horse out of his stable, galloped a dozen miles to the nearest Border Tier camp, where he apparently thundered through the sleeping Joy tracklayers paraphrasing Paul Revere:

"The Katy boys are in Chetopa laying track!"

John Scullin's happy lads, ripe for such a lawless venture as this, were slapping down ties and spiking rail within a score of yards of the Indian Territory line when they heard the thunder of horses' hooves—maybe the mounts of "sojers."

But it wasn't the "sojers." Instead, it was a contingent of about thirty of Joy's hardest characters hastily recruited, not quite sure as yet whether or not the race had been won by the Katy, but determined—if it had—to tear up those tracks. Nobody, it appeared—extraordinary in the light of those wild times—had a lethal weapon. The Katy hammers might have served as such, but Irish John Scullin's men were the pattern of himself and disdained them; they went into action barefisted. It was a gory and glorious fight while it lasted, but before the people of Chetopa, aroused by ancient Irish war cries,

[5] This misadventure has all the earmarks of simple Indian strategy. It could serve no useful purpose in the territory race since the Land Grant Act required that Kansas' Governor Harvey ride over a completed track and certify it, over his seal and signature, as "a first-class completed railroad to the northern boundary of the Indian Territory." Such a make-shift stretch of track touching the border line, however, would serve nicely to quiet the Indian enemies of Colonel Boudinot and Stand Watie who were complaining so bitterly of Katy railroad gangs intruding "before the railroad has reached the territory line." It would end their insistence upon forceful ejection of the railroaders, for which they were importuning both the Indian Superintendent and Washington!

could throw on some clothes and dash out to enjoy the spectacle, it was all over.

One of those so rudely disturbed by the roars of the battling railroad men was James Hammill, lately appointed United States marshal of southern Kansas by President Grant. With two of his deputies he tumbled out of bed. The three of them, armed with two revolvers apiece, arrived on the scene with their shirt tails hanging out of their trousers. They broke up the fight.

The marshal, a very picture of outraged law and order, is said to have roared his demand for the name of the man in charge of the Katy camp.

Our story-teller recited that John Scullin stepped forward—his nose bloody, his knuckles split, his face bearing the smile of a man who loves a fight.

"Mr. Scullin," said the Marshal, "You'll have to tear up that piece of track before you leave. And this business of trying to jump the gun will have to be reported to Washington."

He turned to the Joy men, now beside their horses, cursing, licking their broken fingers.

"And you now," he shouted. "Get you back where you belong!"[6]

On Saturday, June 4, after a long hot day, Bob Stevens swept the papers from his desk in the parlor or business end of his private car, the "Prairie Queen," which for two whole weeks had been riding the construction train. Here he had worked out the strategy of the battle and personally directed tactics. Here he had stimulated—and goaded—his subordinates into almost superhuman efforts to get the track to the Territory line ahead of the Border Tier.

He looked out of the window—and found himself already arrived. Here he was in Chetopa. The construction train blocked Maple Street, and it was nearly true that all Chetopa was gawking at him through the glass.

Hurriedly he got up and called his secretary. Together they shouldered their way through the gaping crowds to the Miller House.

"You'll not be wanting me any more, will you, Mr. Stevens?" the younger man asked.

"Just one thing more," the General Manager told his new aide, who was young Henry Denison, a nephew of the new vice president. "We're going to cross the Territory line at noon on Monday. So wire everybody to be on hand for the great occasion. Get the word to all

[6] Related by Sylvester R. Hurst, Welch, Oklahoma.

the newspapers, all our friends in the legislature, everyone you can think of. Send special invitations, of course, to Governor Harvey and the railroad commissioners, to the Indians, and to Judge Parsons— he's in Sedalia today."

He thought for a moment, then grinning slying he said: "Do you think you can talk the city fathers here into giving us a celebration at the Territory line? Tell 'em I'll give the whole town a free ride to Russell Creek and back if they will."

Good news awaited Bob Stevens at the Miller House. From Washington had come a letter which was balm to his soul. Secretary Cox had finally ruled against Joy's claim, it appeared, for enclosed was a copy of the Secretary's report of May 21 to President U. S. Grant in which he said:

> I therefore find that the Kansas & Neosho Road [the Border Tier] is not authorized, at present, under said legislation, to enter the Indian Territory and build the trunk line aforesaid, and that to complete its right at this time to do so, it would have been necessary for said road to have been completely con- structed to a point in the Neosho Valley at or near the crossing of the boundary-line by the Neosho, and where it could enter the Cherokee country without crossing the reservation of any other Indian tribe. This the said company has not done.

President Grant had concurred in the findings and the sad news had been given to Mr. Joy. Stevens' only worry now was whether Joy's tracklayers were coming down Fly Creek—and if so, how fast and how far had they already come? Things had reached such a stage in southeastern Kansas that Katy people gave the Border Tier a very wide berth, and vice versa.

Alone in his room in the Miller House on Sunday, June 5, Bob Stevens wrote:

> Fortunately I can soon get a rest and relief—As you know, two weeks since last Friday eve, I left Junction to *stay at the front* until the Locomotive left the state for Indian Territory & tomorrow will see it done. Just think, road partly graded, masonry for one bridge (Pier 29 feet high), 2 bridges 150 and 160 feet long put up, and 26 miles of track laid in less than 12 days. Don't you believe that took work? The engine now stands within 1 mile of the State line.
>
> After all the fuss we have *beat Joy*, as the Secy. of Interior

The Katy Wins!

& President decides but one Co. can have right of way thro Indian Territory, and that is the one entering the *Cherokee Country in the Valley of Neosho first with a completed road. That we do tomorrow and he is 17 miles away.*[7]

Representing his newspaper, Mr. Patterson of Ottawa (Kansas) had been bidden to the Katy unveiling—the most important unveiling in the history of the railroad, past, present, or future. Patterson was a poetic soul, proud of his rhyming gift—even if his efforts did owe something to "Hail to the Chief." He sat down at once to write a poem for the occasion, realizing full well that, if he left the work until arriving at the scene of rejoicing, it was quite possible that said rejoicing might well hamper the even flow of verse; besides, the poem, in printed form, could be distributed among the crowds and quite possibly the famous Topeka Quartet (half legislators and half lobbyists) could be induced to sing it to the assembled ladies, dignitaries, politicians, newspapermen, settlers, railroad hands, and sundry Indians. All that Poet Patterson hoped for came to happen—and then some. His song of praise, "Rivet the Last Neosho Rail," has luckily been preserved for us:

> Rivet the last Neosho rail,
> With an iron hammer and an iron nail;
> For over the hill and over the vale
> The Iron horse Is coming!
> Along the prairies wild flowers sweet
> With red lips kiss his flying feet,
> Wild eagles his wild scream repeat;
> His Hymn of praise the bee is humming.
>
> Hail! To the day and deed!
> Hail to the iron steed!
> Hail to the iron rail!
> Hail to the South, all hail!
> From the lakes to the gulf the rail
> Runs over mountain and vale,
> Which echo with blows on the nail,
> Now heard by the list'ning races.
>
> Hail to the pathway of nations here!
> It runs today through a hemisphere,

[7] This letter is in the possession of Mr. Frederick C. Stevens, Buffalo, N. Y., a grandson of Colonel Stevens.

The good time coming must now be near:
It shines on our hope-lighted faces.

Hail to the age of steam!
Hail to the iron team!
Hail to our iron bars!
Hail to our flag of stars!

All Chetopa—whose population had been swollen to some two thousand hardy souls—firm in the belief that their town would be "a second Kansas City", arrayed themselves in their western best and came parading down Maple Street on the morning of June 6, 1870, to sweat, to cheer, to drink and to eat, to strut proudly before thousands of excited "strangers" as the 45-pound iron rail, fresh off the boat from Sheffield, England, was truly laid across the border between Kansas and the Indian Territory, and a little wood-burning engine, a brand-new Grant 4-4-0, chugged across the line. As the train came to a slow halt before what appeared to be a great tribal council of "blanket" and "white-collar" Indians, General Manager Bob Stevens dived into the shack where the telegraph instrument had been set up and sent this message to the waiting world:

We have struck the Territory line and are going like hell.[8]

In the valley of Russell Creek that morning, the Katy tracks had been thrown down directly on the Texas Road. This was a hard-packed, hoof-pounded trail which was already old in 1870. It had stretched over the prairie for nearly fifty years; it began in St. Louis as the Boon's Lick Trail, and grew into the Osage Trace because a Jesuit, Father Lacroix, wanted to bring the word of God to the mighty Osage Nation; he was later to direct other priests in the founding, in 1847, of the famous Osage Mission at St. Paul, Kansas, in the Valley of the Neosho eighteen miles north of Parsons.[9]

As early as 1822 this great highway helped populate Texas and serve important pioneer traffic north and south through what was to be eastern Oklahoma. For almost half a century, until the coming of the railroad and for many years after that, thousands of home-seekers moved along the Texas Road, and millions of head of cattle came to move over it to the northern markets. Lanky drivers walked and popped their long whips alongside creaking and rattling ox

[8] Katy former Passenger Traffic Manager W. M. (Billy) Fenwick, who retired a decade ago after fifty-seven years of distinguished service with the company, reports that this message, framed, hung in the general manager's office in Sedalia before headquarters were moved to St. Louis in 1894.

[9] Grant Foreman, *Down the Texas Road,* 2.

wagons; military expeditions jingled over it; Civil War regiments of both the North and the South explored it and fought over it; herds of wild horses were chased and captured on its confines; buffalo in thousands wandered about it. Where the Katy crossed the border of Kansas and Indian Territory on that June morning of 1870, the Texas Road was almost a mile wide—hard-packed, dry clay.

According to the poetically-inclined Mr. Patterson of the *Ottawa Journal*, all "the Wit, Beauty and Chivalry of Kansas" was gathered for the ceremony of the Katy crossing of the border. According to Colonel Horner's *Southern Kansas Advance*, this was "A Fenian Invasion." The Colonel meant this kindly, having reference to John Scullin's hundreds of Irish-born tracklayers, tiemen and gandy-dancers.

The white tents of the working parties glistened in the sun as far north as the eye could see. On the outskirts of this ever-seething settlement were hundreds of emigrant wagons, the occupants of which moved when the railroad moved, sat still while the railroad consolidated its positions; these were hardy souls enough, but they rightly saw protection in the size and strength of the Katy army. These emigrants were after land along the right-of-way, in Indian Territory if they could get it, and, if not, then on to Texas with the railroad.

Mulling through the several newspaper accounts of this great day, we have come to consider this story printed by the *Southern Kansas Advance* as the best:

> At ten o'clock on Monday morning the M.K.&T. Railway reached the south line of Kansas. The construction train was ordered up to the foot of Maple street by Mr. Stevens and, thru the herculean and enthusiastic efforts of the tin horn band, hundreds of our citizens were soon on their way to the depot —to be in for a free ride later to the land of LO (the poor Indian).
>
> The end of the track is two miles and one hundred rods south of Chetopa. Arrived there we found the Irish Brigade which had hammered and shoveled its way from Junction City, one hundred and seventy miles (actually it was 182 miles) to the Indian Territory in less than nine months, resting their picks and hammers on Cherokee soil, on the grassy slopes looking down to Russell Creek.
>
> Mr. Creighton announced in a few words the order of ex-

ercises and recited the poem, "Rivet the Last Neosho Rail."
[This must have pleased Newsman Patterson greatly.] R. S.
Stevens then drove the last spike on this side of the line. Three
or four false blows of their superintendent amused the Irish;
but in his neat little speech, he hit the nail most happily on the
head. He said:

"It is with feelings of no ordinary interest that we meet on the
spot considered by many as on the verge of civilization—on
the line which divides the red man from the white man. This
gathering augurs that the two civilizations which meet and
commingle here today are to be blended into one and the line
which separates them to be blotted out.

"Enemies an drivals have assailed us with taunts and jeers.
Quietly and unobtrusively [the Katy party still bore the scars
of their midnight fight with Joy's gandy dancers] we have
gone about our business, till today we gladly take up the
gauntlet and throw defiance at those who have maligned us.
We know what we promise when we say that by October the
completion of the Sedalia Road [the Tebo & Neosho, whose
charter had just been taken up by the Katy] will give us unbroken connection between the Atlantic seaboard and the Indian Territory.

"Nor shall we stop here. Our course lies onward to Red River
We shall not pause there but continue to the Río Grande. Beyond this, even, we are casting our eyes—through the chap-
arral and over the steppes of Mexico—till our engine stands
panting in the palaces of the Monteczumas and the halls of
the Aztecs."

Bob Stevens stepped down from his little platform, built directly
on the border line, and handed his spike maul to the tall, handsome
Cherokee attorney, Colonel Elias C. Boudinot, who drove the first
railroad spike into the first railroad tie that ever rested on Cherokee
soil.

"My own people," said the Indian, "along with the Creeks, Choctaws, Chickasaws and Seminoles [the Five Civilized Tribes] have
always been pre-eminent to the wild Indians of the plains by virtue
of what we have learned by contact with the white man. I stand in
no fear or dread of the railroad. It will make my people richer and
happier. I feel that my people are bound closer together and to the
government by these iron bands."

And now came the climax of this great day. "The Beauty, Wit, and Chivalry" of Kansas, the governor's staff, distinguished guests from far-off places, a regular swarm of newspaper reporters, General Stand Watie and Colonel Boudinot with their retinue—all possessed of special tickets—had a path cleared for them through the throng and arrived at the cars sitting behind the little diamond-stacker some few yards from the border.

Everybody got aboard who was entitled to get aboard, and, amid delighted squeals from beauty, tender cautions to beauty from chivalry, and loud laughter from the wits, the little engine, snorting like a score of suddenly stuck pigs, started off on its great journey. Five bands, all playing different tunes, according to Reporter Patterson, made contribution to a splendid din.

Chugging, snorting, and whistling, the little engine and its string of cars made slow progress; the tracks were packed with people who didn't want to move. At 1:33 in the afternoon (the journey from the border had taken twenty-two minutes) the train arrived back in Chetopa.

At the entrance to the Miller House, General William B. Hazen and Enoch Hoag, heads of the Central and Southern Indian superintendencies, who had been appointed by Secretary of the Interior Cox to determine which railroad first complied with the conditions of the Land Grant Acts, approached Stevens. Colonel Bob eyed them warily.

"Congratulations, Mr. Stevens," they boomed in unison so that all might hear. "We'll be happy to report that the Indian Territory has been truly entered."

Before leaving Chetopa for Junction City, Stevens issued orders to strip the Neosho division of every available worker and move them over to the Sedalia division. The iron, ten thousand tons of it, lay in Sedalia and on the levee at St. Louis ready for Scullin's track-layers, and Munger and Frye, subcontractors on grading, were already preparing to haul out.

The trip to Junction was uneventful. There the sly politician, one Bob Stevens, introduced his bosses to Governor James M. Harvey of Kansas, the officer "specified by Act of Congress" to pronounce upon the completion of the road. Once aboard the Prairie Queen, which Stevens took good care to see was beautifully equipped and plentifully supplied with every luxury, it is a fair question whether the Governor saw much of the line either en route to or returning from the border. On Tuesday and Wednesday of that week he was feted and entertained at Council Grove, Emporia, Burlington, and Chetopa as he had seldom been feted before, and on June 9, 1870, he reciprocated all the Katy courtesies when he wrote Secretary Cox:

> On the 6th instant, said road was completed to the south boundary of the State, and on the 7th and 8th instants, I passed over the same, and made a careful and critical examination of its construction and equipment, and hereby certify that said Missouri, Kansas & Texas Railway Company have constructed a first-class railroad, beginning at its junction with the Kansas Pacific Railway at Junction City, from thence in a southeasterly course, to the head-waters of the Neosho River, and thence down the valley of said river to the State line of the Cherokee Nation, south of the town of Chetopa.[10]

Accompanying the Governor's hard-won certification was the formal report of the two Indian superintendents appointed to judge the race. It testified:

> 1st. That the Union Pacific Railway, Southern Branch (recently named the M.K.&T. or "Katy") reached the northern boundary of the Indian Territory, in the valley of the Neosho River, on the west side and about one mile therefrom, at 12 M. on the 6th day of June, 1870, and that at that time there was no other railroad nearer than sixteen miles of that point. [Apparently Joy's men had built only a mile or so down Fly Creek.]
>
> 2d. That on the 9th day of June, 1870, Governor James M. Harvey, of the State of Kansas, the officer specified by Act of Congress to pronounce upon the completion of this railroad, certified over his official seal and signature, that the same was a first-class completed railroad to the northern boundary of the Indian Territory.

[10] This certificate, vital to the race, was secured despite the fact that many of the smaller dry creek beds had been hastily filled without regard to the need for culverts to carry off the sudden freshets which constantly plagued the valley. More obvious to the governor might have been the painfully visible evidence that, in the last desperate rush for the border, Scullin's graders had reduced the width of what little roadbed they had put in to not more than nine feet—just the width of the ties—whereas standard practice called for three-foot shoulders. This was true even across the high dumps, and accounted for much of the terrific maintenance expense that finally toppled Parsons' empire. In that final rush, too, Stevens had used in the track lightweight 45-pound iron he had intended solely for sidings and passing track, because his 56-pound rails had been diverted to Sedalia by President Parsons.

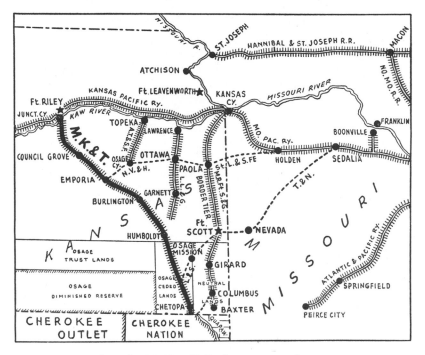

On June 6, 1870, the M. K. & T. Railway won a three-way construction race to the Indian Territory border and earned the sole right to build south through the lands of the Five Civilized Nations to the storied Red River and Texas.

It was a month later before Secretary of the Interior Cox held a meeting to give James Joy and the Border Tier Road an opportunity to show causes "if any there were, why said reports should not be received as conclusive of the fact that the Union Pacific Railroad Company, Southern Branch, now called the Missouri, Kansas and Texas Railway Company, had first complied with the conditions prescribed for securing the right to construct the trunk road through the Indian Territory." The only argument put up by Joy was the assertion that "no satisfactory evidence is before the Department that the character of said Southern Branch Pacific Railway is that of a good completed road." The irate Secretary promptly disposed of this argument by producing Governor Harvey's certificate, and as promptly sent the Border Tier delegation packing.

On July 12, 1870, the Secretary sent President Grant a long report of the race to the border. In conclusion he recommended "that you give the said Union Pacific Railroad Company, Southern Branch [the Katy] in accordance with the terms of the eleventh section of the Statute of the 25th of July [1866] aforesaid, your written approval to construct and operate its line of railroad from said point on the northern boundary of the Indian Territory to a point at or near Preston [now Denison] in the State of Texas."

One wonders what passed through the President's mind as he read the detailed report of what he knew from experience must have been a thrilling race. Enough to say he must have enjoyed the outcome, for in his bold, scrawling hand he wrote across the bottom of the Secretary's report:

Approved, and the recommendations of the Secretary of the Interior will be carried into execution.

U. S. GRANT

July 20, 1870.

Colonel Robert Smith Stevens had finally carved himself a niche in railroad history.

TEN

The Katy Invades Missouri

No sooner had Governor Harvey certified to the winning of the border than Stevens shut up shop on what he was already calling, or miscalling, his Neosho division and moved headquarters to Sedalia, to pit his wits against the Missouri Pacific and to work out President Parsons' "manifest destiny."

It was a good time to leave the fertile, febrile valley. On June 8, 1870, Congress disposed of the vexing Osage Indian question by adopting Senator Pomeroy's amendment providing for the removal of this once numerous tribe from Kansas to a new reservation in the Indian Territory. The entire Osage Diminished Reserve, a tract of some 8,000,000 acres, was ordered sold to actual settlers at $1.25 per acre, and immigrants were soon swarming upon the land.[1]

Isaac T. Goodnow, the former state superintendent of public instruction who was now the Katy's land commissioner, had his hands full. Who, then, could blame him for willing his friend and patron, Dull Stevens: "Squatter, squatter everywhere, and all of 'em fighting drunk." However, all he could do to protect the interests of the company pending receipt of final "patents" on 1,300,000 Kansas land-grant acres was to publish notice that:

> All persons on even sections of railroad lands will have thirty days from date in which to come to the principal land office at Neosho Falls and buy same at the appraised value, or else give place to others who will buy.

Here, perhaps, is a good place to tell what finally happened to the Katy's juicy Kansas land grant which, like the carrot before the donkey, was dangled before the Katy's nose, and was withdrawn, like the Indian Territory grant, after the line was completely built.

[1] *Missouri Democrat,* June 8, 1870.

The 1,300,000 Kansas acres earned by the Katy under Congressional Land Grant Acts, it should be understood, were in addition to the 3,064,390 Indian Territory acres to be awarded by the government to the railroad which first crossed the Indian border and built "a first-class railroad" to the Red River border. Most of these Kansas acres, however, were denied the Katy when, in 1875, the Supreme Court ruled that the government "obviously" had no intention of including the Osage ceded lands in the land grant or the act would have "specifically" said so. A minority opinion, however, shrewdly pointed out that:

> The Government of the United States, through one set of its officers, after mature deliberation and argument of counsel, has issued its certificate on tests, that the lands in controversy were covered by the grant, and has thus encouraged the expenditure of millions of money in the construction of the public highway, by which the wilderness has been opened to civilization and settlement; and, then, on the other hand, after the work has been done and the money expended, has, with another set of officers and all the machinery of the Judiciary, attempted to render and has succeeded in rendering utterly worthless the titles it aided to create and put forth upon the world. Such proceedings are not calculated, in my judgment, to enhance our ideas of the wisdom with which the law is administered, or the justice of the Government.[2]

Fortunately, Bob Stevens that June had no thought of failure; he was riding the crest of success, happy to get away from the disgruntled Indians and bickering settlers and anxious to link up his Neosho line, which "began nowhere and ended in the same manner," with Sedalia and the beckoning East.

It must have pleased the colonel immensely, on his arrival in Sedalia, to learn that John Scullin was laying track "a mile a minit," as the big Irishman himself asserted. Much of the grading had already been done, of course, by his Tebo and Neosho predecessors, but still Scullin had earned a pat on the back if not a bonus by getting the line out of town and out past Keatley's to Parkersburgh (now Green Ridge, Missouri), a round dozen miles to the southwest.

Although construction on the Sedalia division did not quite equal the speed with which the southern end of the Neosho division had been laid down, nevertheless it went at what was then a record clip.

[2] U. S. Supreme Court Reports, 92, U. S. 760.

The track reached Windsor, twenty-one miles west, by June 30, 1870, and entered the thriving town of Clinton, forty miles out, on July 18. Clinton was a popular and populous centre of 640 souls then, the heart of a fine agricultural section.

This was the day Bob Stevens was waiting for. Because of the lagging drive for city and county bonds to finance the Katy's building, the time had come, Stevens knew, to do something to rekindle enthusiasm along the projected route for the coming of the iron horse to southwestern Missouri. How better to do it, thought the resourceful General Manager, than to re-enact in Clinton the scene at the territory line. Stevens did just that—no, he did more; he announced far and wide that the first regular train service from Sedalia southwest would be introduced effective July 18, 1870, as shown by the time card on page 80.

There were big doings that day along the Tebo. Whole populations of the little settlements along the way came to watch the ornately decorated diamond-stacker as it thundered by, tearing the silence of the savannahs forever apart. On the rear of this queer "mixed" freight, passenger, and construction train rode, appropriately enough, the Katy's prize piece of equipment, the luxurious and expensive ($8,000, it cost) "Prairie Queen." It carried, in addition to the railroad officials, Bob Stevens' Indian friends General Stand Watie and Colonel Elias C. Boudinot, here to lend color and invaluable publicity to the day.

Nothing loath, Clinton turned out "her beauty and her chivalry," such as it was then. There was feasting, and merriment, even roistering, that day, probably not quite so rough and uncouth as in southeastern Kansas, but every bit as sincere. And Henry County came through with another $200,000 in bonds![3]

Building went on apace. The track reached the section markers now known as Montrose (Milepost 50) on August 20; Appleton City (M.P. 60) on September 10; Schell City (M.P. 70, named for the great banking family of New York), September 30; Walker's (M.P. 80) on October 15; and entered Nevada, Missouri, ninety miles from Sedalia, on October 26, 1870. En route, the line had crossed innumerable small streams and bridged two considerable rivers, the Grand and the Osage, to make the entire distance in rather less than five months.

Nevada City, founded in 1855, was the Confederate County Seat and a hotbed of secession during the Civil War. Later it en-

[3] Edwin L. Lopata, *Local Aid to Railroads in Missouri*, 136.

MISSOURI, KANSAS & TEXAS RAILWAY.

Sedalia Division.

No. 1. TIME TABLE. No. 1.

TAKES EFFECT MONDAY, JULY 18, 1870.

WESTWARD.		STATIONS.	EASTWARD.	
TRAIN NO. 1.	MILES.		MILES.	TRAIN NO. 2.
Leaves 7:30 A. M.	0	...............SEDALIA...............	40	Arrives 4:40 P. M.
" 8:00 "	7	...........* KEATLEY'S...............	33	Leaves 4:10 "
" 8:20 "	5–25	...........PARKERSBURGH..........	27–75	" 3:50 "
" 9:10 "	8–75	...............WINDSOR...............	19	" 3:00 "
" 10:00 "	7–50	...............CALHOUN...............	11–50	" 2:20 "
" 10:20 "	4	.............* LEWIS'...............	7–50	" 2:00 "
Arrives 10:50 "	7–50	.........CLINTON...............	0	" 1:30 "

GENERAL REGULATIONS.

* Indicates Trains do not stop unless signaled, or to have passengers.

All Trains and Engines must cross Truss Bridges and Trestles at speed not exceeding ten (10) miles per hour, and without steam when possible.

Dampers of ash-pans must be closed in crossing Bridges and passing Wood-yards.

The use of intoxicating Liquors as a Beverage, will be followed by immediate dismissal from the service of the Company.

The Employees of the Company are expected and required in all cases to exercise the GREATEST CARE and watchfullness to prevent injury or damage to persons or property, and, in doubtful cases, to take the safe side.

Trains bound westward will have the right to the Road. Trains bound eastward will wait at meeting places until the train bound west arrives.

☞ Run cautiously down all grades.

SIGNALS.

1. The *Danger Signal* is a Red Flag by day, and a Red Light by night; a lantern swung across the track, a Torpedo exploded thereon, or any object waived violently on the track.

2. A White Flag by day, or a White Light by night, displayed on the road indicates *Caution* to be observed in passing over the track.

3. The Signal for starting an Engine or Train must be given by Ringing the Bell of the Engine which must always be rung before starting the Engine.

WITH THE WHISTLE.

4. One blast is the Signal to apply the brakes.
5. Two "   "   let go the brakes.
6. Three " "   back the Engine or Train.

WITH THE LAMP.

7. A Lamp swung across the track is the signal to back.
8. A Lamp raised and lowered, vertically, is the signal to stop.
9. A Lamp swung in a circle, is the signal to go ahead.

WITH BELL-CORD.

10. One tap of the Bell is the signal to stop.
11. Two taps "   "   "   start.
12. Three "   "   "   "   back.
13. A Red Flag by day, and a Red Light by night, carried in front of an Engine, denotes that the Engine or Train is followed by another Engine or Train, running on the same time, and entitled to the same rights and privileges as the Engine or Train carrying the Signal.

H. HALE,
Superintendent Sedalia Division.

R. S. STEVENS,
General Manager.

[Sedalia Daily Bazoo Print.]

The Katy's first printed time card

joyed an influx of hundreds of loyal Union settlers and had prospered accordingly. Now it was all for putting on a public demonstration to celebrate the Katy's arrival, for "the locomotive was received with joy and delight by the citizens." However, the city fathers voted only $10,000 in bonds to pay for depot grounds and right-of-way through the town, and "at the particular request of the railroad authorities" the big celebration was cancelled.[4]

[4] *History of Vernon County* (St. Louis, Brown & Co., 1887), 358.

The Katy Invades Missouri

So Scullin's Irish Brigade drove on through Nevada without pausing even to slake their thirst, and Bob Stevens "gave the back of his hand" to its innocent and bewildered citizens. The track crossed the Missouri state line fourteen miles west of Nevada on November 30, and the Katy's victory in Missouri—at least the pioneering stage of it —was complete.

So much was happening at this time, it is surprising how President Levi Parsons, busy in the East gathering "the sinews of war," could keep abreast of developments, but he seems never to have missed a trick. He had but recently written his General Manager that the Texas legislature, by an act passed August 2, 1870, had granted to the Katy "the right to extend our road from the point where it shall cross into the State from the Indian Territory through the State of Texas in the general direction of Waco and Austin, to the Río Grande, with a view to a farther extension to Camargo and the City of Mexico." Now he wrote Stevens triumphantly that negotiations were under way to purchase the rights of the Bolivar Point, Eastern Texas and Red River Company, which had been chartered on August 3, 1870, to construct a railway "from the water's edge nearest the mid-channel of Galveston Bay . . . to a point on Red River . . . with the right to vary to meet any railroad coming from Kansas through the Indian Territory . . ." Neither of the Texas acts granted lands other than the necessary two hundred feet for right-of-way, but other inducements, such as the temporary waiving of taxation, were solid encouragement.

At this time, too, Parsons considered the financial position of the Tebo and Neosho (Sedalia division) so satisfactory that, by merger of October 19, 1870, he brought it formally into the Katy family. (Although that part of the main line was locally known for many years thereafter merely as the "Tebo.") He had a right to be pleased with the local assistance he received. The communities served had come through handsomely. Pettis County and Township had put up $250,000 and the City of Sedalia had subscribed another $100,000; Henry County during the entire construction period had kicked in with a whopping total of $600,000; and Vernon County had sweetened the pot to the extent of $300,000.[5]

On December 7, 1870, the Katy entered the thriving City of Fort Scott, Kansas, that "sink of proslavery iniquity" which was now Union

[5] Lopata, *Local Aid to Railroads in Missouri,* 136.

81

headquarters, whence military detachments issued from time to time in futile efforts to keep the Land Leaguers[6] under control. There was the usual celebration, dampened somewhat, however, by the usual bickering of local land speculators irked by the heartless efficiency of the Katy's own land speculators. Bob Stevens' frank letter to Levi Parsons about his Fort Scott difficulties is so revealing that it is worth quoting here:

> By the agreement on the part of the city, you remember, they were to furnish us depot grounds (eight acres in the city, and twenty acres outside) and for this purpose they were to issue twenty-five thousand dollars bonds. In going down there and locating the road, we found that it was impossible to put our depot within the city limits, and had to go under the hill near Crawford's[7] foundry. At this place he had some sixteen or eighteen acres which he offered to sell the city at $1,000 an acre, on which there sprang up a good deal of rivalry on the part of the officers of that city as to where the land should be secured to be furnished us, and a half effort made to send us here, there and elsewhere, and it looked very much as if the Council would get into such a muddle as would result in our getting no ground where we wanted it. I finally proposed, when down last, to the City Council to take their $25,000 and secure our own lands.

Fort Scott's own historian, Goodlander, believed that the grasping attitude displayed towards the road ended any possibility that Stevens might build the Katy's great shops there, and bluntly declared that "Fort Scott can blame the imbecile mayor and council who were in authority at the time that Fort Scott is not a city of 30,000."[8]

Back along the Sedalia division, meanwhile, the property was being intensively "developed," mostly by Levi Parsons' land com-

[6] Hordes of immigrants, many of them honest settlers but a goodly proportion of them tough, land-speculating squatters who hoped to make fortunes by pre-empting railroad lands, were organizing into "leagues" to fight for their "rights" throughout this period. Some of these organizations grew powerful; all were a thorn in the side of the Katy; most were a real deterrent to honest settlement and development, for the "hardest characters" usually obtained control of the leagues and were responsible for many outrages perpetrated during this period.

[7] George A. Crawford, father of Fort Scott, who platted the town around the old fort and had it incorporated in 1855.

[8] C. W. Goodlander, *Early Days of Fort Scott*, 129.

panies. These were a continuing succession of small townsite companies which were generally subsidiaries of the Land Grant Railway and Trust Company of Missouri, a newly formed corporation which, of course, was an extension of Parsons' eastern corporation. The officers of this company were all handpicked by Stevens "out of the Sedalia office." Asked by Parsons why he didn't put himself on the board, Stevens replied: "I could not quite stand being a citizen of Missouri."[9]

Understandably, then, townsite projects on this division were developing very well. At Appleton, where Levi Parsons owned a quarter, something over $20,000 had already been collected from the project, although out of 540 acres costing $13,000, only about forty acres had been sold. Here the Katy already had "a fine depot and freight house" up and was doing a good business.

At Montrose the company had up a good depot and were "building up quite a business." At the Rockville townsite, too, buildings were going up rapidly and a good depot had been erected.

Immediately south of the Osage River, the company had purchased for a nominal sum a tract of 3,500 acres. On this tract it was proposed to put up a passenger depot and a freight house, for a short distance down the river was the old town of Beloit with several stores and "quite a gathering of inhabitants." The idea was to incorporate the depot tract as a town, called "Schell,"[10] show Beloit citizens the obvious advantages of moving their town over to the railroad site and making it one of the most important points on the division. The plan worked perfectly.

At Nevada, Stevens already had a fine depot up and the Katy was hauling considerable freight to that point. Immediately the railroad had arrived, Nevada became the shipping center for the entire area, which included Lamar, Carthage, and the country southeast of the line.

At Fort Scott, where the "imbecile mayor and city council" had "forced" Bob Stevens to build outside the city limits on land of his own choosing, ample terminal facilities were in, but the end of track still hung over the banks of the Marmiton awaiting completion of the bridge.

Back in Sedalia, which after a few years of wartime glory and excitement had gone back to sleep as little more than a whistle stop

[9] Stevens, of course, held Missouri's border ruffians accountable for the tragic sack of Lawrence, and never forgave the state.

[10] Named for the New York bankers, Augustus and Richard Schell.

on the Pacific Railway of Missouri, business was booming again. As the Katy's terminus and only interchange point, its warehouses were bulging with goods for and from the hinterland, its other facilities stretched to the limit. Stevens now reported: "I am now putting in a building 28'x60' for the stationary engine and the machinery being sent me, and a carpenter shop 28'x40' for workmen on repairing cars."

At this time Stevens quietly organized the Parsons Town Company, with himself as president. Just as quietly, on October 24, 1870, the secretary of state for Kansas granted him a charter, and the stage was set for a big-scale land "operation."

No whisper of the location of the proposed junction of the Sedalia and Neosho divisions was allowed to leak out before the township plat had been filed and the lands bought in, but the secret was out the moment Chief Engineer Gunn's survey party, under C. G. Wait, arrived on the scene. On Monday morning, November 7, the party began driving location stakes through "Township 31, Range 19," and the following day the construction gangs of Frye and Pierce broke dirt at the junction. The anticipated land rush was on the moment construction began (and that story will be told shortly) but Stevens had instructed his people to "keep the lid on as long as you can" and to "rush construction of the track all possible."

Superintendent White of the Neosho division, whose job it was to "bull-whack" the builders of the road from the Parsons junction north, took Stevens' orders literally. He drove the grading and track-laying gangs to such purpose that by mid-December the track was at South Mound and the graders were approaching the Neosho River, a dozen miles north. They could easily have visited, had they wished, with John Scullin's southbound construction parties who were grading just north of the Osage Mission and approaching Flatrock Creek.

On December 11, 1870, right on the heels of "Boomer's bridge monkeys," the southbound tracklayers crossed the 160-foot Marmiton River bridge at Fort Scott. Five miles farther on is Marmiton No. 2; Scullin's men reached that point on December 17, were hung up there just three days while Boomer completed the bridge, and were thereafter on their way to Pawnee Creek. At the 100-foot Pawnee bridge, a little north of the present town of Hiattville, Kansas, Scullin's deeply religious if wildly irreverent Irish tracklayers paused to "celebrate" Christmas of 1870.

Just thirty miles to the south, White's "end of track" that Christmas was at the Neosho River, two miles south of the Osage Mission

(St. Paul, Kansas) awaiting the bridge which had been shipped by the American Bridge Company, from Chicago via Kansas City and the Santa Fé to New Chicago (Chanute), thence via the Katy through Parsons. The grading of the link had been completed; Engineer Melville, whose work parties were putting in the small openings, girder bridges and trestle work, was ten miles ahead of the track, so that with completion of the two big spans over Flatrock Creek and the Neosho the gap was about ready for the iron.

From then on the weather began to "close down," and Stevens was reporting: "Between Sedalia and Green Ridge our passenger train ran into a snow drift six feet in depth. Last night, however, this train returned from Fort Scott with a good load of passengers and thirteen in the sleeping cars."

Bad weather continued to interrupt the delivery of materials, chiefly iron, fish bars, spikes, and ties, and Stevens lit out to investigate. In the yards at Sedalia and at the front the General Manager found only seven miles of iron, and to close the gap there were twenty-four miles yet to be laid. Fearing he would be delayed getting more iron over the Missouri Pacific, whose co-operation was, to say the least, no more than lukewarm, he finally went to St. Louis to talk with Superintendent McKissock of the Pacific. His experiences on this trip are so interesting that his report is quoted below:

> On reaching St. Louis I found the river frozen over with the exception of a very narrow channel, through which were plying a couple of ferry boats, taking over, as a matter of course, very little. McMullin told me they had over 800 cars of freight awaiting transportation. Other roads about in the same condition. McKissock told me there were over 200 cars of freight on the East side of the river for our Sedalia division.
>
> On reaching the Pacific Depot, I found that no iron for us was there, but as a telegram informed me that some 4,500 bars were lying at Cairo I immediately went for Capts. Carroll & Powell of the Steamboat Line and asked them if they proposed to do anything towards getting the iron up, and received as reply: "Nothing! We are not bound to fight Providence, frost nor low water." So it seems that if we are to get any iron before the river breaks up, it must be at our own expense and by our own exertions.[11]

[11] This report is especially interesting because it highlights the problems of trans-Mississippi commerce before the building of the great Eads bridge, first to span the mighty main stream, which was not opened to traffic until July 4, 1874. Letter Book No. 6.

When the General Manager got back from St. Louis on Saturday, January 7, 1871, he found everything progressing very well, although "Scullin was nearly out of iron and White had not yet crossed the Neosho River bridge." A thorough search of the line quickly uncovered some extra iron in the Sedalia yards and at Fort Scott, and this, with what could be spared out of side tracks and spurs, was estimated to be enough to close the gap—for White at the south end was "fairly well supplied with light iron."

White's tracklayers crossed the Neosho River bridge on January 9, and on Wednesday, January 11, the construction train chugged laboriously into old Osage Mission.

This Jesuit Mission settlement was the oldest and accounted the most "civilized" settlement in the area, yet even here all was not exactly quiet on the southwestern front. Sheriff Horne, for example, had just shot and killed James Kern, whose friends in turn would have quickly finished off the law man had not the latter's friend, John Ryan of the Irish brigade, got the drop on them first. Clay Livingston, accused of butchering his wife with an axe in a drunken frenzy, was strung up to a limb over Big Creek by indignant neighbors. And when A. W. Fields was found in Miller and Baxter's livery stable with his throat cut, the boys just called it suicide and let it go at that.[12]

No sooner had the "end of track" disappeared north of Osage Mission than the weather closed in again. For weeks work was almost at a standstill. On February 1 Stevens wrote:

> There is not to exceed 4 miles of track unlaid, and I yesterday telegraphed Mr. White, if he could not get his men up to the scratch and lay it, I would send Scullin across the gap to complete same. Am expecting hourly to hear by telegram that a full force is at work today, and about Friday or Saturday (February 3 or 4) shall go down myself, when if it is not done, I suppose it will be necessary for me again to do as I have done in almost every instance previously, strip, and go into the mud myself.

Bob Stevens' red-hot wire to Superintendent White apparently

[12] Items culled from contemporary issues of the sprightly *Osage Mission Journal*.

[13] According to local legend the huge flat rock on the banks of this creek was used from time immemorial as a council table for Osage pow-wows, and as a sort of altar for ritualistic dancing by the painted and feathered warriors.

galvanized that dilatory individual into red-hot action, for as the sun began to set on Flatrock Creek[13] and cast long spidery shadows from the Post's patent bridge onto the long prairie, White's track-layers mingled with Scullin's on the evening of Friday, February 3, 1871, and laid the final rail. Without emotion, with no fanfare on the part of the railroad, without a reporter to record the act for posterity, a joint crew rhythmically but wordlessly drove the last spikes in the last rail a few rods south of the bridge. The link was complete. The Indian Territory was tied irrevocably with a slim silver ribbon to Washington, to the industrial East, and to a cruel, hard world.

ELEVEN

Birth of a City

The story of the birth of Parsons City—its conception, the labor pains of those who bore it, and the painful delivery of a great, squalling, overgrown child—is essentially the story of dozens of towns and cities, from Missouri to the Gulf, that were brought into being by "Katy," the Missouri, Kansas & Texas Railway, in the prolific early Seventies.

When the time came that fall to file the plat of the projected townsite, Levi Parsons, who had suggested the town be named "Stevens," inquired why the tracings were titled "Parsons City." Colonel Stevens, who well knew when modesty was a virtue, replied: "Many of us here are believing that it is only a question of time, and that short, when it will really be a city of the first rank. You will notice by referring to the advertising sheets of the Atlantic and Pacific (now Frisco Lines) 'Peirce City' in glaring capitals. Why should there not be a 'Parsons City' as well?"[1]

Stevens organized the Parsons Town Company on October 17, 1870, in the company's land offices at Neosho Falls, Kansas. Because the organizational setup and the operating methods of this "wholly-owned subsidiary" were typical of the pioneer railroad builders' way of "building up the country," it may be of interest to go into this venture in some detail.

It quickly became apparent that Chief Engineer Gunn had talked without sure knowledge when he had assured the General Manager

---

[1] Andrew Peirce, Jr. was managing director of the Atlantic and Pacific Railway, now part of the St. Louis–San Francisco Railway. He was then feverishly building southwest from Springfield, Missouri, to the eastern border of the Indian Territory. Peirce City, now spelled "Pierce," was intended to outshine Parsons as the "great metropolis" of the area, but is now just a whistle crossing on the Texas Special route, its ambitions long forgotten.

that the site was clear, for already it was becoming much too settled, Professor Goodnow[2] reported, and several titles actually were being contested. Stevens was irked, to put it mildly. Immediately he wrote Levi Parsons:

> I learn that the Northeast quarter of 19 is claimed by a man named Foltze; also, that the Northwest quarter of 19 is claimed by one Kendall who alleges settlement in 1867. This is all new to me, having always been informed by Major Gunn, who claimed to have examined the records, that there was no settlement on it prior to '68.
>
> The great question with me is how to best get rid of the two claimants to the North half of 19. It would be exceedingly foolish to go on there and spend a large amount of money, letting it eventually inure to their benefit, and I am rather inclined to the idea of temporarily abandoning all improvements there and letting them understand that we shall make them at some other point. It would be a very easy matter after crossing the Labette to make a detour, and, with a mile or two of extra track, get the town exactly where we want it.[3]

Truly, the country was filling up fast, as Goodnow had reported. The area newly opened up by the railroad was at this period of the West's growth the Promised Land not only of immigrants, agricultural settlers, and land speculators, but also of that whole tribe of American wanderers best described as the foot-loose and feckless. Various estimates have placed the increase in population in Kansas during 1870 at from fifty to one hundred thousand. Interestingly, the fertile Neosho Valley and the southern border counties took most of the influx.[4]

Horace Greeley, who had told the world through the columns of the *New York Tribune* (and quite correctly) that "the twin

[2] Professor Isaac T. Goodnow was a struggling teacher at Wilbraham Academy, Massachusetts, when he met and married Eleanor D. Denison, of Colrain (Coleraine), Massachusetts, a sister of Katy Vice President George Denison. His appointment to the powerful (and profitable) post of Katy land commissioner was consequent upon his marrying the boss's sister.

[3] Letter Book No. 6.

[4] "At least 60,000 people entered Kansas in 1870, and the first half of 1871—their own statisticians put it at 100,000. . . . The rich valleys of the Neosho, Verdigris, and neighboring streams are fast filling up with an energetic population. In every direction the virgin soil is being turned, and claim shanties and neat dwellings are springing up like magic."—Beadle, *The Undeveloped West*, 220.

curses of Kansas, now that the Border Ruffians have stopped ravaging her, are land speculators and one-horse politicians," was still broadcasting his advice to "Go West, young man." Greeley visited the frontier again as Parsons City was being platted and plotted, and he, too, was infected by the magnificent prospects of this virgin country. On October 9, 1870, he wrote from Kansas:

> Settlers are pouring into eastern Kansas by carloads, wagonloads, horseloads, daily, because of the fertility of her soil, the geniality of her climate, the admirable diversity of prairie and timber, the abundance of her living streams, and the marvelous facility wherewith homesteads may here be created. . . . Having exposed freely the errors, as I see them, of all parties, I hardly need restate that Kansas, in spite of them all, is going ahead magnificently.

Professor Goodnow reported that during 1870 he had disposed of 135,000 acres of Kansas lands at an average of $5.00 an acre. He boasted that a Welsh colony had made arrangements for the acquisition of a tract of 46,000 acres, and that in one month he had sold no fewer than 173 farms for a total of $148,512. The price of Katy Railroad lands in 1870 varied from $2.00 to $10.00 an acre, and acreage was sold on a ten-year annual installment plan, with interest at 10 per cent. "It is the policy of the Company," he virtuously pointed out, "to sell in small farms to actual settlers, and to discourage the acquisition of large tracts by speculators."[5]

There was considerable justification for the mad rush to pre-empt these southeastern Kansas lands. Mr. A. Hall, whose farm was in the valley at the junction of Deer Creek and the Neosho River, for example, harvested in 1870 seventy bushels of oats per acre from a large area; J. C. Clark gathered 4,000 bushels from 65 acres, the entire yield being sold readily at 50c a bushel. Not bad for land selling at a top of $10.00 an acre! But perhaps the wintering and fattening of Texan and Indian cattle, a really profitable business in the seventies, drew most of the newcomers.

Here, then, was good reason for Bob Stevens to worry about the fate of his Parsons townsite. But the Colonel was no man to stand idly by while the populace moved in on his preserves. On December 14, 1870, he gathered his dummy directorate together in Neosho Falls for a council of war, and when it was over everyone there knew Parsons City would come to term—regardless. The general manager

[5] *First Annual Report.*

sat impassively as Goodnow reported the results of his several investigations of the titles of claimants to tracts on the townsite. "A decision had been rendered by the Register and Receiver as to the right of Foultze to pre-empt the Northeast quarter of Section 19," he said sadly, and feared that John Kendall, with the aid of perjured testimony, might succeed in establishing his right to the Northwest quarter. Moreover, some 400 or 500 persons had got on to 19 and 13 and seemed to have an organization like that of the Leaguers on the Joy lands.

Stevens listened attentively, scribbling notes occasionally on the pad before him. When all were talked out he got up, took the pad in his hand, and said: "Gentlemen, I fear there is only one way to solve our difficulty. The same spirit that actuates the Leaguers characterizes these men, and if they become satisfied that we have got them and not they us I think they will quietly disband and scatter." He then presented the following resolution, which promptly passed and was published in every newspaper in the section:

> Whereas, the Missouri, Kansas and Texas Railway Company have decided to locate its machine shops and important buildings elsewhere than at the junction of its Sedalia and Neosho Division, thus rendering the building up of a large town at such junction impracticable, therefore
>
> Resolved, that the Board of Directors of the Parsons Town Company hereby abandon all idea of locating or building a town on sections eighteen (18) or nineteen (19), Town. Thirty-one (31), Range Nineteen (19), or anywhere in that vicinity, the decision of said Railway Company above referred to rendering such action necessary."[6]

Never for a moment, it should be understood, did Stevens seriously entertain the idea of giving up the townsite he'd originally planned. No other tract in the section was so ideally located, so well suited in every respect to his purposes. Furthermore, he and his collaborators—or conspirators—urgently needed the ready money that a great sale of high-priced town lots would bring in overnight. In the eastern money marts signs of uneasiness and of the panic soon to come were distinctly noticeable during the winter of 1870. Even Jay Cooke, the Philadelphia banker who had recently obtained control of the Northern Pacific with its 47,000,000 land-grant acres, was having trouble financing the construction of his "Banana Belt" railroad.

[6] Nelson Case, *History of Labette County, Kansas*, 171.

On the other hand, business was beginning to pick up on the newly built Katy divisions. Stevens reported to Levi Parsons that "Traffic is increasing every day, while our local freights are very largely on the increase. On Thursday the freights over the line amounted to over $1,100, and the passenger business on the same day was about $500."

Immediately the resolution to abandon the Parsons townsite was published, Stevens left for his home in Attica, New York, to spend the holidays with his family and to allow time for the settlers to think over the problem he had set them. On his return in mid-January, 1871, greatly humbled individuals and delegations awaited the great man's pleasure—just as he expected. The claimants, or, rather, the squatters, told Colonel Bob they wanted to do the fair thing and would sell out to the company all the land it wanted for $50 an acre. They ended by coming to the conclusion that if they could get pay for breaking the ground and for what little improvements they had on the land, and a few lots in the townsite, they would be "divilish lucky."

The townsite problem was finally settled on the following basis: Kendall, who claimed the northwest quarter of 19, and Foltze (or Fultz) who claimed the northeast quarter of the same section, agreed to pre-empt the land, and then deed it to the Town Company. In return, the General Manager agreed to pay them $2,000 each. This transaction was completed and registered at the land office in Humboldt, Kansas, immediately and the Colonel's townsite problems were about over.

When the first through train from Sedalia to Parsons, Chetopa, and the Indian Territory, with through sleeping car from St. Louis, rolled into Parsons City station on Sunday, February 5, 1871, the only notables aboard were Colonel Bob Stevens and his lieutenants.

There was an air of expectancy, a touch of excitement, among both passengers and crew that afternoon as the first train slowly puffed up to the unfinished depot and transfer house, "made of lumber in the cheapest manner possible,"[7] which then represented Parsons City. Both engineer and fireman hung out of the cab, searching for the anticipated welcoming committee, prepared to play the role of hero for one brief moment. The lush-bearded conductor, L.

---

[7] "At Parsons, I am putting in a very cheap building 20 feet wide and 50 feet long, with a board roof, as an office (depot) and storehouse, between the tracks, with a platform 50 feet long to roll freight across from one car to another." —General Manager's Report.

S. Hamilton, swung on the front step of the coach, ready to be first
off and first to buss the beauty if not the chivalry of the new city.
However, brakeman A. O. Brown, hanging on the rear, paid little
heed. He, a conductor on the construction train, had been in and out
of this junction many a time, and expected no change from the
monotony of his former trips. And Brown was right. The crowd that
met the first through train that day gave evidence of nothing unusual
—there was nothing unusual by that time in a train stopping at the
junction—and a most important event in Parsons' history passed un-
noticed.

The month that followed the successful joining of the two divisions at Parsons junction was a hectic one for Stevens. Now, since he
had a real railroad to operate and make profitable, he must find business for it, many passengers to carry, much freight to haul. He must
contract with the Southwestern Stage Company and a dozen others
for through rates and convenient connections at points along the
line in order to control the traffic to and from areas far removed from
the railroad. He must make a deal with Sawyer and Ficklin's stages
(El Paso Stage Line) for connecting service to and from all points
in the Indian Territory and Texas.

The Colonel's chief headache, however, was contained in a report that had just come to him from "a friend of mine who had just
had an interview with Governor Fletcher," to the effect that the Atlantic and Pacific people and Captain Brown, who was ambitious to
become president of the Missouri Pacific, were in league with the
Missouri governor and certain St. Louis interests to get control of
the Missouri Pacific. Stevens' informant could not state positively
but thought that Mr. James F. Joy was in the combination. Governor
Fletcher was reported to have said: "If we can once get ahold of the
Missouri Pacific we can then command the trade of the Southwest,
and will shut out the M.K.&T."[8]

The relaying of this information to Levi Parsons brought quick
reaction. The Judge and his colleagues well knew that, with the
Katy's southern terminus still at the Indian Territory border and the
Atlantic and Pacific railhead likewise resting on the Territory border
uncomfortably close on the southeast, any blocking of the Sedalia
interchange point would immediately put the line between powerful
pincers that could—and undoubtedly would—squeeze the life out of
their half-built property. Stevens had written: "I can hardly endure
the thought that after such arduous labors and having got our road

[8] Letter Book No. 6.

now in condition to be profitable and paying that we are to be entirely shut out at Sedalia. It is in my judgment much easier to checkmate the Atlantic and Pacific, and secure amicable running arrangements with the Mo. Pac., and far less expensive, than to secure an outlet Northward via Boonville."[9]

Levi Parsons' decision was to extend the line in both directions, but to build down through the Indian Territory first. Thus he could corner the Indian and Texas traffic, shutting out the Atlantic and Pacific, meanwhile using the threat of an extension of the line from Sedalia north as a club over the Missouri Pacific to hold the Sedalia "gateway" open. So the month of February passed and time ran into March, with Colonel Stevens feverishly organizing another railroad building race. Iron was to be gotten up, and fish plates, and chairs, and spikes, and all the paraphernalia of battle. Ties, hundreds of thousands of them, had to be got out in the Indian country, and no one, least of all Stevens, knew if the Cherokees, the Creeks, the Choctaws, or the Chickasaws could be counted on to co-operate, or even to exercise a benevolent neutrality.[10]

By the end of February the Parsons Town Company had the townsite nicely laid off. Civil Engineer L. F. Olney had his maps and plats ready for filing, and Colonels Bob Stevens and Willard Davis went over every inch of the site, appraising the lots, naming the streets for the president's financial angels, setting aside tracts for railroad and municipal purposes, and reserving choice lots for those in the inner circle. The Town Company had been capitalized at $250,000, consisting of 2,500 shares of beautifully lithographed stock, which Levi Parsons described as "very decent appearing certificates." These were distributed by the President mainly as largess to his backers, and the names of the recipients are preserved in the street names of Parsons today.

On Wednesday, March 8, 1871, Mr. Solomon, a man with the virility and voice of a tobacco auctioneer, stood on the wide platform of the Katy freight house at Parsons junction, back-stopped by a top-hatted and frock-coated group of Parsons Town Company officers, and began to sell off lots in the townsite. There was much rivalry for the privilege of purchasing the first lot. After spirited bidding, the

[9] For February 21, the General Manager reported the following revenues: passengers, $1,108.40; freight, $1,293.93; total revenue, $2,402.33.

[10] In the original line, ties were laid at the rate of about 2,600 to the mile—and Stevens had 250 miles to go in the Indian country.

Public sale at the new "railroad owned" townsite
of Parsons, Kansas, March 8, 1871

honor fell to Abraham Cary, a local hardware man who headed a
group of sensible settlers which on February 22, at the suggestion of
Colonel Davis of the Town Company, had filed incorporation papers
for the town. Thereafter bidding was fast and furious for choice lots,
and by nightfall sales had "netted nearly $5,000" and Parsons City
was definitely on its way. By Saturday Stevens was able to wire Levi
Parsons that outlying tracts were "selling as high as $200 an acre,"
and that "sales in your townsite Thursday, Friday and Saturday were
nearly $18,000."[11]

[11] Letter Book No. 6.

Ten days after lots went on the block in Parsons, sales had soared over $30,000, and ambitious plans were fermenting to make it a city of the first rank. In reply to Director Sheppard Gandy's offer to donate part of his Town Company windfall for a city park to be named in his honor, Stevens diplomatically advised him that, "I have a reservation of twenty acres about half a mile from the depot we intend for that purpose, to say nothing of a most magnificent race track which I propose to get in order by the time you gentlemen shall have sent some of your fast stock."

If Stevens was talking mighty big in regard to Parsons City he might easily be forgiven, for the job he was then doing on the virgin townsite was not small by any rule of measure. He already had persuaded Melville, Plato and Company, a large concern from Chicago, to establish a lumber yard adjacent to the depot, and he had a spur track in and ready to haul their product. He was negotiating with Carney, Fention and Co., to establish a large wholesale grocery and provision store, "agreeing to permit them to put it up alongside the track so as to make the handling of heavy goods exceedingly convenient." Already he had brought in the Southwestern Stage Company and assigned them a couple of lots, "upon which they are erecting large stables," and had a contractual agreement with them to run all their stages in that section of the country to Parsons. In fulfillment of a promise made to himself a year ago, the General Manager brought in his cousin, E. B. Stevens, and started him on the erection of the Belmont House, Parsons' first real hotel.

Illustrating how the wily Stevens kept a firm grip on the vitals of Parsons City was his personal donation of the lot on which Parsons' first regular bank, the First National, was erected. Financed with Katy money, it absorbed the primitive banking facilities first provided by a partnership of Crawford, Matthewson and Company, and Stevens put in as its first president Colonel A. D. Jaynes, his fellow director on the Tebo and his chief financial assistant. The railroad king was now in the banking business.

Within a matter of days, Parsons had grown to a substantial town of nearly two thousand inhabitants. The ill-begotten settlements of Ladore and Dayton, those "cesspools of vice" which had grown up around mileposts 150 and 160, were moved overnight to Parsons. Many other little settlements in the area were similarly torn down, loaded on wagons, and moved to the new town.

So was Parsons born. Today a thriving city of some 20,000 pros-

Parsons, Kansas, in the year of its founding, 1871

The big Katy station at Parsons burned to the ground on March 17, 1912; the company's vital records were among the losses

Motive power of the early seventies. Engine No. 14, a "Pittsburgh" 4-4-0, built in 1870.

A passenger train of the early seventies, from an oil painting

perous citizens, it is exactly what it claims to be, "the metropolis of southeastern Kansas," and a credit not so much to its founder, the man whose name it bears, as to its real father, the irresistible, irrepressible Colonel Robert Smith Stevens, general manager of the Missouri, Kansas and Texas Railway.

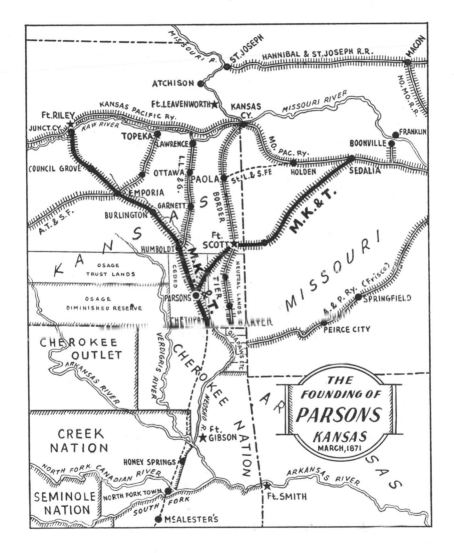

TWELVE

Down Through the Cherokee Nation

The decision to extend the railroad deep into the Indian country instead of sitting supinely by while the Atlantic and Pacific conspired with the Missouri Pacific to throttle the Katy was sound strategy. The coveted Indian and trapper trade beyond the frontier posts in the vast reaches of the West, moving slowly along the time-worn trails which bisected the Territory, would be controlled exclusively by the railroad which first cut south across the trails and established new trading posts at the crossings, shortening the route to the white man's markets. It would also gain, or regain, much of the immensely profitable Texan cattle trade, which by this time had largely veered away westward, coming up the Chisholm Trail through the Cherokee Outlet lands, instead of up the shorter but more dangerous Texas Road.

The prosperity that had followed the tremendous longhorn cattle drives up the Texas trail was but a memory in southeastern Kansas by 1871, for reasons mentioned earlier in this story. Chetopa and Baxter Springs, the original cattle towns of the rip-roaring border, were now down to handling Indian cattle almost exclusively, and by this time the Union Pacific and the Santa Fé were in fierce rivalry for the business that was flooding up the Chisholm. Because the Santa Fé had finally built as far west as Newton, which was on the trail and sixty-five miles south of Abilene, that hell-raising Kansas Pacific Railroad town was fading. On the other hand, the latter road had begun to put up extensive stockyards at Ellsworth with the object of diverting the drives still farther west. This had begun to be desirable because already the squatters along the route pioneered by cattleman Joseph G. McCoy were making it difficult for the drovers to take the great drives through their improvements—exactly as the eastern border settlers had done three years earlier.

Stevens, watching these developments in the cattle trade, could not hide his satisfaction. He had seen McCoy, the shrewdest stock-yards promoter in the West, and had tried to hire him. He had men all over Texas seeing the drovers, promising them to "double their bowls of bacon fat," and in return had received much encouragement for the Katy's building plan. "The only drawbacks we shall meet with," he wrote Levi Parsons, "are the cattle taxes imposed by the Cherokees, Creeks, and Choctaws, some of them levying a tax of 50 cents per head. The gross tax on each animal, after leaving the Texas line, through to Chetopa, is about $1.25." These taxes, he declared with proper indignation, were outrageous.

Another good reason for Stevens to resume the southward surge was the fact that Levi Parsons had just recently completed the consolidation and recapitalization of the railroad property, and funds were now available for the big construction drive. The Katy's progenitor, the Union Pacific Railway Southern Branch, capitalized at $4,250,000, had died quietly as 1870 passed, and its lusty offspring, the Missouri, Kansas and Texas System, was on February 1, 1871, capitalized thus:

On a projected 590 miles of road (located through the Territory to Red River)

Capital Stock	$16,257,500
Bonded Debt	14,000,000
Total	$30,257,500

Amount then issued on 432 miles of road (graded to the Arkansas River)

Capital Stock	$12,257,500
Bonded Debt	10,000,000
Total	$22,257,500

Despite bad weather all through February, the General Manager was not only successful in keeping the railroad running on its brand-new bed of soft, spongy earth and building up a respectable freight business, but he also managed to keep hot, with an amazing energy, all the other irons he had in the fire. By the first of March he had gathered at the end of track, about two miles south of Chetopa, some fifty cars of iron. That was enough for about five miles, but there was more en route at St. Louis, and "sufficient to lay from Chetopa to the end of the grade near the Arkansas River—ninety miles south near Fort Gibson—is on the Mississippi or at New Orleans." He also had piled up enough fish plates, bolts, and spikes for thirty miles, and ties were coming out in driblets all along the grade. Stevens even took time out to boast that he had succeeded in getting the price of ties, as insisted upon by the Cherokees, down from 75 cents to 55 cents. And these ties were of first quality hardwoods, bois d'arc, walnut, and the like.[1]

Grading in the Cherokee country was well advanced by March, 1871. Boomer had finished the bridge over Russell Creek, four miles south of the border, and had his men strung out at every river crossing for nearly a hundred miles into the Indian Territory. As for big John Scullin, with a juicy contract in his pocket to "lay track and surface same from State Line south to Red River," he was joyously fighting the battle of Chetopa all over again. The big six-foot-two son of Erin, with hands like hams and a tongue that lashed like a bullwhip, was in and out of every dramshop, hurdy-gurdy house, and gambling tent in southeastern Kansas by then, rooting his rollicking Irishmen out of their dives and getting them back on the job.

The local newspapers were mirrors of the times. Although the *Southern Kansas Advance* could find no fault with Chetopa proper, it looked with something less than approval at what was going on all around the Katy railhead during these exciting days. An unsigned, sparkling column titled "Men and Things" should bring gasps of envy from present-day columnists, hampered as they are by the libel laws. Here it is:

> Oswego [the County Seat] is full of gamblers.
> The Sheriff of Labette County [Parsons] is still drunk.
> Oswego is trading town lots for votes.
> Texas cattle are being shipped on the MRFtS&G. [This meant that Joy's Border Tier Road, though barred from running rails into Indian Territory, was picking up beeves at the border.]
> The *Baxter Sentinel* publishes a list of twenty gamblers who have been ordered out of that city.
> There is a new hand at the bellows of the *Oswego Register*. The result is an increase of wind.[2]

The viewpoint of the International Council of the Indian Nations and Tribes on the entrance of the iron horse into its domain is im-

[1] Ties purchased by the Katy during 1951 cost an average of $2.83 apiece.
[2] *Southern Kansas Advance,* June 15, 1870.

portant in this record. It is well illustrated in the following letter, signed "Okfuskee," in the same issue of the *Advance*:

The principal chief of the Muscogees [the Creeks] invited a general council to be held at this place, the capital of his nation [Okmulgee]. The Council organized by electing William P. Ross, of the Cherokee Nation, President, and J. N. Perryman, of the Muscogees, Secretary.

Before proceeding to business hands were shaken and the pipe of peace was smoked, after which an address was submitted by the Chief calling the conference. The object of this was to obtain the views of the Nations living in the Territory on "sectionizing" their lands, railroads and territorial bills, and united action in defense of their interests. Upon these important subjects there was entire harmony in the council and they embodied them for promulgation in the form of an appeal to the authorities and people of the United States.

The appeal expresses their desire for peace with all men, their purpose faithfully to abide by the provisions of their treaties; their opposition to a change in their relations with the government; their satisfaction with their own governments and the common ownership of their lands.[3]

Poor Lo! He saw the iron horse as the advance guard of the whites who would overrun his lands. And he was seeking to make the best of things.

In order to get a clear picture of the entry of the railroad into the Indian domain in March 1871, it is necessary to remember that the Congressional acts which gave to the Katy the sole right to build south through Indian Territory did not abrogate the Atlantic and Pacific's right to build *west* through the Cherokee Nation. Like Colonel Stevens, A.&P. General Manager Peirce was no tenderfoot in the railroad and land-grant business, and the feverish activity at the Katy's end-of-track, the building up of the big supply dump south of Chetopa, and the number of grading parties deep in the Territory, soon showed him how Stevens intended to counter the M.P.–A.&P. plot.

[3] The making of treaties with Indian tribes was terminated by Act of Congress approved March 3, 1871. More ominous still was the fact that Colonel Elias C. Boudinot (Cherokee lawyer and Katy undercover man) was then in Washington urging that tribal lands be held in severalty and that territorial government be created for the Indian Territory. See M. L. Wardell, *A Political History of the Cherokee Nation*, 259ff.

Realizing what would happen to his own railhead traffic the moment Stevens succeeded in getting south of him, Peirce set out to beat Stevens to the inevitable crossing point of the two lines, on the flat, fertile prairie somewhere near the junction of the Big and Little forks of Cabin Creek. Right then began another race that kept the Territory in an uproar until it was over and contributed no little to the Katy's reputation as a hard-fighting, aggressively independent railroad.[4]

The first week of March was dry and warm, the sky unclouded. The misnamed and frequently miscalled "Kansas zephyrs" for once were eagerly welcomed and quickly dried out the earth sufficiently to bed the ties.

At seven o'clock on Monday morning, March 6, 1871, Bob Stevens and John Scullin stood on "the last Neosho rail" which lay across the Indian borderline. The sun was just beginning to light the long valley of Russell Creek, high-lighting the grade and giving a golden, somehow heroic touch to the momentarily statuesque line of figures, Scullin's Irish brigade, strung out ready for work. The General Manager said little, but as the tracklaying boss glanced at his stem-winder and threw a high hand-signal to Dick Yost, the young easterner who had been appointed engineer-on-construction at end-of-track, Stevens and Scullin shook hands solemnly. As the general manager turned away, big John spat on his hands, picked up a spike maul and started out for Texas.

The Katy's first objective on the drive south was the Big Cabin, some thirty miles beyond the border, where the Old Military Road coming up from Fort Gibson split off from the Texas Trail and bore away to the northeast. Unless Stevens reached this fork of the trail before the beginning of the first cattle drives, he would lose much of the business—and practically all of the stage coach travel—to the Atlantic and Pacific and to the Border Tier Road at Baxter.

By mid-month, the track had crossed the bridge over Russell Creek and had split the motley Indian tent town and camping ground on the prairie nearly a mile beyond. Intermittent rains, attributed to "the Ekynosual stawm," then hampered the work, so that by April 1 the end of track was only ten miles out, and Colonel Stevens, who thought his bull-whacking days were over, was back at

---

[4] Except for one unfortunate period in the eighties when the ruthless Jay Gould temporarily wrested the line from its owners, the Katy has ever been an independent, self-sustaining railroad.

the railhead to give the job, as he himself expressed it, a little bit of old fashioned speed to Cabin Creek. He couldn't stop the rains, however, which all during April rendered the prairie and bottom lands almost impassable. An added burden was the fact that, although he had over four hundred men getting out ties and hauling them to the grade ahead, they couldn't keep up with the work. Timber suitable for ties, it turned out, was not quite so near the railroad as had been hoped, and much of the timber land had been quickly fenced in by enterprising Cherokees, making it necessary for Stevens to trade and barter with the wily redskins individually instead of through the National Council as originally agreed upon.[5]

Nevertheless, Boudinot's spur track was in by the middle of April. Another siding was completed at end-of-track fifteen miles out from the border, to serve the wild tent and shanty town that materialized almost overnight in spite of hell and weather. Here "Shawnee Tom" Blue Jacket, now become a Cherokee by virtue of tribal agreement, decided he need look no farther for a homestead to replace the one he'd lost in Kansas—and the "improvements" he put in at that railhead tent town gave birth to the thriving little agricultural community which still bears his name today.

Tom Blue Jacket, and the Methodist preacher, Uncle Charley, and their wives and families, had found their happy hunting ground. But there were hundreds of other prairie wagons whose owners were ever ready to pull up stakes and push ahead; their pot of gold would always be at the end of the rainbow. There was plenty of work for the menfolk on the railroad as the iron rails slowly snaked their way down through the Cherokee lands. And these men were bound together by an all pervading faith in this enterprise. True, there was drinking and gambling in the railroad camps, and clean fist fighting. The general make-up of this great advance guard of railroad workers, however, was just about summed up in that word— clean. The livid-faced professional gamblers, the "terminus men," the dive-keepers, the prostitutes, the gunmen and the thieves were

---

[5] Under Cherokee law, an individual Indian might hold as his own as much of the tribal lands as he could fence and improve. However, if he neglected or deserted his homestead, it automatically reverted to the Cherokee Nation. Many shrewd Cherokees lived a life of ease merely by fencing great prairie pastures and leasing them to enterprising whites who had gained entry into their country, legally or illegally, and stayed by taking out annual work permits issued by the Cherokee National Council. These permits usually were sworn to and paid for by the Indians who leased their lands, but the many desperadoes and "terminous types" who flaunted permits were living indictments of venal officials, both Indian and white, who trafficked in these valuable passports.

not workers, no part of the railroad clan, but they started the towns. Just as soon as portions of the army of wagon drivers, tracklayers, graders, and engineers decided that HERE was a place to pause, then shacks would go up and a town would spring out of the fair prairie, like a bed of toadstools, built by "the scum of creation."

By the middle of May the track was over the bridge at Cabin Creek, had reached the big double plank cabin with stairway running up between that gave this fork of the trail the local name of Big Cabin, and was stopped for the moment awaiting completion of the trestle over White Oak Creek, thirty miles out.[6] Here the Katy's Cherokee friend and counsellor, Elias C. Boudinot, who had profited from his association with the company's land operators, undertook to go into the townsite business for himself.

As a Cherokee national in good standing, Boudinot was entirely within his rights in fencing off unoccupied tribal lands and improving them as he saw fit. So, with the expert advice and covert assistance of Katy officials and workers, who knew that the Atlantic and Pacific survey crossed the Katy here (the location stakes were easily traced), he quickly fenced something like two miles square with posts and lumber and undertook to "own" the entire townsite and more. With admirable taste, he named the townsite "Vinita," in honor of the beautiful and talented sculptress Vinnie Ream, who was then the toast of society in Washington and, rumor had it, a very close friend of the tall, handsome, arrow-straight Cherokee Colonel.[7]

Perhaps something should be told of this ultracivilized and educated half-blood who had cast his lot with the Katy. He was a son of the famous fullblood Buck Oowatie[8] who had taken a white man's name in honor of his patron, Elias Boudinot of New Jersey, and married a prominent Connecticut girl, Harriet Ruggles Gold. Elias Boudinot, Sr., had been gruesomely butchered back in 1839 when several leaders of the Treaty Party were massacred by the fanatical full bloods of Chief John Ross's following. Although Elias Sr.'s brother, Stand Watie, had bloodily avenged that deed time and time

[6] This point, in the delta of the two creeks, should not be confused with the present location of the town of Big Cabin, which is five miles south thereof.

[7] J. D. Benedict, *History of Muskogee and Northeastern Oklahoma*, Vol. I, p. 661.

[8] Brother of Stand Oowatie, who changed the name to Watie. The only fullblood Indian to become a brigadier general, Stand Watie had command of all the Indian forces of the Confederacy during the Civil War, and he handled them superbly, as many a Union commander testified to his own mortification. He was a great power in the Cherokee Nation, and universally respected, until his death on September 9, 1871. See H. F. and E. S. O'Beirne, *The Indian Territory*, 76–77.

again, the young Elias still fought the Ross faction tooth and nail at every opportunity.[9]

An eastern-schooled, university-bred lawyer, Boudinot was the man who had done more than any other of his race to bring the railroads into Indian Territory. In the three-cornered rush, for the right-of-way and for the land grant, Boudinot had always been on the side of the Katy. Before the opposition of a great majority of his people had been broken down, he had been practically exiled by his tribe—which may have suited his purpose, for he took up his residence in Washington, fought Chief Ross in the Halls of Congress, and lobbied indefatigably for the coming of the iron horse.

Overnight, a typical tent town sprang up on Boudinot's hand-picked acres. Bob Stevens had hired a smart freight agent by the name of Prescott away from the Atlantic and Pacific and had given him a contract to "Keep along with the railhead, and at its southern terminus, as the track progresses, put up all your own buildings and handle all the freight except such as belongs to the people at that point." Here Prescott's installations alone were nearly enough to start a town. He was also permitted to receive from the consignees ten cents per hundred dollars in the way of storage; thus, to make any money, he had to secure freight to and from the south over the Katy. Smart as a whip and well acquainted both in the Indian country and in Texas, Prescott already had "runners" out in the Territory, directing his old customers to ship their cattle, cotton, hides, and pelts to such points in the Cherokee country as the Katy should reach.

Messrs. Graham and Maurice, heavy overland freighters, had been given a contract for hauling from the end of the railroad southward, and their great wagon grounds, set up to facilitate the loading and unloading of the long wagon trains that already were plying between the railhead and Texas, gave this end-of-section settlement a bustling appearance of importance and the illusion of permanence.

By May 22, 1871, the Atlantic and Pacific track had succeeded merely in penetrating the Shawnee and Wyandotte reservations, a matter of some ten miles, and had reached the banks of the Neosho River, which served as the eastern border of the Cherokee's Delaware district. Peirce was still twenty-five miles short of the junction point of the two lines and was just beginning the erection of the first span of the Neosho bridge, so Bob Stevens with proper contempt dismissed the A.&P. from his mind and resumed the drive southward.

For all practical purposes the race with the Atlantic and Pacific

[9] Wardell, *A Political History of the Cherokee Nation*, 9, 17.

was won, but Stevens still was faced with the necessity of letting the world know it. Back East, the Missouri Pacific and the A.&P. were confidentially—but confidently—whispering the news around that they had the Katy shut out, that henceforth traffic to and from the Indian Territory and Texas must move over the A.&P., and that the southeastern Kansas business would be handled exclusively by the Missouri Pacific and the Border Tier Road. Worse still, they had instituted "a campaign of lies and vilification" and were "filling the air with so many stories and allegations in regard to our financial status" that the company's bond and stock position was being seriously weakened, and money was getting tight.[10]

Giving substance to the whispering campaign, the Missouri Pacific immediately began a series of moves inimical to the Katy. Rates through the Sedalia gateway to points on the Katy were held high while they introduced a series of reductions through the Kansas City gateway which enabled Joy's Border Tier Road and the Leavenworth, Lawrence and Galveston to undercut the Katy and take the traffic right out from under Colonel Stevens' nose. Furious, the Colonel wrote Judge Parsons: "The understanding had with Mr. McKissock (general superintendent of the Missouri Pacific) was that in case any reduction was made between St. Louis and Kansas City we should have a corresponding reduction to this point [Sedalia]. On the 10th of this month they reduced the rates from St. Louis to Kansas City to 55c, 32c, and 25c, and refused to give us any corresponding reduction, so we are now paying on 4th class rates 30c to Sedalia and they are carrying it to Kansas City for 25c."

Even now it is difficult to discern the hand of the man who initiated the moves designed to pull Judge Parsons' southwestern empire down around his ears. It is strongly indicated that the villain of the piece was Bob Stevens' old enemy, James F. Joy, the would-be empire builder of the Chicago, Burlington and Quincy, still plotting and maneuvering to control southwestern business. The General Manager certainly thought so, and he had sound reasons for thinking so, because he knew that the mayor of Quincy, J. G. Rowland, had been in Sedalia recently, as Joy's avowed emissary. He had been sent to ascertain the condition of the Northern Extension of the Tebo Road, which had been located and partly graded through Boonville to Fayette and Moberly, on the North Missouri Railroad, and to see on what terms the franchise could be secured.[11]

[10] Letter Book No. 6.
[11] Frank Skiddy, of course, held the controlling stock of the Northern Extension of the Tebo and Neosho, so Judge Parsons had the franchise in his hip pocket.

Mayor Rowland had let it be understood that it was the desire of the C.B.&Q. to build from Palmyra or Munroe through to Sedalia. Joy understood the Katy was under contract with the Northern Extension of the Tebo Road, Rowland confided, to make fair running arrangements and give them rates of freight and fares equally as low as any other company, and the Burlington was ready to "put the iron on" at the earliest possible date.[12]

Knowing the wily "James F.," Colonel Stevens wondered whether Joy was really in earnest and honest in what he had told Mayor Rowland, or whether, having aided the A.&P. to secure control of the Missouri Pacific, he now, by getting control of the Northern Extension, would shut the Katy out entirely. Stevens considered it outrageous that the Missouri Pacific should attempt to deprive the city of St. Louis of the potentially enormous southwestern trade by closing the Sedalia gateway to the Katy, and he thought it quite unfair of them to work covertly to turn St. Louis sentiment against the company at the same time by accusing the Katy of trying to divert the traffic from St. Louis to Chicago.

An explanation of the sudden change in Katy plans, the quick switch in destination from Chicago to St. Louis, is, of course, to be found in the fact that Joy, president of the Burlington, was in control of every gateway to Chicago and was out to crush the Katy by blocking it at every turn. Under the circumstances, Stevens had no alternative but to take his licking at the hands of the Missouri Pacific or to build north to a junction with the North Missouri Road, say at Moberly, and reach St. Louis through that connection.

Especially embarrassing for Judge Parsons was the success of the "campaign of vilification" in the eastern money marts. It effectively prevented him from peddling enough stocks and bonds to enable him to extend the railroad at both ends at the same time—and both extensions were vital. Stevens, in fact, had been instructed to reduce expenses to a minimum and to "ease up your drafts all you can."

In compliance with these instructions some strange things happened. For example, he had declined to pay county taxes in Kansas, justifying this action on the very sound grounds that the counties had refused to pay interest due on their bonds. A shrewd lawyer, the General Manager knew he had a fine legal point here, but he reckoned without the rough-and-ready pioneer spirit possessed by the Kansas frontiersmen, which made naught of fine legal points. The company received a painful lesson in Kansas law when a sheriff's

[12] General Manager's Report.

posse held up a Katy train at Council Grove, removed the crew at gun point, and fastened the engine to the track with a chain! Kansas had levied upon the Katy with a vengeance, and Stevens meekly paid the $8,491.41 due and got his train back. As to what became of the bond interest, due from the county, the record is silent.

In St. Louis, the perplexed General Manager had a long visit with his very good friend Dan Garrison, recently retired vice president and general manager of the Pacific, who was not too happy about that road's subservience to the A.&P. and had little respect for Andrew Peirce and his devious ways.[13] The "Commodore," utterly honest, held out no hope that the Katy could effect any practicable working arrangements with the M.P.–A.&P. combination, which, he declared, was obviously out to ruin the line and then acquire it after foreclosure.

"Bob," said Mr. Garrison finally, "tell Judge Parsons there is but one solution of this trouble for the M.K.&T., and that is to go right ahead and build to Fayette or Moberly. This will bring the Missouri Pacific to their knees. The Judge knows Peirce, and knowing him can but be conscious of what Peirce will do if he has the opportunity." Colonel Ray, who was with the Commodore, broke in with: "Your people have been sold down the river, and I know who got the money!"[14]

Greatly troubled in spirit, Bob Stevens returned to Sedalia, to the now almost open hostility of the Missouri Pacific people at that key point in the Katy's plans, and to the dreary prospect of still more fighting before his new-born railroad—be it ever so strategically located—could be made to pay its way. Steadily the situation deteriorated all along the line of road. Each day's developments proved to Stevens that Garrison was right, and Colonel Ray's hint convinced him that Joy was the "nigger in the woodpile."

[13] A man of many parts and a powerful influence in the development of St. Louis in his day, Daniel Randall Garrison was a builder of the Bob Stevens type, a constructor in a world of "projectors." As general manager of the Ohio and Mississippi Railroad, he had successfully brought that struggling line west to the Father of Waters, giving St. Louis its first rail service to the East. During the Civil War he had taken the Pacific of Missouri in hand and as general manager of that line finished it from Sedalia to Kansas City by October, 1865. He was who set some sort of record in 1869 by reducing the Pacific's track gauge from 5 feet, 6 inches to 4 feet, 9 inches in sixteen hours flat. By 1870, however, when he was 55 years old, he had temporarily lost patience with the political trickery (and treachery) in which the state's railroads were steeped, and had returned to his first love, the iron foundry business. In 1871 he was busily building up St. Louis' Vulcan Iron Works.—J. Thomas Scharf, *History of St. Louis City and County,* 1170.

[14] Letter Book No. 6.

After his visit with Commodore Garrison, the General Manager declared: "At first, the prospect of being closed in, after a year of such hard labor, was, I must confess, annoying, but it has ceased to trouble me, and I am now ready to roll up my sleeves and, strength being given, go in for another gay fight."[15]

Judge Parsons, no mean fighter himself, adopted his general manager's ideas with enthusiasm and immediately set about the business of gathering the sinews of war required to build the line north. While the end-of-track still reposed at Big Cabin in the Indian Territory, Parsons and Stevens quickly organized and operated what was certainly the first and probably the greatest "investment bankers' excursion" in Katy history. Publicity-wise even then, Katy officials had nearly as many newspapermen on the train as there were investors, and their glowing reports, reprinted all over the nation, improved the Katy's stock and bond position remarkably and did much to offset the damage caused by the Missouri Pacific's intensive campaign of vilification.

Newspaper reports of this trip, obviously written with an eye to pleasing host Stevens, are dull, drab things when compared with employees' notes on this pioneer tour. The intention was to stay overnight at the railhead (Vinita), but disturbances there persuaded the general manager that he'd better get his precious cargo back to civilization as quickly as possible, before somebody important got hurt.

It seems that some ignorant, unlettered Cherokees, who had fenced in some fine timber land and secured themselves a "bond right," sold a lot of trees to Loring and Company, who had the local contract to provide ties. Guilelessly the Indians padded around, quietly notching on sticks the number of ties taken out. The workmen, aside from curious glances, "paid them no mind." When the time came for Loring to settle up, lo, the notches did not agree with the count made by the contractor, and LO, the poor Indians, pointed out the discrepancy. Loring and Company, however, brushed them off, probably with unnecessary roughness, and proceeded to forget about the whole matter until, as fate would have it, some of the distinguished visitors decided to wander over towards the timber for a closer inspection. Greeted with blood-curdling war whoops and a fusillade of shots, the terrified visitors turned tail and fled helter-skelter back to the train, never to leave it again until the embarrassed Bob Stevens had it under steam and headed north.

15 *Ibid.*

It was then decided to spend the night in Chetopa, that "model" frontier cowtown with which Colonel Horner and the *Southern Kansas Advance* could find no fault. What happened there is best told by the train conductor, A. O. Brown: "They intended to stay in Chetopa overnight, but after supper they went out to see the city. At that time it was mostly built of tents and tepees. Of course they ran into a roughhouse, and one man was killed. So the New Yorkers wouldn't stay any longer. The train came up to Parsons and stayed all night. There was no Parsons there, only a few little houses."[16]

The lone prairie, it seems, was safer than the settlements!

Fortunately for Colonel Stevens, no other bloody encounters marred the trip. Filled with enthusiasm and Ike Cook's champagne, the junketeers were taken up the fair Neosho Valley, to be feted and fawned upon at every whistle stop enroute to Junction City. They saw at first hand the hundreds upon hundreds of settlers swarming upon the land; they saw the raw towns mushrooming up all over the luxuriant Indian prairie, and they found all of it good. The Osage Ceded Lands, once the haunt of the buffalo and the coyote, already were showing the marks of the plow; rude shanties—and some not so rude—were beginning to dot the landscape.

Steaming grandly through the Kaw Diminished Reserve just beyond Council Grove, the easterners had their first taste of Indians in the primitive. Here the Katy tracks follow for some miles the Kaw trail to Junction. At this point, "A band of vagabond-looking fellows, bedecked in dirt, paint, and feathers, rode up on diminutive ponies." According to Conductor Brown, "We stopped the train to let these New York men see the Indians. It being a special train was all decorated with U. S. Flags. [A gaudy sight, that old diamond-stacker!] As soon as the train stopped, the Indians swarmed over it, stole all the flags, and tried to get in the coaches, which we locked. The New Yorkers were frightened and requested that the train move on. Whooping and hollering, the Indians jumped on their ponies and chased the train."[17]

[16] Excerpted from employees' reports, May, 1871. Conductor Brown's report was made available through the courtesy of his widow, Mrs. A. O. Brown, of Parsons, Kansas.

[17] Concerning the Kaw tribe, the newspapermen reported: "The Kaws are the only tribe within the state and number less than 700 souls. In 1860–61 Mr. R. S. Stevens had the contract for erecting 150 stone dwellings for the Kaws, which we passed. The buildings are now (1871) mostly deserted. The Indians, instead of living in them, sold the windows, roofs, and flooring, stabled their ponies in the deserted dwellings, while they lived outside in miserable bark huts. The reserve contains about 230,000 acres, including the Trust Lands,

Down Through the Cherokee Nation

By all modern standards, the Katy's first "Investors' Special" was an unqualified success. Everything that could be done had been done to counter the Pacific's drive on Judge Parsons' southwestern empire, and the relieved Colonel Stevens was well content to get back to the peace and quiet of the end-of-track.

which are now worth from $25 to $30 per acre where settled up."—*St. Louis Republican*, May 26, 1871.

Katy inspection train stopped by Kaw Indians
just north of Council Grove, Kansas, May, 1871

THIRTEEN

The "Trail of Tears"

Back in Sedalia, later, Colonel Stevens thought he could afford to overlook the discourtesies not only of the Missouri Pacific but also of the "landed gentry," the so-called City Fathers, and the local newspaper people, all apparently "in the know" about the imminent demise of the Katy. It was not generally known, however, that Joe Seligman's withdrawal from the Katy directorate, a natural consequence of his company's large holdings in the Pacific combination, had been neatly offset by the addition at the annual meeting in May of J. Pierpont Morgan, a fairly new but already powerful figure in the railroad banking world.

Despite the danger signals, the Colonel drove steadily ahead with his plans, laying new rail ever southward, plastering the entire Southwest with his "dodgers" announcing "the shortest, cheapest route to the Beautiful Indian Territory & Texas," and pleading with Judge Parsons for new equipment to handle an anticipated enormous increase in business. At the Annual meeting on May 17, he had reported the equipment of the road as follows:

Locomotives	24
Passenger Cars	23
Baggage and Mail Cars	10
Box Freight	200
Flat Freight	300
Cattle	250
Coal	56
Other	32

Since then, the General Manager had received four more Grant locomotives, Nos. 25, 26, 27, and 28, and additional baggage and mail cars, coaches, flats, coal cars, and cars "designed expressly for Texas other road." These were forerunners of the Katy's famous Palace Stock Cars, featuring individual stalls for each animal, which were first introduced in 1873.

Arriving at the end of track on June 4, Colonel Stevens found the horny-handed John Scullin forging ahead at his customary "mile a minit" pace. The track had crossed White Oak Creek, and the Irish Brigade, despite the heat, mosquitoes, malaria, cholera, surly Indians, and miscellaneous pestilences, had laid over twelve miles of track in ten consecutive days. They were then crossing the domain of the famous Cherokee subchief, William P. Adair, who was no friend of the railroad.[1]

Although the Cherokee 'bloods and 'breeds committed no overt acts in an organized way, their miasmic lands scourged the Katy's builders worse, perhaps, than any human agency. Sickness was rife, and the workers, particularly the wagon drivers, quit in droves. Major Gunn and young F. O. Marvin,[2] who had been newly appointed to the post of assistant on superstructure on both tracklaying and bridge building, complained to the General Manager with tears in their eyes that conditions at the railhead "were fearful in the extreme," and strongly urged that work be postponed for a month, when conditions might improve.

It was utterly impossible to do work on the prairie during the day, Stevens was told. The stock were nearly eaten up alive. Scullin had his horses and mules covered entirely over with Burlaps; he had made leggings for them, and rubbed every exposed portion of their flesh with fish oil, yet blood fairly dripped from them at times it was reported.

Regretfully, for Stevens was a humane man although a hard driver, the General Manager ordered the work to proceed without respite. Time had him by the forelock again. The workmen cussed him profanely, they cussed Scullin and all his forebears, they cussed the Indians, the flies, the sun, the red-hot iron rail, and they drove their spike mauls with such concentrated bitterness that by mid-

---

[1] The remarkable Adair family of Cherokee-Scots gave many illustrious members to the Nation and are deservedly honored not only by the Cherokees but by all of the Five Civilized Tribes.

[2] Mr. F. O. Marvin, nephew of H. L. Marvin, then bridge engineer, was for many years dean of the school of engineering, University of Kansas, Lawrence, Kansas. In his later years, Dean Marvin recounted the hardships and perils of his early railroad building years with the Katy in Indian Territory.

June the end of track had progressed another ten miles to Pryor's Creek,[3] fifty miles south of the border and halfway to Fort Gibson.

The task of Stevens' men, that hot summer of 1871, was a grueling but monotonous one. They graded dirt, they built their bridges and their trestles and their culverts, and they laid track, but before they could do those jobs they had to cut and slash their way through countless malaria-infested "bottoms," and across miasmic sloughs, splitting the canebrakes that grew almost as thick as the jungle in places and frequently thirty feet high. Here the Texas Trail, which they had paralleled all the way from the border, was known as the Gibson Road, and at Pryor's Creek it lay, hot, hard and dusty, a scant three miles east of the grade. Here the sweating workers could see in the distance interminable lines of white-covered wagons with their great hitches of oxen or mules creaking stolidly over the prairie, some destined for the military posts at forts Gibson, Sill, Richardson, or Griffin, but many of them immigrant trains bound for Texas or "Californy." Frequently the workers would stop to watch handsome stages bowl smartly over the hard packed earth behind spanking teams of spirited horses, and listen enviously as other knights of the road "hoorayed" them along with outlandish shouts, the cracking of bull whips, and the enthusiastic if dangerous firing off of rusty fire-arms. At nights they could "light out" and join the campfires of the cowpunchers who were riding herd on the great drives of longhorn Texan or Indian cattle now coming up the trail to the Katy's rail-head, but mainly the workmen stayed close to the track and found their relaxation in card games, story-telling, and drinking with their fellows in the tents and shanties they knew as home.

The Katy railhead was now "nearly twenty-four hours nearer St. Louis than by the Atlantic and Pacific," yet the Texas mails were still being staged to the A.&P. railhead and sent over that route, evidence that the two Pacific railroads were using their political power in St. Louis and Washington. In retaliation, Colonel Stevens made satisfactory arrangements with the North Missouri Road (Wabash) for the transportation of Government freight from St. Louis to New Chicago (Chanute, Kansas), thence via his Neosho Division to the Indian Territory and Texas, by-passing the Pacific lines entirely. Here, of course, he was short-hauling himself between Sedalia and Parsons—and the former city would feel the loss of the business

[3] The prosperous town of Pryor, which now occupies this site, was named for the redoubtable Nathanial Pryor, pioneer Indian trader and subagent to the warlike Osages.

severely—but the "outrageous rates" charged on Katy traffic between St. Louis and Sedalia made this route economically feasible.

Except for the Pacific set-back the general manager had everything running smoothly on his new line. Freight business was increasing daily as the road crawled slowly south. Receipts for May exceeded April, and with its new cattle and grain traffic the line was doing even more business than had been anticipated.

By the time the end of track had reached Pryor's Creek, the Cherokee National Council was mustering all its strength against the railroad, and, of course, against the Stand Watie-Boudinot faction which favored it. The Indian Treaty had promised little more than the right-of-way through the tribal lands, and the Ross Party was determined not to provide (or permit) one iota more. The workers were harassed, the officials baffled, at every turn. The leading "councillors" of the Nation interposed every objection, every difficulty, they could devise, to obstruct and delay the railroad's progress. Successfully they stirred up the ignorant full-bloods and meaner 'breeds to a menacing antagonism that more than once threatened the success of the enterprise.

Actually the tracklayers saw little of the Indians except for occasional small parties galloping over the prairie on their diminutive ponies, headed no one knew where and bent on designs of their own. Their villages were not on the prairie but mostly along the timbered banks of the Grand (or Neosho) River, which here flowed parallel to the grade but about ten miles to the east, away out of sight beyond the Gibson Road. Such "diviltry" as was worked here was done under cover of the night, and none knew by whom hand or order the evil was perpetrated.

A considerable number of small settlements had grown up along this river in the half century since the Cherokees had reached this happy hunting ground and ejected the wild Osages with the help of the Great White Father. Here had been the famous Chouteau trading post, headquarters for Auguste Pierre Chouteau's far-flung fur and Indian supply trade; here Frère Pierre Chouteau had reigned as resident manager and U. S. Indian agent for the Osages. This was the "Inden Cuntry" made famous by Washington Irving in his immensely popular *A Tour on the Prairies,* a romantic account of a trip he had made through this territory in company with Auguste Pierre Chouteau back in 1832. Incredibly, here on the river's brim had been a magnificent "white log house with piazza" where Colonel Chouteau had lived with his Indian wife and raised a tribe of half-blood children in wild but munificent splendor, waited upon hand and foot by dusky slaves. Here had been built a private racecourse, complete with blooded stock, hundreds of miles from "civilization," for the royal entertainment of Chouteau's friends: all the perquisites of a lordly baron who wielded sovereign power deep in a savage wilderness. Here was the Grand Saline or primitive Indian saltworks which had been worked, off and on, for fifty years; and this was the vale of the Cherokee Nation's "Trail of Tears!"[4]

Irked by the grasping proclivities of the self-seeking near-whites of the Cherokee National Council who were perpetrating what the general manager considered "highway robbery" upon all who crossed their domain, Colonel Stevens suddenly decided to by-pass Fort Gibson, the only settlement of consequence in the Nation, and head for the Creek (Mus-co-gee) country just as quickly as possible. Unburdening his resentment, he told Judge Parsons: "One great drawback to all lines seeking the cattle business in this vicinity is this 'devilish,' unjust, 'unconstitutional' and unwarranted tax on cattle levied by the 'noble red man,' amounting to $1.75 each. You may rest assured I will make every effort possible to get out of Mr. Cherokee's country at the earliest day possible into that of the Creeks, and save 50c per head."

So it was that instead of following the Texas Road and the course of the Grand River to Fort Gibson, the railroad track was laid due south, making a beeline for the northeastern corner of the Creek Nation a dozen miles away. From that moment the legendary Fort Gibson, perhaps the most important military fort on the western frontier, began to wither and die, and the vision of a great city within the confines of the Creek Nation, perhaps to be named Mus-co-gee, began dimly to take form.

In Fort Gibson, Colonel Stevens revealed his new plan to General William Tecumseh Sherman and got his approval of the slight change in route. Vastly interested in the military value of the railroad, the famous commander of the Civil War accompanied Stevens on a brief inspection tour of the new survey, and the two became very good friends. To clinch the friendship, an invaluable one for the road, Stevens ordered up a special train for the old warrior and sent him happily on his way to Leavenworth, not, however, before beguiling him with visions of the great depot it would be necessary to erect at the Three Forks of the Arkansas, and the great city that surely would

[4] John Francis McDermott, *The Western Journals of Washington Irving,* 108–10.

arise on the site.[5] The General was thoroughly in accord with the idea and immediately issued instructions for the improvement of the old military road which ran from Fort Gibson to old Fort Davis, the Civil War fort at the Three Forks, and continued on southwest to Fort Sill. Thus Fort Gibson was dealt a blow from which it was never to recover.

The trestle over Pryor's Creek was not ready for the iron until June 28, and Bob Stevens was impatient to press on into the Creek country. Despite the warnings of Boss Tracklayer Scullin and the engineers, the order went out—drive on! "I don't intend to let up unless the flies and pestilence drive us plumb out of the country," he told his harassed subordinates.[6]

With the new location of the track approved and the crossings of the Verdigris and Arkansas rivers lined in, Boomer's bridge gangs were already hard at work. Boomer had promised to have the trestle across the Verdigris finished by September 1 and the great 840-foot bridge over the Arkansas by October 1. He had a force of one hundred men on the bridges, with dozens of heavy ox teams hauling masonry for the piers, and all around the Three Forks was hurry and bustle.

Despite the Colonel's drive and his explosive impatience, the end of track crept south with a slowness that was maddening. Myriads of "flies" drove the tracklayers to distraction and to sick beds. Although ties were abundant in the timber, the bull whackers were frequently unable to get their teams on their feet, the whip and the picturesque curses for once useless. The only cheering note of this time was that "all Texas is now alive to our railroad," and the railroad was receiving more than its full share of cattle. Long wagon trains of the Overland Transit Company, organized by Maurice, McDonald and Company, were beginning to arrive from the south with great quantities of cotton. These prairie schooners were strikingly marked:

OVERLAND TRANSIT CO.

M

M. K. & T. R. W.

[5] Thomas Nuttall, the famous English naturalist who in 1819 ascended the Arkansas River to the very heart of Indian Territory, wrote prophetically of the Three Forks: "If the confluence of the Verdigris, Arkansas and Grand rivers, shall ever become of importance as a settlement, which the great and irresistible tide of western immigration promises, a town will probably be found here, at the junction of these streams."—*A Journey Into Arkansa Territory*, (Philadelphia, 1821), 272.

[6] General Manager's Report.

The Texas trail between Pryor's Creek and Chouteau's
(Cherokee Nation), I. T., July, 1871

The name stood out brilliantly against the white canvas tops of the wagons and the verdant green of the prairies, and the endless lines that strung out all along the trail between the end-of-track and the Red River were balm to the Colonel's soul. Agent Davis, the General Manager's runner in the south, reported every hamlet in northern Texas bulging with cotton and awaiting the freighters from "our line."

By the end of June, 1871, Colonel Stevens claimed to have "hauled more stock into Sedalia than the Kansas Pacific have to Kansas City —I think by 2 to 1."

At this time, Stevens couldn't resist the temptation to renew his plea for a new northern connection. "Our great drawback, however, to all this business," he told Judge Parsons heatedly, "is the doing of anything that is reasonable with Peirce. Brown and Bridge of the Mo. Pac. are mere nonentities. The entire controlling spirits of the whole concern are Hayes & Peirce, together with their advisors of the Atlantic & Pacific. The Missouri Pacific exists merely in name."[7]

By July 20, the end-of-track, doggedly pushed forward by hundreds of gaunt and sallow tracklayers, half sick, fevered by dysentery, typhoid, and "chills," reached the northern border of the Creek country, and the entire organization heaved a collective sigh of relief. The terminus was moved that day down from Pryor's Creek to Chouteau's (they folded their tents like the Arabs). Then the trains commenced running to and from that point, sixty miles deep in the Indian Territory.

[7] Letter Book No. 0.

FOURTEEN

Into the Creek (Mus-ko-gee) Country

The end-of-track was moving so fast during the summer of 1871 that the "terminuses" had little chance to grow into the wild, dangerous robbers' roosts that developed a short time later. In southern Kansas, however, where the might of federal justice theoretically reached right down to Chetopa, all was not well. With the flood of eager homesteaders pouring into the coveted Osage Ceded Lands had come also the riffraff of the West and the offscourings of the big eastern cities—all those on the wrong side of the law who had discovered that the Indian Territory line was a grand refuge from pursuit.

Conditions soon became so bad that the Osage District Protective Association and similar vigilante organizations were formed by the settlers to combat the outlawry. They were successful in one instance at least, in a case so celebrated in its day that a mere mention of it here should serve to illuminate the whole ghastly period.

The mystery of the Labette Hills, ever since known as the Bender Mounds, really began in the early weeks of 1871, when newspapers from as far away as Kansas City and St. Louis began publishing accounts of men reported missing in the Southwest. Patient tracing by relatives and by the law narrowed the search down to the area of the wagon trace which ran between Old Osage Mission and the new settlement of Independence, a few miles west of Parsons. This mail-stage road crossed the Katy tracks just north of the Parsons junction, and everyone in the mushrooming tent town was suspect.

It was not until Dr. William York, a widely known and greatly respected border physician, was reported missing that a determined effort was made to unravel the mystery. A posse of sixty hard-eyed frontiersmen began a minute search of the suspected area. They visited every shack, every cave, every cabin, no matter how carefully tucked away; and they grilled every bad actor on the border. Eventually they came upon the Bender place. This was a sixteen by twenty-four foot shack which William Bender and his wife, his surly son John, and his pretty red-haired daughter, Kate, had built on the 160 acres they had homesteaded back in October, 1870.

The Benders were frugal Germans, thick of speech and thick of body, slow in their actions, and exhibiting none of the spontaneous friendliness that was typical of the newly settled Irish and of the early French traders and trappers of Kansas Territory. Their home was a reflection of themselves; they had partitioned off the front part as a store, where they offered for sale a pitifully small stock of groceries. The partition consisted of rough hewn boards except for a wide space from roof joist to floor that could be curtained off by an outstretched wagon sheet, and behind this was the family living quarters.

The luscious nineteen-year-old Kate Bender seemed hardly to be one of the family. The flame-crowned daughter was a clever girl who frequently traveled around the settlements promoting spiritualist meetings and giving seances. Her striking beauty and her undoubted accomplishments attracted business to the Bender store for some time, but the surliness of her menfolk soon antagonized the neighbors, so that by the time the posse visited the area, not only the Bender men but Kate herself was suspect. Many of the settlers, urged on by their women, were beginning to murmur that perhaps Kate Bender was the siren that lured travelers to the port of missing men.

Although the posse found nothing amiss at the Bender store, a few days later Leroy F. Dick, a neighbor, learned that the Bender stock was wandering about the farm, unfed and untended. Investigation revealed that the place had been hastily deserted. Mr. Dick and a quickly summoned posse broke into the shack and, urged on by the evidences of sudden flight, soon uncovered bloody evidence of foul play.

In the vegetable patch at the back of the house, and in a shallow well that had recently been filled in, they dug up the horribly mangled bodies of Dr. York and seven other missing persons. Each had been stunned, perhaps killed outright by a blow from a claw hammer which had fractured each skull. Then a heavy shoe hammer had been used to bash them almost out of recognition. Soon three more bodies were found in the neighborhood, making a total of eleven bodies recovered. By popular account the fate of some thirty or more victims, missing in the same area at the same time, never did become known.

The murder plot was easily reconstructed. Apparently it had been the custom of the Benders to seat lone travelers, inveigled by the lovely Kate, with their backs to the wagon sheet partition which screened the living quarters from the store. While the victim was engaged in talk by one of the family, another casually disappeared behind the makeshift curtain, and, as opportunity offered, delivered the fatal stroke from behind the sheet.

In spite of many clues and a nationwide search—with the poor facilities for such a search that then existed along the frontier— neither Kate, whose pretty hands may have actually committed some of the murders, nor any of her family were ever found.[1]

In the few short months since the iron horse had invaded the Indian country, a vast transformation had taken place along the Cherokee Strip.[2] Whereas the border previously had been delineated merely as a line on a cartographer's tracing, by mid-Summer of 1871 it was startlingly visible. From east to west it appeared as an even line, with fence nearly all of the way—on the south side an unbroken prairie, on the north, farms, orchards, pleasant dwellings, and every evidence of civilization.[3]

At Parsons, focal point of the area's development, the settlement was in a fair way to becoming a bustling city overnight. Already it was beginning to fulfill Bob Stevens' prophesy that here would rise a city that would quickly become a metropolis. Great mountains of goods were daily being loaded and unloaded at the Katy's makeshift station for reshipment to and from the Indian Territory, Neosho Valley points, and the East. Immense piles of trade goods were changing hands daily on the boardwalks, offered by merchants who had not yet had a chance to build their stores; and the verdant prairie was rapidly disappearing in a great sea of canvas tents and board shanties that lapped in every direction.[4]

[1] Mrs. Will Cunningham, a native Parsonian and daughter of Leroy F. Dick, one of the principals in the investigation, is authority for this version of the Bender Mounds murders.

[2] Not to be confused with the much larger Cherokee Outlet lying south of the thirty-seventh parallel. The Cherokee Strip, approximately two and one-half miles deep, extending from east to west north of the thirty-seventh parallel, was ceded in trust by the Cherokees to the United States after the Civil War, and as part of Kansas was sold to settlers in 1872.

[3] Beadle, *The Undeveloped West*, 362.

[4] In the spring of 1871, Parsons was a "town of magical growth . . . the

Into the Creek (Mus-ko-gee) Country

Back in April, the General Manager's closest collaborator, Land Grant Company President Frank Skiddy, had discussed with Colonel Stevens the idea of publishing a newspaper at Parsons. Such a paper was sorely needed, they felt, to fight the local sheets which were blossoming virulently in every new hamlet along the line of road. Especially was it needed to challenge the scurrilous Land League paper, the *Anti-Monopolist*. "It is not that we need the paper to blow for us," the General Manager virtuously asserted, "but to disabuse the minds of the people of seditious[5] articles published in the *Anti-Monopolist* simply for the sake of stirring up troubles."

Sometime during May, Colonel Stevens arranged to start the *Parsons Sun*, and quickly a prospectus was issued on it. In glowing terms it predicted a magnificent future for Parsons and promised "a first-class paper, one that will do credit to the town and company."

By the first of June, a "large building twenty-four by sixty feet" had been put up to house this "infant wonder,"[6] and on June 17, 1871, Volume I, Number 1, came off the press. The masthead carried the names of Milton W. Reynolds and Leslie J. Perry as editors and proprietors, but actually the railroad was the proprietor. The *Sun* was an immediate success and dutifully reflected glory upon its creators. It did Trojan work not only for the "town and company" but for the entire border country. Eventually, the Katy retired from its covert management and direction, and that step strengthened, perhaps, rather than hurt this influential organ, for it has survived many vicissitudes through the years and today is one of the most respected daily newspapers in the Southwest.

Down at the railhead south of Chouteau's Creek, typhoid pneumonia and "chills" were taking their toll of the tracklayers. It was the general belief that this particular section of the Indian Territory would never be settled because "white men could never survive in such a poisonous atmosphere." Half the force was disabled by malarial diseases, and soon it was reported that "one in every eighteen" of the whites along the line of road had died of the miasmic sickness. Nevertheless, building went on steadily if a trifle shakily all through July, chiefly because big John Scullin, the peerless construction boss, was replacing casualties about as quickly as they oc-

avenues and the great public square are still paved with the original green sward and prairie flowers."—*St. Louis Republican*, May 26, 1871.

[5] Note empire builder Stevens' royal choice of adjectives. All opposition to him was "seditious!" Letter Book No. 6.

[6] This soubriquet was early applied both to Parsons City and the *Parsons Sun*.

curred. By August 1, he was able to wire the General Manager that they were laying track at the rate of a mile a day again, and would reach Flat Rock Creek by Saturday night. That would be August 5, so the Irish Brigade had advanced the railhead another ten miles in fewer than fourteen working days.[7]

Much relieved by Scullin's progress, Colonel Stevens happily wrote Vice President Denison (who at this time was acting president in the absence of Levi Parsons, who had gone to Europe in an all-out effort to interest English, Dutch, and French capital in Katy Railroad bonds) that:

> From Flat Rock creek to the Verdigris, where we shall establish our station for all business until we shall cross the Arkansas [this was the notorious Gibson Station], is but 12 miles distant, and it is only 3½ miles from there to the Arkansas River. Boomer tells me he has sent additional forces and will have the bridge over the Verdigris River done by the 15th of September & the Arkansas by the 1st of October.[8]

Right at this moment, however, an ominous thing occurred to upset the equanimity of the General Manager, and, much worse than that, to undermine his self-respect and somewhat dampen his enthusiasm for the entire enterprise. Major Frank J. Bond arrived in Sedalia with written authority to "consult and advise on matters generally connected with our enterprises." This stuffy, self-important little major immediately began to assume authority over the choleric Colonel Stevens, but quickly he found he had caught a tartar! The General Manager wasted not a moment in making it crystal clear that he would bow to no such authority—and he insisted on carrying on like the empire builder he undoubtedly was. Here was the first faint indication that there might be a schism in the financial ranks, and with President Parsons absent in Europe, it smacked of treachery. Since the split developed slowly, however, we leave it for the moment and return to the end-of-track.

On August 27, the railhead reached the Verdigris River bank, Scullin's men having come a distance of fourteen miles in eighteen working days. In addition they had put in a 2,000-foot side track at Flat Rock (now Mazie, Oklahoma), and a similar terminus facility on the high ground about a mile and a half north of the Verdigris crossing point, which quickly became known as Gibson Station. The tracklaying gangs immediately crossed the river and began laying

[7] General Manager's Report.
[8] Letter Book No. 6.

rail on the three-and-one-half mile finished grade through the Three Forks settlements to the Arkansas River. General Hazen's military detachment from Fort Gibson was strung out over the prairie busily completing a wagon road between the terminus and the fort, and by September 1 Gibson Station was a busy terminal, indeed.

With the fulfillment of the railroad's commitment to "connect the military posts," the company promptly notified the commissioner of Indian affairs that:

> The Missouri, Kansas & Texas Railway Company, having completed its road through the State of Kansas, into and through the territory of the Cherokee Indians, into the Creek Country, to the Arkansas River, having its roadbed ready for iron nearly to the Canadian River, its line located to the Red River, to which latter named point it will be entirely completed and cars running by July 1, 1872, I would respectfully state that said Company is now ready and desirous of negotiating with the various tribes of Indians through whose territory its line of road passes, between the southern boundary of Kansas and the Red River, viz: The Cherokees, Creeks, Choctaws and Chickasaws, for the purpose of acquiring title to lands necessary for railroad purposes, in accordance with the provisions of Section 10 of an Act, entitled "An Act granting lands to the State of Kansas to Aid in the Construction of the Kansas & Neosho Valley Railroad, and its extension to Red River"—approved July 25th, 1866 (See U. S. Statutes Vol. 14, page 238). And also in accordance with Article 1866 (See U. S. Statutes, Vol. 14, pages 787 & 788.)

At this juncture, the trail-breaking railroaders had amply earned the plaudits of the multitude. They had done a magnificent job in the face of mountainous difficulties. The moment the end-of-track reached the Three Forks, the frontier automatically receded hundreds of miles to the westward, and henceforth this was civilization —of a sort.

But for Bob Stevens the fruits of achievement were many miles and several years away; the laurels perhaps never to be his. At Gibson Station, where all was excitement and disorder, he learned that emergencies which demanded his personal attention were arising all along the line. There was some comfort in the knowledge that the Overland Transportation Company, a heavy freighter outfit formed by the general manager to absorb and expand the wagon train company of Graham and Maurice, had been awarded the contract for the hauling of government supplies to forts Richardson, Griffin, and Sill. This meant that thereafter the movement of all quartermaster's stores, government, and Indian supplies into and through the Southwest would be controlled by the Katy. On the other hand, strange things were happening several miles north of Boudinot's Vinita townsite.

Superintendent Eddy, recently placed in charge of the Cherokee division, urgently telegraphed the General Manager that the Atlantic and Pacific people had "commenced the erection of a passenger and freight house within seventeen feet of our track" and were pushing it forward with great rapidity. He had notified the foreman it was being constructed within the Katy grade and asked him to desist until his chief could be heard from, but the foreman said his orders were to go ahead. This wire sent Colonel Stevens hurrying north, with fire in his eye, to find out what Andrew Peirce was up to at Vinita. There he ran into one of the most amazing instances of sharp practice in railroad building and townsite planning that he had yet encountered, and in this the General Manager was no slouch himself. At Big Cabin Creek, Stevens found Colonel Boudinot's terminus town of Vinita almost deserted. There was a rush on to a brand-new townsite some three miles to the north at a point where the Atlantic and Pacific graders had just crossed the Katy track and now were busy with their drags west of the crossing. Peirce's tracklayers were only a couple of miles away, slapping the iron down with feverish speed, and as the General Manager watched this birth of an A. and P. town on his own railroad, his gorge rose and his face went red.

The Atlantic and Pacific, it was plainly evident, had gained the co-operation of several officers of the Cherokee National Council by promising to by-pass Elias Boudinot's cleverly fenced townsite tract at the crossing originally surveyed. Obviously Peirce had agreed to "let them in" on the new townsite to be platted at the intersecting point of the new survey, and apparently had the blessing of Principal Chief Lewis Downing. Bearing out this theory was the fact that Peirce had relocated his line to cross the Katy some three miles north of the Big Cabin terminus and had laid out at the point of intersection the townsite of Downingville. Here he had fenced in a thousand valuable acres, all around the Katy main line, and by the time the hot-tempered Colonel Stevens arrived on the scene, Peirce's men were feverishly proceeding about the business of pre-empting the Katy's acres and building their facilities squarely on the general manager's right-of-way. By design, the Katy's own facilities were to remain high and dry on the prairie three long miles to the south. The naming of the point of intersection for the Principal Chief was a gracious touch, of course, and doubtless Andrew Peirce chuckled about it every time he thought of the Katy's discomfiture.

The Atlantic and Pacific had rather underestimated Colonel Boudinot's political sagacity, however, for the fact that Boudinot was finally "cut in" for one-third of the new townsite is ample testimony that the shrewd Indian lawyer made Andrew Peirce pay for his victory. He even gave the knife a twist by insisting that the name "Vinita," which he had originally chosen for the junction, be given the new site, and this was eventually done.

Furious with the double-dealing Indian, Bob Stevens sent Milt Reynolds out with instructions to hunt up Boudinot and call him to account. The Indian lawyer was sauve and apologetic, Reynolds reported, and told him to tell Colonel Stevens that the Atlantic and Pacific furnished the means for fencing the thousand acres of land surrounding the crossing. The A. & P. were to have four-sixths and he two-sixths, of which, he said, the Katy could take any amount it desired. (At his price, of course.) He still professed unbounded friendship for the Katy, Reynolds reported, and a great desire to co-operate, although he was, without doubt, in the hands of the Atlantic and Pacific.

Reynolds went on to report that Boudinot was concerned with his safety in the Indian Territory. "My life is threatened," he told Reynolds, "but my temper is up and I am determined to see the thing through although action good will result therefrom, though some Indian blood may flow.

Although the Indians played no prominent part in the railroad struggle for the Vinita townsite, some good Irish blood was spilt before the issue was decided. The first skirmish took place between the rival engineers. Otis Gunn peremptorily ordered A. & P. Engineer L. Kellett to get his forces, his equipment, and all his "damned buildings" off Katy property—forthwith! He ordered Katy crews to begin immediate construction of side tracks to occupy the area held by the A. & P. "squatters."

Superintendent Eddy engaged a party to take his teams and men there and go to work, but for some unaccountable reason, after a short delay, they informed Eddy they could not come. The next effort was the employment of a man by the name of Hart, one of the old A. & P. contractors, whose force was there at the crossing, but next morning he, too, withdrew because, he explained nervously, "threats had been used and he could not attempt to do the work."

When Gunn reported this state of affairs to Bob Stevens, the touchy Colonel went into such a rage as the quaking engineer had never seen before. "We've got to have action. We can't sleep upon our rights," the General Manager roared. It was about six o'clock in the evening and everybody had quit work for the day, but Stevens issued a general order for all hands to get back on the job and stand by for an emergency. He telegraphed his best fighting man, Long John Scullin, who was then at the Arkansas railhead, to move up his entire force and get ready to grade new Vinita sidings and lay rail overnight.

Wind of this move must have reached Peirce, for on Thursday night Kellett's men laid about a thousand feet of iron on each side of the Katy main line and next morning informed the engineer in charge that they would not permit the Katy to grade any sidings or to cut through their track.

On Friday morning, Scullin's construction train, loaded to the guards with track material and hundreds of wild veterans of the Irish Brigade, puffed laboriously into the original townsite at Big Cabin Creek and picked up Colonel Stevens and his staff. En route to the "Downingville" intersection, the General Manager held a council of war. "Here's what I want you to do, John," he said to Scullin. "Follow Gunn's tracings to the letter. Run your side tracks clear through their buildings if they won't move 'em. Level everything for our siding, and don't stop unless you are intimidated or driven off by superior numbers." Here Scullin laughed outright, but Stevens, still serious, added: "The law might move in. If the marshal serves you, stop, but not otherwise. Then Peirce will not be able to accuse us of having slept upon our rights."

Just as the outfit train reached the intersection, he drew Scullin aside and said quietly: "When your grade is ready for the sidings, John, lay down the ties, put on the iron, and so arrange the grading as to put our tracks directly over theirs." Then he added: "One thing more. Get rid of that damned crossing—I don't want it in my line!"

Big John Scullin did as bid. His fighting Irish swept everything and everybody before them, and by sundown the Katy side tracks were in, the grade more than a foot higher than that of the A. & P., whose stub track was effectively buried under Katy ballast, ties, and rail. With Peirce's main railhead still a mile and a half away, Stevens

Vinita (I. T.) townsite battle between Atlantic & Pacific
(Frisco) Railway and Katy construction gangs, October, 1871

felt amply justified in his action, and showed no concern when informed that Kellett had sent to Arkansas for a marshal.

The crowning insult was heaped upon Andrew Peirce shortly
after midnight Friday, when Scullin's pickets gave warning that an
A. & P. force was approaching to undo their labors of the day. Big
John's shock troops met them head on in the moonlight and routed
them in one of the bloodiest axe-handle fights in railroad construction history. Then to cap the climax, the Katy tracklayers, their

tempers thoroughly aroused, tore up the crossing points, loaded them in a wagon, and dumped them at Andrew Peirce's railhead just east of town. When Saturday morning dawned, the Katy construction train was discovered, rumbling leisurely back and forth on a straight, uninterrupted line of rail where the crossing used to be, with all aboard peacefully sleeping the sleep of the just.[9]

From Vinita south, down the old Texas Road, were fought some of the bloodiest and most exciting battles of the War in the West. Every creek crossing, every park-like prairie, every teepee, village, or timbered hide-out along the Texas Road between Cabin Creek (Vinita) and the Three Forks (Muskogee), has something to contribute to the history of the developing West. Grant Foreman, the Oklahoma historian, reports that along "this great thoroughfare there are more historical locations, features, and associations of historical interest and significance than are to be found on any other highway of even much greater extent west of the Mississippi River."[10]

The Vinita problem was just one of many that Bob Stevens was called upon to solve at this time. At Paola, Kansas, for example, there was the devil to pay because the end-of-track on the "Holden Line" was fast approaching Paola, and neither the County of Miami nor the City of Paola would pay. The county had voted a bond issue of $75,000 to bring the road in, and the city had added $25,000 additional. By September 16, with the railhead within eight miles of the city limits, the time had come for delivery of the bonds. An unidentified group of "cheats and swindlers," however, had secured an injunction to prevent issuance of the bonds, alleging various shortcomings in the road's specifications, and other objections. Thus the funds on which Colonel Stevens had counted to satisfy the railroad's creditors were suddenly tied up for an indefinite period. "I am fast arriving at the conclusion that there is no faith in man," the harassed General Manager wrote Judge Parsons that day. "It seems that all 'save us' are a set of cheats and swindlers."

On Sunday night, September 24, 1871, church-going Paolans stopped to gawk at hundreds of sweating Katy tracklayers, working a double shift, who, racing to beat an injunction, had advanced the railhead eight miles in a week and were then spiking the last rail, some four hundred feet inside the city limits. There was excitement

[9] See also Benedict, *History of Muskogee and Northeastern Oklahoma*, 661. The principal sources for the "Battle of Vinita," as related above, is Letter Book No. 6 and the General Manager's Reports.
[10] Foreman, *Down The Texas Road*, 9.

in the air, for everyone knew that a big celebration was in the making to signal the triumphant arrival of the iron horse on the morrow.

Colonel Stevens, himself a registered voter from Paola, entered the city on the first train with all the pomp and circumstance he could muster. The Board of County Commissioners, Mayor Smith, the Common (City) Council, and a large delegation of friends and citizens, met the General Manager and paraded him into town behind the Paola Silver Cornet Band which probably played the "Conquering Hero" march. Somebody made a welcoming address and Colonel Stevens rose to make the reply. Here was his opportunity, of which, the record indicates, he took full advantage.

"Not being in very good humor," Stevens candidly told friends later, "I talked very plainly. I gave them a brief history of that line of road, telling them of the great hesitancy with which it had been taken up by our company, and the urgency with which the Paola people insisted upon our taking it in hand. I also made emphatic reference to the constitutionality of the bonds, and reminded them of the unanimity with which they had endorsed the action of their commissioners."

The peppery Colonel's speech apparently was a classic, because it resulted immediately in emergency meetings of the Board of County Commissioners, the mayor, and the Common Council. Quickly they passed an ordinance waiving the necessity of the governor's certificate, the county commissioners declaring the road completed and accepted by them, and "directing the delivery of the bonds to the M. K. & T. forthwith."[11]

Back at the end of track, which was halted at Gibson awaiting completion of the great bridges over the Verdigris and the Arkansas, Colonel Stevens found the Three Forks a scene of almost indescribable activity that last week in September. Major Bond had got the turntable in, completed the side tracks, and by mid-month had erected two great yards for the loading of cattle. The station building, with a long rough addition for freight, was completed by Monday, September 18, and on that day regular passenger train service began operating between Gibson and the north.

A rough survey of the traffic potential revealed "that there are at least 75,000 head of cattle in the vicinity of the Arkansas," a fact which caused Stevens to anticipate a tremendous increase in business even before the river crossings were effected. The Overland Transportation Company were getting in fine working order, he

[11] General Manager's Report.

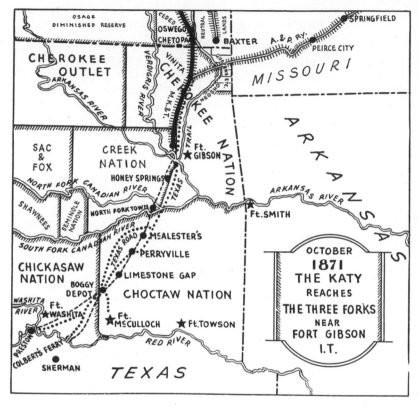

OSAGE
DIMINISHED RESERVE
CEDED
OSWEGO
CHETOPA
BAXTER
A. & P. RY.
SPRINGFIELD
PEIRCE CITY
CHEROKEE
OUTLET
ARKANSAS RIVER
VERDIGRIS RIVER
M.K.&T.
NEOSHO
MISSOURI
SAC
&
FOX
CREEK
NATION
HONEY SPRINGS
NORTH FORK CANADIAN RIVER
SHAWNEES
SEMINOLE NATION
NORTH FORKTOWN
Ft.
GIBSON
TRAIL
TEXAS
ARKANSAS RIVER
Ft.SMITH
ARKANSAS
CHICKASAW
NATION
SOUTH FORK CANADIAN RIVER
TEXAS ROAD
McALESTER'S
PERRYVILLE
LIMESTONE GAP
BOGGY
DEPOT
CHOCTAW NATION
WASHITA
RIVER
Ft.
WASHITA
Ft.
McCULLOCH
Ft.TOWSON
PRESTON
COLBERTS FERRY
SHERMAN
RED RIVER
TEXAS

OCTOBER
1871
THE KATY
REACHES
THE THREE FORKS
NEAR
FORT GIBSON
I.T.

boasted, and were loading trains almost every day. They had now caught up with the accumulated freight except for forty-eight cars and had teams enough to ship it without fail on arrival.

Accompanied by Major Bond and Chief Engineer Gunn, the General Manager inspected the Verdigris River bridge and, almost incredible in the light of what happened less than a week later, found that "The masonry is of a very superior class, all completed, and the falsework for one span up."[12] This bridge was being erected in three spans, two of 150 feet each, and one of 200 feet.

Just about quitting time on October 1, Boomer's men were swarming over the bridge, making all fast for the night. Suddenly the great structure began to sway, and before the workers, paralysed with fright, could do more than scream in terror, the great centre span, 200 feet in the clear, tore loose with an ear-rending crash and plunged into the river, taking nearly all of Boomer's men with it. The hand-

[12] Chief Engineer's Report.

ful of fortunate workmen on the remaining spans and on the banks were struck dumb, frozen stock-still for a moment, but they quickly recovered and began the work of rescue.

It was a heart-rending task for those who had been in the clear. Two bodies were quickly recovered from the river, another was removed by frantically manhandling an enormous iron girder out of the way, and eighteen critically injured workmen were tenderly carried up the steep banks and laid in a long row at the railhead to await medical attention. Scores of others, more or less severely injured, many of them suffering from shock, wandered vacantly around the prairie like whipped and bewildered children.

Three of the critically injured bridge builders died during the night. Train No. 2, out next morning, was transformed into a hospital train to rush dozens of the severely injured to hospitals in Sedalia and St. Louis.

FIFTEEN

The Three Forks Settlements

The wreckage of the Katy bridge lay just a stone's throw west of the famed Falls of the Verdigris. Here the river curves south to join the broad and muddy Arkansas, three miles below, and to mingle its waters with the limpid Grand (Neosho) River. This meeting place of the waters, looked upon by the Creek Indians as their Promised Land, and chosen as their agency headquarters, was perhaps the best known section in the Indian Territory, at least by hearsay. Variously known as the Three Forks, Falls of the Verdigris, or Creek Agency, it long was "farthest west" in the Indian country for daring traders and trappers who in the early years plied their trade under the guns of Fort Gibson.

Colonel A. P. Chouteau, the man who so impressed Washington Irving with the magnificence of his living in what the great essayist was pleased to call "the wilderness," once owned a "port" at the Three Forks. To this landing, keelboats and even an occasional paddle-wheeler plied from New Orleans and from St. Louis; here vast shipments of baled furs, incredible boatloads of the West's most valuable crop, were gathered and floated to eastern markets. Back in the 1830's, there was rather more water here, at the head of navigation, than there is today.

During his visit with Colonel Chouteau at the Three Forks, Irving met and was escorted about by Sam Houston. At the time of Irving's visit (1832), Houston was living primitively among the Cherokees in a log cabin about three miles east of the Katy's Verdigris crossing. His wilderness home, which he called Wigwam Neosho, was always well stocked with whisky, hauled from the East in keelboats, and assuredly it was convivial headquarters for the army officers stationed at near-by Fort Gibson.[1]

Forty years later, in this romantic setting, the frontier railroad, which had signalled its arrival with disaster, established the notorious Gibson Station. This short-lived terminus town soon achieved doubtful fame as the wildest, wickedest spot in the West.

Gibson Station was set up as a base of operations to serve for some little time, for it was expected that track laying would be delayed several months by the difficulties of passing the Verdigris and Arkansas river barriers.

With track laying temporarily halted Scullin's Irish brigade had time on their hands, money in their pockets, and opportunity to do little with either. As a consequence, Gibson terminus began to take on a deceptive air of permanence; it began to grow and flourish, wildly. Great, tented gambling hells went up, big enough to hold most of the riffraff in the territory—which they did. Gaudy ladies from the "dovecotes" of Sedalia and St. Louis set up establishments capacious enough to flatter a respectable sized city, and did a land-office business.

By the end of September, 1871, Katy Traffic Manager H. D. Mirick was beginning to be much concerned about conditions at Gibson. He reported that large quantities of government supplies were lying there awaiting shipment to military posts throughout Texas, more than the Overland Transit Company would be able to move forward for some time. His chief concern was "the horde of parasites" in the form of drunkards, robbers, terminus men and gamblers who had collected at the end-of-track.

Mirick had good reason to be worried. On September 13, the government had ordered the abandonment of Fort Gibson, and by the end of the month only a corporal's guard was left to keep order in the vast territory. With the removal of the soldiers, all hell broke loose, for the white man's law had no application in the Indian country. An anonymous reporter for the *Fort Scott Monitor* has given us a good description of Gibson terminus at the time. He wrote:

> It has fifty or sixty structures in which human beings live, sell whiskey, bacon, blankets, and such other articles as frontiersmen call for. There is more cloth than wood in these habitations, some being tents and some having sides made of boards, while the roofs are of canvas. Ruder stores and residences could not be made, and most of their occupants and

1 J. F. McDermott, *The Western Journals of Washington Irving,* 111. Marquis James, *The Raven,* 157.

inhabitants seem to be equally rude. We have seen much of new towns and rough life, but Gibson Station is "the worst card in the deck."

It is needless to add that there is gambling and drinking, shooting and killing going on here at nearly all hours of the day and night . . .[2]

A "Terminus Type"
—from *Scribner's Magazine*

Despite the best efforts of the Overland Transit Company, goods continued to pile up at the end-of-track. The hastily constructed warehouse was soon packed to the roof, and mountains of freight lay stacked around it, around the modest station building, in the wagon yards, and along the tracks. It was poorly protected against the elements by wagon sheets, and scarcely protected at all by the few railroad guards who found themselves well-nigh helpless against gangs of bold, heavily armed robbers. On October 6, President Levi Parsons, who had been fully advised of the situation at the railhead, urgently requested some government relief. He wrote the War Department:

There is an intense animosity among the Cherokees and Creeks, existing and demonstrating itself in various forms, between the full-bloods and the half-breeds. Naturally at the end of our Road there congregates a large number of white people

[2] *Fort Scott, Kansas, Monitor*, November 8, 1871.

—some well disposed, and others not so well disposed. There being no force to preserve order between the Indians and the white men, it leads to collisions constantly.

[Fort Gibson] at night is dangerous, and halfbreeds and whites are drinking, gambling and shooting all night long. Women of bad character are also in full force.[3]

The Katy President urged that a force of twenty-five or fifty soldiers be stationed at the Katy's railhead, to move forward from time to time as the road was extended, to preserve order and protect property.

Some idea of the volume of merchandise arriving at the railhead at this time is to be had from the October report of William C. Graham, heavy freighter. It indicated he had "overlanded" to Fort Sill, 582,880 pounds; to Fort Richardson, 246,882 pounds; to Fort Griffin, 277,174 pounds. He had engaged in this service 190 teams.

The United States government apparently was in no hurry to answer the Katy's frantic call for help. Perhaps rumors that the railroad was not wholly blameless slowed official action. True it was that Levi Parsons was having difficulty peddling his bonds, chiefly because of the "campaign of vilification" being carried on by agents of the Pacific lines, but a potent cause of trouble along the line of road was the financial unreliability of subcontractors.

Contracts for grading, hauling rock, and getting out ties were let piecemeal to small private contractors, usually in five- or ten-mile sections. Some of these small businessmen turned out to be fly-by-night operators who swindled their workmen, their suppliers, and the railroad—playing no favorites. Others were merely inefficient, shoestring financiers, who hadn't the means to carry their payrolls or their suppliers for the week or two necessary to clear their own drafts upon the railroad. Invariably the company was blamed for the contractors' sins.

Sam Frye, who had the contract to grade the ten-mile section south of the Arkansas River, was scrupulously honest but notoriously impecunious. He was well liked by both Bob Stevens and John Scullin and admired by Chief Engineer Otis Gunn for the quality of the work he got out of his graders. He had done a great deal of work, off and on, for the company since the beginning of construction. It is told of Sam Frye that one day, while he was giving his foreman some instructions, he took a step backwards and inadvertently

[3] Traffic Manager's Report.

put his heel on the business end of a long-handled shovel. The handle whipped up and dealt him a resounding blow on the back of the head. Without turning, Sam hunched his shoulders, cringed a little, and cried, "Come back Sattiday—I pay off Sattidays!"

Point is given to this story by the following article, briefed somewhat, which appeared in several contemporary newspapers:

> Major O. B. Gunn, chief engineer, and Maj. Sam Frye, contractor on the M. K. & T. railroad, had an adventure down at the front a few days since which came near ending very tragically . . . on account of a small arrear in pay.
>
> The hands, about sixty in number, conceived the idea of seeking redress for their imaginary grievances. . . . Under the impulse of revenge and bad whiskey they resolved to seize and lynch Messrs. Gunn and Frye.
>
> [Warned of their peril], Gunn and Frye mounted their horses, and by a swift and hard night ride they made good their escape.[4]

The agent at the new station, Mr. Hudson, was swamped with business. September earnings showed an increase of $10,000 in freight and $4,000 in passenger traffic receipts over the preceding month; and October assuredly would break all records. The cattle traffic, which recently had been slowed by a poor market, began moving to winter ranges and to feeder grounds in Kansas, Missouri, and farther east. Texas merchandise traffic was rapidly increasing, and Agent Hudson's freight house, 140 feet long, was scarcely big enough to handle the local business!

It was time to do something spectacular, Stevens thought, to attract national attention to his railroad activities. Promptly he extended an invitation to the Kansas Editorial Association to inspect his pioneer line. On October 25, in a body, they took him at his word.

A special train, luxurious in its appointments for that era, reached the end-of-track at Gibson Station on the morning of October 26. There were 140 editors and legislators in this Kansas party, including Senator Caldwell, Governor Harvey, and Congressmen Lowe and Sidney Clarke. En route, their Katy hosts casually but constantly called attention to the deserted appearance of the country so far as humanity was concerned, the entire absence of improvements, and the area's wild beauty and adaptability for agricultural purposes.

[4] From undated clippings, 1871.

The junket was a glorious success from the point of view of the road. The journalists wrote reams about the "B. I. T." (Beautiful Indian Territory) and the politicians were most positive in their statements that no effort would be spared to open up the country to settlement and development.

SIXTEEN

Mus-ko-gee

The paralyzing effects of the great Chicago fire, which started on Sunday, October 8, 1871, and raged unchecked for three days, were felt throughout the nation. When Mrs. O'Leary's cow kicked over the fatal kerosene lamp, the Katy's construction schedule through the Creek domain to the Choctaw country was knocked into a cocked hat. The General Manager fretted because no word came from Boomer and Rust about the fate of the American Bridge Company. Finally, Vice President Rust telegraphed that, although the bridge company's offices had been gutted and all their records destroyed, the plant had been spared; as quickly as some sort of order could be restored, the shipping of bridge structures would be resumed.

On Monday, October 16, Katy bridge carpenters, paced by George (Cap) Shannon, completed the falsework across the 200-foot gap in the wrecked Verdigris structure. Fortunately, the first span for the Arkansas crossing had just arrived, and Chief Engineer Gunn decided to use it to finish the Verdigris bridge. Working against time and foul weather, he completed the structure by the end of the month.

Post and Smith, architects who had the contract for the masonry on both bridges, finished work on the Arkansas piers November 1. Half of the superstructure had arrived, permitting Stevens to be happy in the expectation of soon crossing that great barrier, too. It was less than four miles from the Verdigris to the Arkansas, but heavy rains had been falling, and these bottom lands, now a quagmire, were ruining his business.

Towards the latter part of October, the traffic flooding up the Texas Trail had been avoiding the Katy's ferry crossings. The mile-long cavalcades of prairie schooners could not negotiate the soaked delta lands. They were swinging east when they reached the Fort Sill–

First railroad bridge across the Arkansas River,
at the Three Forks (Muskogee, Creek Nation), I. T.,
completed December, 1871

Fort Gibson Trail (at old Fort Davis) and crossing the Arkansas to Fort Gibson, using the old Nivens ferry just below the Three Forks junction of the rivers.

This situation resulted in a considerable loss of business because the A. & P. had dozens of agents in Fort Gibson competing for the traffic. They were "offering big rebates to all who would take their wagons up the Texas Trail to Vinita and ship over the A. & P." They even offered fat rebates, both on freight and passenger traffic, to all who would ship locally on the Katy from Gibson Station to Vinita and there transfer to the A. & P., instead of using the Katy all the way to Sedalia and St. Louis.

These agents were openly charged with inciting the Indians, the 'breeds, and even the "white trash," to do injury to the line. Traffic Manager Mirick, particularly, was disgusted with the tactics of his opposition at this time. "You have no idea," he told Colonel Stevens, "of the stories circulated, and slanders disseminated, by emissaries of the A. & P. in this country. Down in this wild country, with neither military nor civil law to protect us, a few vagabonds can make a great deal of trouble on small capital."[1]

In the following days rain fell in torrents and it was not until November 11 that tracklayer Scullin was able to report the line completed from the Verdigris to the Arkansas. Here on the north bank, Colonel Stevens had hoped to build a big dump of supplies for his next jump forward. This proved impracticable, however, for the entire area was under water. It became necessary to ferry everything across the river and to make the dump about a mile beyond, near the intersection of the Texas Trail and the Fort Sill-Fort Gibson Road.

Just east of this new dump were the ruins of Fort Davis, the Confederate stronghold captured and destroyed by Union forces on December 27, 1862. Here, during the completion of the Arkansas bridge, grew up another mushroom town of tents and shacks. This short-lived settlement ambitiously called itself Fort Davis and aspired to permanency; but the road had other plans.[2]

On November 17, a superabundance of rain made a raging torrent of the Arkansas, on whose crest piled-up driftwood washed out all the falsework that had been erected. The work went on, however, despite adverse weather conditions all through the period. The bents were replaced, the great spans of the 840-foot structure settled slowly

[1] Traffic Manager's Report.
[2] Grant Foreman, *Muskogee and Eastern Oklahoma*, 47–50.

into place, and on December 7, big Charlie Knickerbocker, now maintenance-of-way engineer, told tracklayer Scullin the structure was finished, ready for the iron. The Irish Brigade went back to work that day, and on December 8, the construction engine passed over to renew the race to Texas.

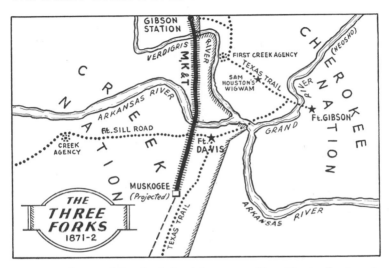

From the south bank of the Arkansas to Fort Davis, the terrain was almost as flat as a pancake. It was typical Oklahoma "bottom" land, a thick, almost impenetrable canebrake, which that December was thoroughly waterlogged, a veritable hellhole for track workers. Almost every day it snowed; snow changed to sleet, and then it rained in torrents. Beyond Fort Davis, however, the grade makes a long, slow rise, then levels out again for many miles to the south.

By December 23, Sam Frye's graders were about twenty miles south of the Arkansas near Honey Springs (Ok-ta-ha), but Scullin's tracklayers had just succeeded in laying track enough to get out of the hole. Thereafter, conditions improved a little, and by December 30 the track was some five miles south of the Arkansas. Stevens was now ready to found another metropolis in Levi Parsons' empire.

It was too bad that Judge Parsons had recently sailed for Europe, else the city that Bob Stevens planned that day—now a thriving metropolis of 50,000 people—might have been named "Stevens," in honor of its founder. Vice President George Denison, however, was at the throttle in New York on December 30, when Bob Stevens wrote:

I send you herewith tracing showing the line of our road from the Arkansas River down a little over three miles to a point where I propose to establish a station to be called *Musko-gee*. It will be the end of an operating division first below Parsons, being 113 miles or thereabouts.[3]

In accordance with treaty stipulations, F. S. Lyon, United States agent for the Creek Nation, had posted an order forbidding anyone to raise, construct, or build any tent, house, cabin, or other building, or to reside or do business along the line of the railroad. How the orders of the Indian Agent were respected by the hard characters at the Katy's railhead is best illustrated in the words of Locating Engineer F. O. Marvin, who later became the greatly respected dean of the School of Engineering at the University of Kansas. Dean Marvin wrote:

I myself located Muskogee. One afternoon about four o'clock I picked out a place for a new siding and drove stakes marking the railway's reservation for depot and wagon ground adjacent.

The town literally sprung up in a night. In the case of Muskogee, the first morning after I drove my stakes, there were several tents and board shacks up and ready for business. Before breakfast, one man was dead and the murderer was being chased over the prairies by a lot of men. So Muskogee was born in blood.[4]

Muskogee's first citizens were the same "terminuses" who had infested Gibson Station and Fort Davis. George Reynolds,[5] a Katy special agent in the Indian Territory, used to tell graphically the story of Muskogee in its earliest days. In January, 1873, Agent Reynolds was host to Edward King, a *Scribner's Magazine* reporter, who had been commissioned to do a story about the newly built frontier railroad. Sitting one night in their special car, parked at Gibson Station, Reynolds reminisced while reporter King took notes:

Three men were shot about twenty feet from this same car in one night at Muskogee. Oh! this was a little hell, this was. The roughs took possession here in earnest. The keno and

---

[3] Letter Book No. 6. .
[4] Letter dated February 16, 1908, in company files.
[5] Brother of Milt. Reynolds, publisher of the *Parsons Sun*.

A dance hall in new-born Denison, Texas
—from *Scribner's Magazine,* July, 1873

"Good Bye."
WE'RE GOING TO KANSAS AND TEXAS.

Scene in one of the Through Cars running to Kansas and Texas from Hannibal, St. Louis, Moberly, Kansas City and Sedalia, over the Great Emigrant Route, the Missouri, Kansas & Texas Railway.

monte players had any quantity of tents all about this section, and life was the most uncertain thing to keep you ever saw. One night a man lost all he had at keno; so he went around behind the tent and tried to shoot the keno-dealer in the back; he missed him, but killed another man. The keno man just got a board and put it up behind himself, and the game went on. One day one of the roughs took offence at something the railroads folks said, so he ran our train off the track the next morning. There was no law here, and no means of getting any. As fast as the railroad moved on, the roughs pulled up stakes and moved with it. We tried to scare them away, but they didn't scare worth a cent. It was next to impossible for a stranger to walk through one of these canvas towns without getting shot at. The graveyards were sometimes better populated than the towns next them.[6]

Writer King noted with curiosity Mus-ko-gee's boot hill, where eleven men were buried with their boots on. "Each grave," he wrote, "is a monument to murder."

Brad Collins, a half-blood Cherokee outcast, was a typical terminus type. Collins was nearly white, a smuggler of whisky, a desperado, and a dead shot. It was said that he could throw a pistol in the air, causing it to make half a dozen turns, catch it as it fell, and strike an apple at thirty paces. He was reported so quick on the trigger that all the other "shootists" in the the Indian Territory were in awe of him.

In the spring of 1872, this rosy-featured, athletic young man was then under bond to appear at the May term of the Federal Court in Fort Smith, for shooting at a United States marshal with intent to kill. Many excused him for a previous incident in which he actually had killed a marshal, inasmuch it was a private quarrel. Collins' gang included a dozen or more young Cherokee 'breeds.

Amazement at the lawlessness of Muskogee impelled one visitor to inquire about the condition of the government in the Territory. "The fact is," he was told, "there is no government actually, but lots of trials. If both parties were Indians—that is, had 'head rights' in the Nation—it's tried by Indians under their laws; if either's a white man, it's tried at Fort Smith, and that's just no trial. My protection and government is in these stone walls, a shot gun and six-shooter."[7]

6 Edward King, *Scribner's Magazine*, July, 1873, p. 271.
7 Beadle, *The Undeveloped West*, Chapter XX.

As a frontier town, as a terminus town, Muskogee was unique. Other terminuses quickly settled down to become quiet, respectable communities, or faded away altogether. Muskogee alone remained rip-roaring and lawless for twenty years or more. The reasons for this condition will become apparent later in the story.

It would be doing a grave injustice to the embryo city of Muskogee not to mention that here, as at every end-of-track community created by the railroad, many of the tents and cotton-cloth shacks which struck the casual observer as pitiful beginnings were put up by resolute, God-fearing men of genuine pioneer stock.

James L. Barnes, proprietor of the "Pioneer Boarding Car" and the "Pioneer Dining Car," was typical of the better element. He had moved his rolling hotel successively from Gibson Station to Fort Davis and to Muskogee in something less than four months. By January, 1872, his hotel consisted of five cars installed on a side track at the new site, and he was providing comparatively luxurious food and quarters to all who took the Texas Trail. He was a capable hotel operator and enterprising business man, and he was liked for his ability to conjure up "a magnificent dinner." Barnes, of course, had the materials for delicious meals readily at hand. On the short stretch from Gibson Station, travelers often saw great flocks of prairie chickens in a leisurely flight; wild turkeys waddling away; deer fleeing across the roads; and rabbits jumping painfully in the snow.

J. S. Atkinson was another of the genuine pioneer stock, a trader who could move as quickly as the dive-keepers! Atkinson was a legitimate merchant, a supplier for the Katy workmen at the rail-head, and here at the Three Forks he had reached what was for him the end of the trail. He applied for permission for J. S. Atkinson and Company to establish themselves as forwarding agents, first at Gibson Station, then at Fort Davis. Here he erected a large establishment next to the Katy freight house, and thus founded Muskogee's first business house.

These enterprising men, and many others like them, created the Muskogee that is today a cultured city, a city of fine homes, schools and churches, full of God-fearing, well-doing people who have wiped the memory of the city's lurid beginnings forever out of mind. But in January, 1872, law and order for Muskogee were still twenty years in the future.

When the Katy reached the Three Forks in the fall of 1871, the United States agents for the Five Civilized Tribes were headquartered individually with their tribes. The Cherokee agent had his offices in Tahlequah; the Choctaw and Chickasaw agent was located at Boggy Depot; and the Seminole agent was at Wewoka. On July 1, 1874, the government ordered the consolidation of these agencies, and thereafter the United States Agency for the Five Civilized Tribes was known as Union Agency.

After two years of negotiation, the consolidated agency was finally located at Muskogee, and on or about January 1, 1876, the agent for the Five Civilized Tribes moved into a brand-new Union Agency building. The choice of Muskogee as headquarters for these land-wealthy Indian tribes was probably the decisive factor in Muskogee's survival. Otherwise, in its earliest days, there was little justification for its existence.[8]

[8] Grant Foreman, *Muskogee: The Biography of an Oklahoma Town*, 24.

SEVENTEEN

Breaking the Pacific Strangle Hold

The cotton and the corn, the cattle and the hides which came flooding up from Texas with the establishment of the "New Route to the Gulf," daily increased the cupidity of the Katy's competitors. The great volume of manufactured goods which began to flow into the Southwest through the road's ever-advancing railhead, was driving Andrew Peirce frantic with envy. Peremptory instructions were issued cancelling all traffic agreements with the Katy. Confiscatory rates were applied on Katy traffic, and orders given to break connections with all Katy trains and strangle the line at the Sedalia gateway. All this, and more, in order that the A. & P. might secure the long 340-mile haul between St. Louis and Vinita on all southwestern traffic. Colonel Stevens, understandably enough, declined to be "shorthauled," and the battle between the two general managers began to assume serious proportions.

The Missouri Pacific hiked the carload rate on cattle to $30 between Sedalia and St. Louis while maintaining the rate between Kansas City and St. Louis at only $25. Nonetheless, Stevens continued to deliver cattle at Sedalia—as many as 514 cars in one month—and ignored the very existence of Vinita.

The common rate on cattle from Vinita to St. Louis was established at $75; Peirce ordered a kickback of $10 to all who would drive one station east of Vinita and ship over the A. & P. Colonel Stevens' man, General F. C. Armstrong, who then was heading the El Paso Stage and Mail Line which operated between Fort Gibson and Sherman, reported that the A. & P. were offering a cash rebate of $10 to all St. Louis passengers who would transfer from the Katy to the A. & P. at Vinita, and this rebate caused all kinds of complications.

Passenger fares between St. Louis and Sherman had been set at
$50. Of this amount the stage line got $30 for the haul between Gibson and Sherman, leaving $20 to be divided between the railroads
north of Gibson. The Missouri Pacific charged their local fare, $8.50,
between St. Louis and Sedalia, leaving the Katy $11.50 for the haul
between Sedalia and Gibson. This was a fairly equitable arrangement. The A. & P., however, charged $19.15 between St. Louis and
Vinita, leaving the Katy but 85 cents for the sixty-mile haul between
Vinita and Gibson. Immediately Bob Stevens boosted the local rates
in Indian Territory to ten cents a mile (there was practically no station-to-station travel anyway), and Peirce was caught again.

Since the only through rate was made over Sedalia, Stevens' action meant nothing if a passenger went via Sedalia. If he went via
Vinita and the A. & P., however, the Katy got $6.00 for the sixty miles
between Vinita and Gibson instead of 85 cents. The railroads' $20
proportion of the through fare between St. Louis and Texas was
changed overnight to, Katy $6.00, A. & P. $14. And with the advertised $10 rebate, Peirce began to receive only $4.00 for his 340-mile
haul!

The City of St. Louis quite properly was very much interested in
the fight. Given to believe that the Katy had no interest in St. Louis

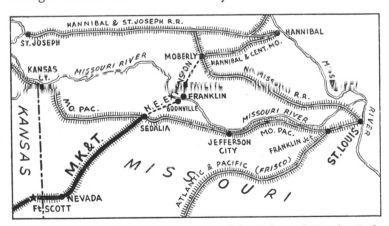

The projected Northeastern Extension of the Tebo and Neosho Railroad (the Katy) from Sedalia to a junction with the North Missouri
Railroad (the Wabash) at Moberly. The construction of this line
in 1873 forced open "the Sedalia gateway" and gave the Katy access
to St. Louis.

and was headed for Chicago—as originally planned—the St. Louis Board of Trade gave the A. & P. every support.

Thus encouraged, Mr. Peirce made another move. The Katy's offices in St. Louis, established at Second and Pine under the able direction of Mr. Holmes, had been doing a remarkable business. Peirce put an end to that. He issued stringent instructions to the M. P. and A. & P. ticket sellers to cut the Katy out completely. Thereafter Mr. Holmes could not buy or sell a ticket. Overnight the Katy was out of the passenger business in St. Louis.

The situation deteriorated rapidly. Bob Stevens broke all connections with the A. & P., and his trains went through Vinita as though that junction didn't exist. The A. & P. began the practice of parking a thirty-car freight drag squarely across the track whenever Katy trains were due, which caused Stevens to brusquely warn that if the practice was not stopped forthwith he would again tear up the frog crossing. It was stopped forthwith.

Finally, Colonel Stevens told President Levi Parsons that the strangle hold by the Pacifics on the north end of the line must be broken or the road would be ruined financially. "Every day is telling fearfully against us," he warned the Judge. "Our only course lies in going to Boonville with all the speed that we can put on."[1]

Fully apprised of the danger, and galvanized into action by the abrupt drop in revenues following the adoption of Peirce's shut-out policy, Judge Parsons (still in Europe on a bond-peddling tour) cabled George Denison to go ahead with the Northeastern Extension. Bob Stevens, given the news of November 1, was, in his own language, overjoyed.

On January 1, 1872, contracts were awarded for building of the Northeastern Extension—still under the name of the Tebo and Neosho Railway—to Boonville in Cooper County, to Fayette in Howard County, and on to a junction with the North Missouri (Wabash) at Moberly in Randolph County. Notwithstanding the actual beginning of construction, representatives of both Pacific lines in St. Louis had no hesitancy in telling members of the St. Louis Board of Trade that the Katy was bluffing—that they did not have the financial backing to build north.

Accuracy compels the admission that the calamity howlers were not very far from right. Judge Parsons was unable to provide the funds to finance construction at both ends of the line at the same

---

[1] The Katy's struggle against the Mo. P.–A. & P. combination is covered in great detail in Letter Book No. 6.

time—for, it should be remembered, there were no counties in the Indian Territory eager to vote bond issues. Bob Stevens was instructed to push to the Red River with all dispatch, and to do only such work on the Northeastern Extension as would convince the Missouri Pacific and St. Louis interests of the seriousness of the Katy's intentions.

With a great flourish of publicity, Colonel Stevens called in the directors of the Tebo and Neosho Extension—all local land-owning "projectors"—and closed the contract to construct the line and operate it as part of the Missouri, Kansas and Texas Railway. Boonville thrilled to the news and staged one of the noisiest celebrations in its history to signal its gratification.

The contract was to build the line, and a million-dollar bridge across the Missouri River to Old Franklin, within eighteen months. So Colonel Stevens had plenty of time to do the actual construction. However, he wanted publicity, and he wanted it *Now*. The very threat of his building to a connection with the North Missouri gave him "a rod of terror" to hold over the heads of the Missouri Pacific. Now they would not dare to slam the Sedalia gateway shut. The rod was being fashioned to his hand, and Stevens knew well how to use it.

No real effort was made to construct the Northeastern Extension until after the main line had reached the Red River and the beckoning goal of Texas. The general manager's rod of terror, however, effectively held the Sedalia gateway open.

EIGHTEEN

Through the Choctaw Nation to McAlester

The new year dawned bright and cheerful for Bob Stevens. Rested and optimistic now, he was eager for the fray. Scullin's tracklayers were back from the Mus-ko-gee terminus, nursing their hangovers, licking their wounds, ready to go to work again. The Red River and Texas lay straight ahead, only 150 miles. There was nothing much between, except the Choctaw and the Chickasaw nations and the twin forks of the Canadian River.

Sam Frye's graders already were twenty miles away, down past Chimney Peak mountain and Honey Springs (Ok-ta-ha). Boomer's bridge gangs were at work at the crossings of the two Canadians (the Nawth Fo'k and the South Fork), where the masonry was going up "finely." The weather was cold but clear; perfect weather for ties to be got out all the way to Perryville (McAlester), some sixty miles south of the Arkansas. Chief engineer Gunn had the line located all the way to the Indian Agency at Boggy Depot (soon to be moved to A-to-ka), while Major Walker was out surveying for a good crossing of the Red River into Texas. Stevens was impatient to get on with the work, to cross the "Indian Bridge" and reach the Lone Star State.

The General Manager's impatience was understandable. He was in country where his genius as a city planner, a founder of great metropolises, had no room for expression. Here was no opportunity to pre-empt mile-square sections of prairie, to build stations, to designate them as regular stops for all trains, and then sell off town lots at fantastic prices. No, sir! Here was nothing but the treaty-prescribed two hundred feet for right-of-way. Not a foot of the sacred Indian soil was available for civic betterment! No wonder the irreverent Bob Stevens had his eyes fixed on Texas. Those eyes had a golden gleam in them.

Incidentally, the General Manager's townsite properties in Kansas and Missouri were developing marvelously. Stevens and his associates were getting rich merely by having faith in the railroad, and by being on the ground first. The city of Parsons was only one example of the Colonel's Midas touch. The story was repeated at Neosho Falls, at New Chicago (Chanute), and at Burlington on the Neosho division; repeated again at Appleton, at Schell City, at Fort Scott, and a dozen other points on the Sedalia division.

At Parsons, the modest little station (constructed as cheaply as possible) which the General Manager had first put up, already had been replaced by a handsome two-story brick edifice, into which "a respectable force" moved on January 12, 1872. Work had been begun there in November on the first eight-stall section of the great roundhouse; foundations, too, were in for machine shops to serve the entire railroad. As a consequence, lots were still selling like hotcakes. It would be a long time before the struggling little railroad made any money for its owners, the bond and stock holders, but its managers were already doing quite well, thank you!

During the latter part of January, 1872, track laying was hampered by a sudden change in the weather. Snow, sleet and rainstorms lashed the high prairie, so that by month's end the railhead was stalled at Elk Creek, thirteen miles south of Muskogee. This was at the old Indian stomping grounds known as Honey Springs, then nothing more than an Overland Mail stage post on the Texas Trail. Here grew up another little terminus town, named Ok-ta-ha, after the famous Creek full blood Oktarharsars Harjo, the vindictive leader of Indian uprisings who answered to the name of "Old Sands."

Honey Springs, a flat and fertile meadow nestling in the foothills of the Rattlesnake Mountains which rise away to the east, was a popular gathering place for the Indians in the early days. Here, between Wolf Gap and Elk Creek, was fought the greatest battle of the Civil War in the Indian country. Pouring down the Texas Road in July, 1863, General James G. Blunt's Union forces met General Douglas H. Cooper's Confederate brigades entrenched in the timber of the creek and routed them with tremendous losses. General Stand Watie's Indian battalions fought valiantly here, but a pitiful marker in the old Oktaha cemetery over the grave-trench of 150 southern soldiers tells the bitter tale of defeat.

By February 13, the end-of-track was advanced another ten miles, and at the railhead the Creek town of Checotah, named for Principal Chief Samuel Checote of the Creek Indians, came into being. This quiet little town once competed with Muskogee for the honor of housing the Union Indian Agency—which, of course, would have made it the most important center in the Indian Territory and assured its future.

The rivalry of the two little settlements was seriocomic. It centered around the water supply. Before Muskogee had completed its first year of existence, the water problem became a serious one for that settlement. Charley Willy, a fierce looking character noted for his many eccentricities, had a monopoly of the business of hauling water for the stores and homes, but his barrel-and-bucket service quickly proved inadequate to meet the ever-expanding demand.

"Water Works Willy" was a large, husky, bearded individual, inclined to alternate heavy bouts of drinking with equally heavy bouts of hard work, who, apparently, had arrived in Muskogee as a gandy dancer for the Katy. It might be well to explain that a gandy dancer's job was to pound down hard earth between the railroad ties as these were laid, preparatory to the spiking down of the iron rail. The term "gandy dancer" is said to have originated in the hopping movement of the workman as he skipped from tie to tie with his mallet-shaped, high-handled pounder. Early Muskogee stories had it that Charley Willy was the disinherited son of a fine English family. However that may be, he apparently had nothing to worry him when sober but the peddling of water by the barrel; when on a bender, he concentrated on the consumption of whisky—by the barrel!

When the water shortage at Muskogee became acute, George W. Ingalls, the first Union agent for the Five Civilized Tribes, who had his Union headquarters out at Agency Hill, had an idea. Smarting under the impression that the merchants of Muskogee were not extending to him that degree of courtesy to which the dignity of his office entitled him, he decided to look for a suitable source of water supply farther south. If he found it, he would move the Agency and ask the railroad to move its depot. This meant, of course, if his plans matured, that the merchants would have to move, too, and obtain new licenses for new town lots from the Creek Council—but only with his approval.

The consummation of Ingall's scheme would have meant the quick death of Muskogee. The merchants were well aware of this. The Agent made arrangements to have a deep well dug at the present site of Checotah. The excavation of this great well was vigilantly watched by the Muskogee merchants, and when it reached the depth where water was beginning to seep in at the bottom, some enterprising citizens, whose identity the old pioneers have ever since refused to divulge, purchased a barrel of salt at the Patterson store, had it hauled down in the nighttime, and quietly poured its contents into the new well. Whispers, still echoing after the passage of three quarters of a century, have it that the barrel of salt was brought to the mouth of the well by Charley Willy, who could hardly be blamed for protecting his own interests.

When the Indian Agent learned that his big well had struck salt water, his scheme for moving the Union Agency headquarters from Muskogee was abandoned and the citizens were thoroughly convinced of the efficacy of salt as a remedy, when properly applied, for it saved Muskogee's life.[1]

At the time of the salting of Agent Ingall's well, Katy terminus towns had no municipal government, no officials, and no authority to raise funds by means of taxation. Taxes levied by the Indian tribes went to support the Indians themselves and were not squandered on terminuses. When the white leaders of a settlement, voteless and landless, needed any public improvements, the money had to be gathered by voluntary contributions.

The track reached the North Fork of the Canadian River on March 25, and by mid-April had crossed that turbulent stream and reached the romantic old Creek Indian settlement of North Fork Town, forty miles out from Mus-ko-gee. Bob Stevens was now about ready to leave the Creek country. The main Canadian marked the northern boundary of the Choctaw and Chickasaw domains, and there the General Manager could get out from under Creek cattle "taxation without representation." Henceforth the beeves would ride in style along through both the Creek and Cherokee nations, nonstop. When the road reached the Red River, Stevens would be rid of his cattle tax problems entirely.

Two miles south of the "Nawth Fo'k" and just west of the Indian settlement, Bob Stevens set his "dump" of materials in preparation for the next jump forward, which included spanning the main Canadian. Major Gunn's engineers had recently run into some trouble there. Just as the superstructure was about completed, the southern abutment had given way and the entire pier had to be rebuilt.

The delay at North Fork Town, sacred site of the old Asbury Methodist Mission destroyed by fire in 1869, here resulted in the growth overnight of a wild terminus town that quickly ranked with

[1] John D. Benedict, *History of Muskogee and Northeastern Oklahoma*, Vol. I, p. 342.

Gibson and Mus-ko-gee at their worst. At the Indian agent's suggestion, Bob Stevens had named the temporary station Eufaula, which was an important village name in the history of the Mus-ko-gee tribes. Before the sidings were in at Eufaula, or the warehouse and wagon yards had been laid off, a typical cotton-cloth town had mushroomed up out of the prairie.

The outlaws collected here in ever increasing numbers. All the white trash from the country's hellish backwaters, all the murderers, robbers, gamblers, gangsters—all whose names were written with the notorious symbol G. T. T.[2] attached—seemed to gravitate here on the way to anonymity. Here they settled down temporarily to pursue their various arts of chicanery. Whisky was smuggled in and peddled to railroad workers as well as to Indians.

Soon huge mocks of supplies began to pile up at the Eufaula terminus. Indians and "terminuses" made almost nightly raids on these goods, and several guards were shot in their defense. Faro, keno, and poker games were in progress in shacks and tents twenty-four hours a day.

Gangs began tearing up the newly laid track and setting fire to piles of ties, anything to delay construction and hold the railhead at the terminus town. Scullin's workmen were becoming demoralized, and Bob Stevens was helpless. The pistol totin' half-blood, Brad Collins, and his outcast gang sifted down from Muskogee on the first train to the new terminus. It was well known they had a load of smuggled whisky with them but no one dared challenge them. At Eufaula, they were uproariously greeted by the other "terminuses" who had preceded them, and the whisky was opened and passed. Before the day was out, the liquor-crazed 'breeds were galloping about the town, brandishing pistols, and yelling like demons.

Secretary of the Interior Cox chose this untimely moment in April of 1872 to visit the Indian Territory in person, to see for himself whether the reports of lawlessness in the Indian country were not exaggerated. Bob Stevens extended him the courtesy of a special train, and General Superintendent Woodard, who had timed the arrival of the Secretary's special train to coincide with the opening of the bridge over the Canadian River, accompanied his distinguished guest.

The bridge opening went off smoothly enough, but on their return to the tent town terminus they found things rather lively. Right

---

[2] G.T.T. Gone to Texas!—beyond the reach of the law. A popular catch-phrase used to describe those "on the run."

next to the Secretary's private car, that afternoon, four terminus toughs "stuck up" a passing stranger and relieved him of eighty dollars in gold. Later in the evening, there was much promiscuous shooting and the Secretary learned that one man had been killed. One of the government men accompanying Secretary Cox was taken ill, whether with the news of the killing or not the record is not clear, and Superintendent Woodard ventured into the tent town to find a doctor.

Report has it that Woodard, by mistake, poked his head into the tent of a gambler named Callahan (probably one of Scullin's men), who happened to be a little out of humor. He thrust a six-shooter into the General Superintendent's face, and growled menacingly: "Air ye lookin' for me? I'm ready if y'are!" Woodard returned without a doctor.

Next morning, Secretary Cox made an inspection of the collection of dives and brothels that called itself Eufaula. The man who had been killed the night before "for a mere caprice," still lay in a tent that the Secretary was invited to enter. Several of the toughest characters at the terminus boldly spoke to the Secretary, blustering that they had a good right to stay in the Creek Nation, and they meant (with an oath) to stay. Within the Secretary's hearing, they boasted of their murderous exploits, practiced at marks with their pistols, and apparently had no fear of the consequences.

Returning to his private car, Secretary Cox attempted to address the unruly crowd from the steps. Some ruffian cut into his talk by firing a pistol, the bullet from which passed through the roof of the car about three feet from his head. Mr. Cox dived into the car and emerged no more. A few minutes later, however, when the crowd had dispersed, Superintendent Woodard came out, went to the telegraph shack and filed a dispatch from the Secretary to Washington. It announced that neither life nor property was safe in the Territory, and that the Indians should be aided in expelling the roughs from their midst.

Immediately, the Tenth Cavalry went into active service in the Territory. Reporter Edward King tells what happened then:

> [The ruffians] got together at the terminus, armed to the teeth, and blustered a good deal. When one of the terminuses was asked his name, he usually answered that it was Slim Jim, or Wild Bill, or Lone Jack (with an oath), and that he was a gambler or a "pounder," as the case might be, and further-

Secretary of the Interior Cox fired upon at Eufaula
(North Fork Town), April, 1872

more, that he didn't intend to leave the Territory. Whereupon the officer commanding would say: "Well, Slim Jim, or Wild Bill, or Lone Jack, I'll give you twelve hours to leave this town in, and if you are found in the Territory a week from this date, I'll have you shot!" And they took the hint.[3]

It might be well at this point to go into some detail regarding the Indian problem as it existed while the Katy was building its tracks across the Indian Territory. The Territorial area was 52,780,000 acres, but the population was not enough to make a city of the tenth rank. The tribes scattered over the prairies and in the mountains numbered as follows:

Cherokees	14,682	Sac and Fox and	
Creeks	13,000	Shawnees	1,118
Choctaws	15,000	Eastern Shawnees	600
Chickasaws	5,000	Kaws	627
Seminoles	2,300	Apaches	378
Osages	3,375	Delawares	311
Cheyennes and		Kickapoos	296
Arapahoes	3,390	Quapaws	225
Comanches	3,218	Wyandotts	169
Kiowas	1,776	Weas, Peories, Miamies	184
Pottawatomies	1,336	Senecas	155
Wichitas	1,216	Ottawas	[4] 149

These tribes (the first five being the civilized tribes), numbering some 68,500 frequently quarreling people, were separated by great distances, by barriers of language and of custom, so that there was little intercourse between them. The rich and fertile land was often waste because there were not hands enough to hold plows, and if there had been, the Indians in general preferred hunting to agricultural pursuits. The country was a lush wilderness because the Indians refused admission to the white man unless he married into a tribe or was adopted, in which case he was required to forswear allegiance to the United States and make his oath to the chief of his tribe. Many intermarried whites did just that, and profited enormously.

Yet, there was something both brave and pathetic about the way the Indian of the 1870's clung to the last of the strongholds deeded

[3] *Scribner's*, July, 1873, p. 272.
[4] *Report of the Commissioner of Education for the year 1872*, p. 412.

to him by treaty for "as long as water shall flow, as long as grass shall grow." The intelligent, educated Indians knew that their people were in process of slow but sure absorption, but they were out to delay the action of the melting pot as long as possible. Men like Stand Watie, John Ross, Chilly McIntosh and, particularly, Elias C. Boudinot, saw clearly that the building of the railroad meant not only the opening up of Texas to emigration but also the opening up of Indian Territory to white settlers. And they feared for the future.

But this is the story of the Katy Railroad and not the story of the Indian treks, of the Trail of Tears. These latter can be found, and many more of the same nature, in the vivid writings of Oklahoma's great historian, Grant Foreman, who served the Dawes Commission, the agency which brought land in severalty to Oklahoma. So, we follow Bob Stevens' railroad builders as they lay the track southward. Later, we can return to see how Muskogee and other Katy-created towns fared.

Here in the fork of the two Canadian rivers is the location of the notorious swirling backwater of the river, subsequently called "Posey's Hole," which has claimed a steady toll of lives over the years. A year after the Katy men had truly laid their track through Eufaula, there was born, in that Creek village, Alexander Lawrence Posey, considered the greatest of American Indian poets; his mother was a Creek full blood, his father a white man adopted into the tribe. The poet was drowned while endeavoring, during floodtime, to cross the "hole" in company with three companions, two of whom were drowned along with him. For two hours, before his strength gave out, he clutched the branch of a tree which hung into the river. Some months before his tragic death in May, 1908, he seemed to foretell the manner of his passing in a brief verse entitled, "My Fancy":

> Why do trees along the river
> Lean so far out o'er the tide?
> Very wise men tell me why, but
> I am never satisfied:
> And so I keep my fancy still,
> That trees lean out to save
> The drowning from the clutches of
> The cold, remorseless wave.

Posey's Hole seems to possess a strange power, causing deaths since the first tragedy; up to this time of writing, eight men, one woman, and a seven-year-old boy have drowned there in a period

The wild waters of the Canadian River at "Posey's Hole" have given the Katy Railroad infinite trouble over the years. Here a Katy work train holds the bridge down during a flood at the turn of the century

Two of the Katy's first locomotives, both Grant 4–4–0's, built in 1870, were caught in an extraordinary wreck near Orrick, Missouri, on June 14, 1873, and crashed between trains of the St L.K.C.&N. (now Wabash Railway). They were being "deadheaded" to Moberly, Missouri, to inaugurate service on the Katy's newly completed Northeastern Extension, scheduled for June 20, 1873.

The Munson-owned cotton compress at Denison, Texas, which contributed much to the development of the area

Muskogee depot in the seventies

of forty years. The Indians and not a few whites are firm in the belief that the place is haunted by the soul of the Indian poet-philosopher.

In recent years, the Katy Railroad has spent nearly a million dollars to raise the grade of the line here several feet and to erect a great new bridge to beat the jinx that seems to hover over Posey's Hole.

As quickly as the bridge was completed over the Canadian, and as soon as the Tenth Cavalry moved in, the hardest characters in the Territory moved out of Eufaula and into a little colony of their own. It was hidden in the canebrakes south of the river. This den (it could not be called a settlement) at various times rejoiced in the names of "Sandtown" and "Buzzard's Roost." Its denizens for months made life miserable for Katy Railroad workers and for all who passed that way. They robbed and they murdered; they pillaged the company's stores; they tore up the tracks, derailing work trains.

Work went ahead, nevertheless. The railhead slowly advanced. By the end of May, the line had been laid through the high rock hills south of the Canadian; it was over the trestle at Rock Creek and was pushing south through the beautiful Reams Valley. By mid-June, Scullin had his rail laid all along the Boag Luxy, better known to the tracklayers as Roast Terrapin Creek, and had reached the vicinity of the coal-rich region that was soon to be the considerable City of McAlester.

At this point, the Irish Brigade was laying track almost directly on the great Texas Road and had reached that vague spot on surveyors' maps then known as the Cross Roads. Here the legendary California Trail from Fort Smith, Arkansas, worn deep by the countless thousands of prairie schooners that took the forty-niners into the Golden West, crossed the older Texas Road. Here J. J. McAlester had the pioneer store which gave the present city of 25,000 its name.

McAlester's first citizen, a native of Arkansas, was a shrewd operator. He had served with the Confederate forces during the Civil War and had learned from a certain Captain Oliver Weldon of coal outcroppings that had been observed in the area of the Cross Roads. When he heard of plans of the Atlantic and Pacific railroad to build west from Fort Smith along the route of the California Trail, he went into action. He quite properly reasoned that where the A. & P. line would cross the projected route of the M. K. & T., then building on down the Texas Trail, a busy terminus was sure to build up, and coal would find a ready market. As final evidence of his long-headedness, McAlester married the daughter of Chief Burney of the Chickasaw Nation and thereby established his right to become a citizen of the Territory and own property therein.

Today the Katy's Wilburton branch meanders east from McAlester, serving the productive mine fields of the area. The substantial town of Wilburton, and all the little coalmining centers that now line the branch, owe their beginnings to J. J. McAlester. He it was who first mined a wagon load of the highly volatile coal that still contributes to the prosperity of Pittsburg County. And he almost gave his life to the cause.

During the administration of the aptly named Chief Cole of the Choctaws, in the early Seventies, Captain McAlester was doing so well in the supplying of coal to the railroad that the Katy agreed to build a branch line out to one of his mines near the present town of Krebs. Chief Cole, however, sullenly refused his permission for the building of any additional track through his domain; but, encouraged by McAlester who knew his "head rights," John Scullin went ahead and started the branch. This flouting of Indian authority so angered the chief that he ordered the Choctaw Light Horse, the Indian police, to arrest all who were connected with the enterprise. McAlester and two others were picked up immediately and ordered shot. Fortunately for McAlester and his associates, the light horsemen delayed the execution while they looked for additional victims, and the prisoners seized the opportunity to escape north to the Creek Nation on a Katy handcar.[5]

When the Katy was building through the Territory, Indian law was simple—but summary. Frequently it clashed with white man's law and the results often were spectacular. East of the Katy railhead, in the Cherokee Going Snake District, a clash occurred between the Indian Light Horse and United States marshals that is spoken of to this day. It appeared that a "bad" Cherokee named Proctor shot at a white man, missed him, and killed the latter's wife, a Cherokee woman. As to the murder, both parties being Cherokees, the United States courts had no jurisdiction and left the trial to the Cherokee Nation; but a warrant was issued against Proctor for shooting at the white man with intent to kill. The greater crime took precedence, and the Cherokee court proceeded to trial.

It was whispered about that Proctor would be cleared, whereat the friends of the dead woman gathered, determined to kill him the moment he was released. The court, fearing an attack, had a strong guard. Meanwhile, United States Marshal Owens showed up with a

[5] Hiram Impson, *McAlester Golden Anniversary Celebration*, October, 1949.

warrant to arrest Proctor as soon as the court should discharge him. Most unwisely, he yielded to the clamors of the party hostile to the prisoner, took them as his posse and started for the courthouse.

As the United States Marshal entered the court, a nephew of the murdered woman jumped in front of him and began to draw a bead on the prisoner. Somebody knocked the gun down and the bullet entered the floor. The Indian police then began firing on the Marshal and his posse, who returned the fire. When the gunsmoke cleared, the leader of the attack and United States Marshal Owens were found mortally wounded and seven of the posse dead. Judge Alberti, the prisoner's counsel, was killed in his chair, as were two of the jurymen. Several others inside the court were wounded, including Judge Sixkiller and the prisoner, Proctor. The total casualties were eleven killed and eighteen wounded, two mortally.[6]

The "civilized" tribes sometimes betrayed all the weaknesses of white civilization!

[6] Beadle, *The Undeveloped West*, 408–409.

NINETEEN

Last Span of the "Indian Bridge"

The moment big John Scullin's ham-handed spike maulers reached the California Cross Road with the track, Colonel Stevens delegated the supervision of the work to his assistant, Henry Denison, and turned his attention to more important things. Major Gunn had the line definitely located as far south as Boggy Depot, early capital of the Choctaw and Chickasaw tribes, but the vital crossing of the Red River had not yet been decided upon. The General Manager had some interesting plans which he hoped would bear fruit immediately the track crossed the storied stream, but he was of no mind to speak of them yet—that is, publicly.

From Boggy Depot, Locating Engineer Northway already had run a line which closely followed the western branch of the Texas Road all the way to Preston. That one-time fort of the Texas Rangers, at the northernmost tip of Grayson County, was now the hospitable site of Colonel Coffey's far-famed Glen Eden, a place of solace for harried travelers. The Preston Bend cattle crossing here was a favorite with the Texas drovers, no matter whether they were taking the Texas Road or driving up the Chisholm Trail. Here was the obvious spot for a railroad crossing, and Stevens wished the world to think so.

Engineer Northway was at this moment deep in Texas surveying a route by way of Dallas and near Waxahachie to Waco. He was called back. It seemed that the Houston and Texas Central was building fast up that way and would pre-empt all the best locations before the Katy could get there. The General Manager had two charters in his pocket, however, the "Camargo to Mexico City" route and the "Bolivar Point" line to Galveston. Quickly he came to a decision.

When Northway returned, he was ordered to run a new line from a practicable crossing of the Red River in the neighborhood of War-ren, which was at the northeastern border of Grayson County. This survey was to run southwardly to the center of Kaufman County, from which point it was intended to diverge. One line, Stevens told the surveyor, would run to Crockett and Galveston, the other via Waco to Austin.

When Northway had gone on this apparently genuine assign-ment, Stevens, the city planner, revealed himself to the Chief Engi-neer. "Major," he said, and his eyes lit up with the golden gleam that Otis B. Gunn had come to know so well: "Major, I'm not going to try to impress upon you the importance of securing a large tract of land at the Red River crossing, on both sides of the river, nor with the need for keeping our plans to ourselves until arrangements are com-pleted." Here the Colonel paused: "With that in view I wish you would direct George Walker to run three lines to the river bank. Run one to Preston Bend again, another to Warren, and a third—the most important—straight south midway between the two. I think you can find a good spot for a crossing somewhere above Colbert's ferry."

"That's the place where we'll get the land," Gunn observed thoughtfully.

"Plenty of land if the middle survey is kept within our own knowledge," the General Manager returned pointedly.[1]

Major Gunn and George Walker casually dropped off the El Paso stage at Chickasaw Ben Colbert's place a few days later and had a very enjoyable visit with the shrewd ferryman, who was also a tribal chief. He solemnly told how in 1850 he had secured from the Chickasaw Tribal Council permission to establish a ferry across the river and how the venture had prospered from the very beginning. The Butterfield Stage Line, spanning the vast and dangerous dis-tances between St. Louis and San Francisco, began using his ferry that year, and business had been booming—particularly since the war.

As the three men smoked quietly, sitting on the comfortable front "gallery" of Colbert's home on the bluff overlooking the crossing, they could see for themselves the tremendous business that Colbert was doing. A veritable little town had sprung up on the south bank at the ferry landing opposite. Long wagon trains loaded with heavy freight were coming in or going out all day long. Up from the south trailed great herds of wild-looking longhorn cattle, to splash across

[1] Letter Book No. 6; General Manager's Report.

the shallows or wildly swim to the north bank, there to take up the long drive to the Katy's railhead. Someone had the temerity to name this disreputable little tent and wagon-sheet settlement Red River City. Although its ephemeral citizens were largely the passing bull whackers, cowboys, and the buffalo hunters, who were then butchering great herds of American bison on the plains, Red River City, too, aspired to permanence.[2]

As Chickasaw Ben reminisced and his guests quietly gloated over the traffic (and the business opportunities) so apparent at this bottleneck in a great trade route, Walker's location crews were just as quietly making a complete survey for the crossing, all along the northern edge of Colbert's chartered head right. And when Gunn and Walker crossed the river the following day to find the location of the road which was coming up to meet the Katy, who was to know that their men were also making a painstaking survey for the Katy railroad, which here might parallel but certainly would not join the Houston and Texas Central.

Some five miles to the south, on the high, wild Texas prairie that was overrun with scrub brush, Walker's men squinted through their theodolites, took field notes for the platting here of another great metropolis. Maybe here would rise a bustling city named for its famed founder, Robert S. Stevens. And maybe not!

It was June, 1872, and Judge Parsons was still lingering in Europe. No doubt he was desperately trying to peddle Katy bonds, but he didn't seem to be having much success. The great panic of 1873 was only a year in the offing, but already the clouds were considerably bigger than a man's hand. Vice President George Denison, at the helm in Judge Parsons' absence, was frantically instructing Bob Stevens to cut expenses to the bone, to get more and more revenue traffic for the road at less and less expense.

The General Manager was soon thoroughly annoyed by Denison's persistent calls on him to get the road built without spending any money. Already he had reduced the wages of trackmen to $1.50 a day and droves of them had quit. Because of the general financial depression and confusion, however, enough eventually returned to work to keep the railhead moving forward, although at a slower pace than formerly.

On one occasion, Stevens was really vexed by a letter he received from Denison after he had paid a bill following a dun that was piteous in its appeal for aid. "How in God's Name can I press

[2] *Denison Guide,* American Guide Series (W.P.A. Writers' Program), 13.

work, hurry up masonry and grading, together with bridges and ties," he queried sourly, "unless I pay the estimates?" He then put the quietus on Denison by volunteering to step out and give the directors an opportunity to get a better and cheaper man.

Already it was safe to say that no great cities would be named for the pugnacious general manager if George Denison had any voice in the matter.

It was sweltering hot in late June when Bob Stevens came down to the end-of-track at Milepost 160, a few miles south of Perryville, Indian Territory, to meet his lieutenants and plan the strategy for the crossing of the Red River. Perryville had been an important supply base for General Stand Watie's forces during the Civil War, but on August 25, 1863, shortly after the Union victory at Honey Springs, General Blunt's cavalry had come pounding down the Texas Road after the fleeing Indians and had captured and burned the place. When the Katy tracks passed this way less than a decade later, little remained. The settlement was vanishing.

The General Manager's car, stifling hot on the long unsheltered prairie that gave this end-of-section its name, Savanna, offered the only shade for miles around. A rough board table set up under the lee of the car served as Stevens' conference room. Present for the meeting were Engineers Gunn and Walker, Henry Denison, and George Reynolds, the former Indian agent and brother of Milt Reynolds of the *Parsons Sun*. George was by this time the Colonel's ace trouble shooter in the Territory.

Also at the terminus for the meeting, but not yet participating, was a small delegation from Sherman, Texas, shepherded by General F. C. Armstrong of the El Paso Stage and Mail Line. This group included General Pfeiffer, who recently had been retained by the Katy as canvassing and soliciting agent for the Bonham and Paris territory in northeast Texas. He had been hired on his own representations that the freighting and passenger business being done by Jefferson could be turned to the Katy. Naturally, Texas Legislator Connor was in the party, for he had recently assured the General Manager that, should it be deemed advisable to run via Sherman, he was confident that a very handsome subsidy could be secured therefrom. Completing this delegation was a short, stocky young man of about twenty-five who answered to the name of Munson. Powerfully built, with dark hair and dark flashing eyes, Munson incongruously wore a flaming red beard which gave him a striking appearance. The Colonel speculated about him briefly.

Before greeting the Sherman delegation, Stevens conferred with his associates. Gunn and Walker unrolled upon the table the long tracings of what, for want of a better name, might be called the middle survey. It was just what the General Manager had ordered. As formerly, the line led straight south along the Texas Road to Limestone Gap, but instead of veering off westwardly along the trail to Boggy Depot it shot through the Gap, leaving the Limestone hills on its right, and headed straight for old Fort McCulloch and Colbert's ferry. Stevens nodded approval.

"We come down to the river along the west line of this Chickasaw's head right, along here," Gunn said, indicating the route. "It's all open land. There are good rock footings for the bridge, and with the high banks there the approaches are short—practically no fill needed."

The General Manager's eyes glistened. "Good! And now, about the other side?"

Gunn unrolled more tracings, more profiles, explaining how the line must be taken south of the river about four miles—a long, slow grade—to get out onto the high prairie. "And here," he said with pardonable pride, "is the ideal site for your big terminus town." With that the chief engineer unrolled another big tracing and spread it out on the table.

Already George Walker had a townsite neatly platted. Capacious station grounds were indicated, and plenty of land set aside for yard and terminal facilities—for here would grow one of the most important railroad cities in the entire Southwest. The plat covered several thousand acres, and the General Manager studied it carefully. Then with a keen look at Walker, he asked: "What about the land? All pre-empted years ago, I expect; but can we get it cheaply and quickly?"

"Yes," said Walker without hesitation. "We've brought a young fellow up from Sherman with us—no, he's not a native—who can handle the whole deal for you, and nobody the wiser.

"Who is he?" Stevens asked.

"That red-bearded man talking with George Reynolds," Gunn said. "Name's Munson. He's a civil engineer from Illinois. Just came to this country last fall. He has settled in Sherman and is dabbling in land just now. He's had some railroad experience, and Reynolds thinks he is just the man to handle the land deals in Grayson County for us."[3]

[3] Letter Book No. 6; General Manager's Report.

Last Span of the "Indian Bridge"

Because William Benjamin Munson played an important part in the development of the Katy Railroad, and an even more important part in the development of the whole southwestern section of the country, it might be well here to tell something of him. Born in Fulton County, Illinois, in 1846, Ben Munson was one of three brothers, all of whom became prominent in north Texas. He was educated at the Agricultural and Mechanical College of the University of Kentucky, received a degree in engineering, and helped locate and lay track for the Rockford, Rock Island and St. Louis Railway extension. Later he had done some contract work for the line and had made enough money out of it to stimulate his business imagination. When railroad building came to an end in Fulton County, Ben Munson decided that the Indian Territory frontier, where the Katy railroad was then feverishly building, was the land of opportunity for him.

He had stopped briefly in the new town of Parsons when he first arrived out West, and then, apparently, had made a careful survey not only of the projected line of railway but also of the business opportunities which its coming would create. Thinking somewhat along the same lines as City Planner Stevens, Ben Munson had chosen Sherman, the southern approach to the Katy's "Indian bridge," as his best field of operations, and now he was ready to operate.[4]

The General Manager was assured by all who were interested, particularly by George Reynolds and Major Gunn, that Munson was a reliable man. Favorably impressed from the very start, Bob Stevens soon was giving Munson his fullest confidence. The red-bearded young engineer was delighted with the former's plans for a Texas border townsite, and before the day was out William Benjamin Munson had been retained as land agent for the Missouri, Kansas and Texas Railway.

By the middle of July, 1872, the end of track was at Milepost 170, now the thriving little town of Kiowa. On August 1 the line crossed Ward's Creek and three days later reached Limestone Creek, deep in the once dreaded Limestone Gap. The Gap was once more to become a dreaded spot, mainly because the deep and narrow railroad cut through its forbidding timbered hills made it an ideal ambush spot for the gangs of desperate train robbers which infested the Territory for many years after the coming of rail transportation. But that tale comes later.

The end-of-track reached and crossed the North Boggy River by the end of August. Here at Milepost 190, another little settlement,

[4] Munson biography, *Ten Million Acres*, privately printed.

named Springtown for its pure, clear springs, came into being. Spring-town (now officially "Stringtown" by post office error in registering) was expected to become one of the great lumber markets of the future. Instead, only its great rock quarries have given the community a precarious existence. An outpost of the McAlester State Penitentiary is now located there.

Although this was the land of the Choctaws, it was definitely the country of creeks. To build the fifteen-mile stretch of track from Stringtown south, the construction crews had to cross no fewer than four good-sized streams and dozens of nameless creeks. There appeared to be a paucity of names here; all the rivers were designated "Boggy." First came North Boggy, then Middle Boggy, then South Boggy, and finally, Clear Boggy! The railhead reached A-tok-a, between the Middle and South Boggies, by mid-September and paused here to gather strength for a renewed drive to the border.

As soon as the railhead reached A-tok-a, the inhabitants of Boggy Depot, the Indian settlement on the Texas Trail several miles to the west, moved in a body to the new terminus, and that old capital of the Choctaw and Chickasaw tribes simply dried up and disappeared. These two factors, the coming of the railroad and the transfer of the Indian agency, made A-tok-a an important settlement overnight. Historian Grant Foreman writes:

> From here [A-tok-a] a tri-weekly stage service was maintained with Fort Sill and other western forts and Indian agencies, and enormous shipments of military and Indian supplies were freighted over the same route. During that time the road from Atoka to the Red River, fifty miles, was crowded with teams, passengers, and freight, so much was business stimulated by the extending of rail transportation; Colbert's ferry crossed hundreds of teams daily. The El Paso stage line had been forced to double the number of stages running from there to Sherman, Texas, to care for the greatly increased passenger traffic. Ice from Kansas was brought down and delivered three times a week at Sherman and retailed at twelve and one-half cents a pound. Cattle buyers were swarming into Texas in order to be ready to profit at the earliest opportunity by rapid transportation of live stock to market.[5]

Here—pushing our history a little ahead—Tams Bixby, chairman of the Dawes Commission, signed the Atoka Treaty with the Chicka-

[5] Foreman, *A History of Oklahoma*, 179.

saws and Choctaws, on June 28, 1898, which was later followed by similar treaties with the other three civilized tribes, the Cherokees, Creeks, and Seminoles.

Tams Bixby was chairman of the Commission from 1897 to 1905, succeeding Senator Henry L. Dawes of Massachusetts, who had resigned because of ill health. The problem of the commission was to treat independently with each nation, to determine the number of citizen heirs belonging to each tribe or nation, and to allot and deed to each citizen his proper share of the estate. In a word, his job was to dissolve the Indian nations. Under the laws in effect prior to the establishment of the commission, the land of each nation was held in common, owned jointly by all the citizens of the nation or tribe.

The commission also had the job of purging the citizenship rolls in each nation of names of persons not Indians by blood, adoption, or intermarriage, not entitled to be enrolled as such and therefore not entitled to participate in the allotment of lands; there were many thousands whose claims to heritage proved to be false.

Tams Bixby walked into an atmosphere of bristling hostility; he not only encountered vicious opposition from the Indian by blood but also from the intermarried citizen. He aroused the enmity of the great cattle barons, who had been using vast, inexpensive acres as grazing lands for their herds, the businessmen in various settlements or towns in Indian Territory, and, to a great extent, the white tenants scattered over the Indian Territory engaged in farming in a small way. These were practically a unit against any change in existing conditions.

Bixby realized that his first job was to break down the barriers erected against the commission's proposals. His patience and diplomacy brought about the Atoka Treaty but it was many years before his purpose was accomplished.

Prior to acceptance of the treaty, it should be understood, no one could own real estate in the Indian Territory. Despite the fact that, since the advent of the Katy Railroad, quite a number of towns and trading points had sprung up in each nation, no man had title to the lot on which his improvements had been placed. The Atoka Treaty established the right of a noncitizen owner of improvements in a surveyed town to purchase the lot on which he had made bona fide improvements—the first time it became possible to acquire title to real estate in the Indian Territory. Out of the treaty grew the organization of townsite commissions, the surveying, platting and sale of town lots of the Indian domains, and official recognition of a white man's title to property of this character.

Following the negotiation of treaties, the work of determining the value of these five tribal estates and distributing the lands among the individual heirs thereto was the next move. Under Bixby's direction, headquarters for the commission were set up in Muskogee, and there he began to form his allotment appraisement, legal, and survey organizations. A force of engineers prepared new and complete maps of each nation, and on these maps were shown the railroads, the acreage occupied by towns and villages, and the areas set aside for schools, churches, and other institutions.

At this time the legal forces of the Katy Railroad took vigorous exception, as they had done several times before, to the proposed distribution of sections reserved to the railroad. They formally notified all persons concerned that at the proper time all such occupancies would be contested. The railroad injunctions were ignored and Bixby proceeded to allot all the land, including the Katy's "alternate sections."

Tams Bixby was the executor of perhaps the largest estate known in western history; it comprised 31,400 square miles, or more than 19,000,000 acres. It was larger in area than the states of Connecticut, Delaware, Massachusetts, New Jersey, and Rhode Island combined. The opportunities for what politicians call "honest graft" were the greatest ever dangled before a public administrator; but when he resigned on the completion of his job, he was as poor in the world's goods as he was when he had started his public service. He bought a small weekly newspaper, the *Muskogee Phoenix*, and built it until it became one of the soundest properties of its kind in the Southwest, and merged other and smaller papers with it. As the *Muskogee Phoenix and Times-Democrat*, it is now edited and published by his son, Tams Bixby, Jr.[6]

South of A-tok-a, construction was over trestle-work of the most difficult character to Caney, at Milepost 210, and Caddo Hills, at Milepost 220, reached on October 26, 1872. This terminus quickly became a town of some importance, for there the Fort Sill trade was concentrated, and the cotton from Paris and other points in Northern Texas came in on the Fort Sill road.

It was to Caddo that a broken-spirited chain gang of wild Indian prisoners was taken after the bloody uprisings two years later, in 1874,

[6] *Tams Bixby Biography*, (privately printed), 45.

for shipment over the Katy Railroad to prisons in the East. The wanton and wholesale destruction of the buffalo, their main dependence for food and coverings, had so alarmed the plains Indians at this time that thousands of braves had left the reservations and gone on the warpath. Screaming Comanches, Kiowas, Cheyennes, and Arapahoes scourged the western prairies, marauding and murdering, but finally General Nelson A. Miles quelled the insurrection. On the recommendation of General Philip H. Sheridan, the ringleaders, 33 Cheyennes, 26 Kiowas, including the famous Lone Wolf, and 13 Comanches—72 in all—were placed in irons and started on their long journey to Fort Marion, in St. Augustine, Florida.

These proud Indians were shackled in a degrading way. Heavy rings connected with chains were riveted on their ankles, and many of them were also handcuffed. At the Katy station they were loaded into two cars attached to a puffing, snorting fiery monster that most of them had never seen nor heard of before. When the train began to pull out, these pathetic captives covered their heads with blankets in terror. Droves of their relatives and friends crowded the high points, coming as near as they were permitted, and the squaws wailed and gashed themselves with knives. Even the hardened railroad workers felt pity for the Indians that day.[7]

Ben Munson, the Katy land agent, was much in evidence at the end-of-track now. On October 26, 1872, he proudly announced that "a new depot will be established today at Caddo Hills, near Blue Creek, Chickasaw Nation, 40 miles from Sherman."[8] He carefully neglected to mention that the depot would consist of an ancient box car that soon "looked like an old mud turtle that had crawled out of the Creek to sun himself." Munson's interests, however, were in land —as much as he could get for the railroad—not in local facilities.

By November 1, Scullin's Irish Brigade had got over the trestle at the Blue River and were passing Armstrong Academy and old Fort McCulloch, not far to the east. By mid-month the railhead reached Durant's place, just fifteen miles from the border. Back in 1832 Pierre Durant, a French-Canadian trapper and trader, had made his home with the tribes and married an Indian maiden. With his wife's people he had made that melancholy journey west to the Territory best known as the Vale of Tears, and here he had chosen his head right.

Late in November, 1872, the brawny tracklayers, putting on a

[7] Foreman, *History of Oklahoma*, 195.
[8] *The A-tok-a Vindicator*, October 26, 1872.

spurt in order to get through to Boomer's men the heavy superstructures they needed for the Red River bridge, went by Chickasaw Ben Colbert's jealously held ferry landing at a record-breaking clip. Here, as at the northern border of the Territory thirty months ago, they laid the ties mostly on the hard-baked, hoof-pounded earth, slapping the iron on with little regard for "fill."

It was getting late on Saturday, November 23, 1872, when they laid the last rail on the northern approach to the bridge—right up to the falsework—and big John Scullin, happy as a devil-may-care Irishman can be, drove the spike that put a period to the pioneer railroad drive down through the Indian Territory. With two strong arms and a spike maul he had written an epic in railroad construction.

___

TWENTY

Denison, the Gate City

While Scullin's crew were tearing down the Texas Trail that fall, Colonel Stevens was by no means idle. He worked harder than they did, but in a much, much different way. Daily he perspired over a hot pen, using his generalship to circumvent the Pacific lines in the north and his craftiness to forestall the Texas Central in the south.

Ben Munson was invaluable to the General Manager at this time. He ran the titles on all the lands that Stevens needed for his Texas townsite. It was just as Stevens expected; every foot of ground he needed had been long pre-empted. All this had been white man's country ever since Dan Dugan, the first settler in Grayson County, had arrived in 1836. There was trouble with the Indians at first, and for a few years the issue was in doubt. Dugan himself was killed in a "broth" of a fight with the thieving redskins, but his Celtic sons more than evened the score. The matter of ownership in this section was definitely decided when Dugan's Irish-tempered daughter Emily shot a marauding Indian, calmly chopped off his head with an axe and set it up on a pole as a bloody warning to the tribes to "leave her be!"[1]

After his first visit with the Katy General Manager, Ben Munson had returned to Sherman with his companions fully determined to throw in his lot with the railroad, for here was progress and the immediate prospect of enormous development. Valiantly he and a handful of other farseeing Shermanites fought the city fathers in a fruitless attempt to stimulate their enthusiasm for the coming of the iron horse from the north. Munson urged, beseeched the City Council to put up the trifling sum of $50,000 in bonds to subsidize the building of the Katy Railroad into their fair city.

[1] *Denison Guide*, 11.

Sherman's officials were adamant. Close-fistedly, they pointed out that already the Texas Central had been voted the bonds that would insure the coming of that railroad to the city. They had merely to wait and the Katy would be compelled to come in—at its own expense.

Munson, Connor, General Armstrong, and a few others knew better. The Katy would be the dominant line the moment it reached Texas, and where that line set its end-of-track, there business would gather. Ben Munson was sorry; had the bonds been voted, the Katy would have built into Sherman and land values both at the new townsite and in Sherman would have skyrocketed at once. Thereafter he concentrated his efforts on the development of the townsite and its environs.

Although Ben Munson's purchases of land and transfers of titles for Bob Stevens—and others in the know, including himself—totaled several thousand acres, the townsite proper as platted by Major Walker covered only 393 acres. How Munson and Stevens acquired this valuable real estate without arousing suspicion is quite interesting.

One day a tall, distinguished old gentleman with carefully knotted string tie, frock coat, and courtly manners accompanied Ben Munson out to the 102-acre tract owned by Mr. and Mrs. L. S. Evans. It was indicated to the worthy couple that Mr. Smith (a good name) was thinking about settling down here and raising blooded stock as a hobby. Evans demurred; it was a good farm and he had some valuable improvements on it. What with the railroads coming to the country soon, this land would be worth good money some day. Ben Munson talked, and cajoled, and perhaps belittled; and finally Evans agreed to sell at $20 an acre. The deal was made. Augustus A. Smith of Wyoming County, New York, paid over $2,000 in gold and the 102-acre tract was his.

Mary S. Stevens, the beautiful and cultured wife of the Katy's General Manager, had a tall, handsome and distinguished father. He happened to be visiting in Sherman at the time. His name was Augustus A. Smith.

So it was with other parcels of land needed for the townsite. Henry Denison, the General Manager's assistant, was the straw man in deals involving two adjoining tracts owned by the Johnson and Stoveall families. Realtor Munson had a little trouble in only one or two instances. The Miller and Layne families evidently had got wind of something, for they couldn't be persuaded to sell to blooded-stock raiser Smith.[2] Finally Bob Stevens had to come down himself. Joe Layne's 62 acres and John Miller's 50 were vital to the townsite scheme. He and Ben Munson finally turned both deals, each at $50.00 an acre, an outrageous price, they thought.[3]

The moment the land problem was solved, Stevens fired off a tracing of the townsite plat to Vice President George Denison. Although the site proper showed no ownership by the Land Grant Railway and Trust Company (every foot was owned by the general manager personally) the wily colonel again demonstrated the virtue of humility by having the townsite prominently lettered DENISON. It was a sop to the vanity of the financier now in power, and it cost Bob Stevens not a penny.

George M. Walker, C. E., filed the plat for the city of Denison immediately, and on September 20, 1872, Colonel Stevens organized the Denison Town Company, with himself as president, to sell off the lots. As it was in the founding of Parsons, the moment Major Walker filed the plat of the Denison townsite the rush was on. Shermanites, chagrined to find themselves outwitted, yet anxious to get in on the ground floor, were further dismayed to find that all the good land was gone. Now they turned to Ben Munson and his new partner, Jot Gunter, ready to listen to reason. But it was then too late. Munson had that faraway look—and a certain golden gleam—in his eyes.

On September 23, 1872, Denison town lots went on sale. Harrison Tone, a clerk of the townsite company, has left us a good word-picture of the community's first birthday, and of its birth pangs. One year later he wrote.

> One year ago today the city of Denison was in a chaotic, unorganized state, a thing wholly of the future. All told there were perhaps 50 men who had . . . erected booths, tents, and in half a dozen cases, temporary box houses, in which they had already commenced business. Here, too, was Gov. Owings [former governor of Arizona Territory] who had the honor of being Denison's first Mayor. Other than these few primitive improvements, there was not a board or a stone to mark the present city of Denison. Main street was a part of a rough pasture covered with brush; Skiddy (now Chestnut) street was a

[2] The Smith-Stevens Stock Farm near Attica, Wyoming County, New York, boasted some of the finest blooded stock in the country in the seventies.

[3] Records of the Munson Realty Company and the Tone Abstract Company, Denison, Texas.

ravine, from which the undergrowth had never been cut, while the rest was unbroken forest.[4]

The enmity and opposition of the citizens of Sherman was bitter in the extreme. According to Tone, the enterprise was belittled and derided, both by the people and the public press. It was declared that the titles to the lands were in dispute and the Town Company's claims were no good. Little did they know that their own townsman, Ben Munson, had run the titles carefully and well. It was claimed that the M. K. & T. Railway was a bankrupt concern (they were not too far wrong) whose aid and influence could never build a town. Finally, it was said that the railroad had no charter and could never enter the state of Texas.

On the day of the sale, one hundred Katy graders were leaning on their shovels between the Red River and the townsite, restrained from working by an order from the District Court, which denied the M. K. & T. Railway the right to build a road through their own lands. Moreover, a determined group of settlers had assembled to prevent lots from being sold at anything more than nominal prices.

Undaunted, the Katy auctioneer went to work. Despite threats and blusterings of a gang of rowdies, bidding was brisk from the start. The first lot was knocked down to S. A. Cook for $250. Thirty-one lots in all were disposed of that day at an average price of $155. Stevens, in a word, had taken in $4,800.

Someone nailed a board between two trees that morning, set some bottles on the makeshift counter, and opened up the first bar in Denison. Probably it was J. J. McLauchlin, first operator of the notorious "Sazerac" honky-tonk. Former Governor Owings made a speech to the crowd, calling for decency and order. These two little incidents were significant in the light of Denison's destiny.[5]

The ineffectual injunction issued by the District Court had been secured by chagrined officials of the Houston and Texas Central Railway. Earlier in the year the Katy General Manager had attempted to come to an understanding with the Texas Central people, whose railroad, begun in Houston in 1853, had reached Dallas by June, 1872. They had paused to receive the plaudits of the multitude in that great city of almost 3,000 population, and as a consequence were still many miles short of the border when the Katy reached the river. Stevens had been willing to come to some mutually satisfactory agreement for a common meeting point and, if possible, for a division

[4] *Denison Daily News,* September 23, 1873.
[5] *Denison Guide,* 14.

of the cost of erecting the Red River bridge. There had been no meeting of the minds. Mr. William M. Rice, the Central's largest stockholder and representative of the company in New York, was not inclined to dicker. The reason soon became plain; Andrew Peirce, the Katy's arch rival had become a large stockholder in the Texas line.

Concurrently with Ben Munson's real estate activities in behalf of the Katy, the H. & T. C., it was reported, had bought up more than two thousand acres on the Texas side of Colbert's ferry crossing. This tract included the ground on which the cotton-cloth shack settlement of Red River City, at the water's edge, had come into being. And here the H. & T. C., proposed to establish a great common terminus. As we have seen, Bob Stevens ignored the invitation to make his terminus here, just as the Central had ignored his invitation to participate in the cost of the Red River bridge. Cooly he built right on past their dearly bought acreage.

Frank Bond, the Katy's bustling little major, who had wormed his way into a vice presidency of the company in Judge Parsons' absence, came down to Sherman to talk with the H. & T. C. On October 7, he and William T. Hutchins, the Central vice president, got together importantly and worked out what they considered a practicable solution of their problems. The injunction was then dissolved.

Since the Central was determined to build through to Red River City and make that their great northern terminus, and since Bob Stevens was determined to do likewise at Denison, the two vice presidents drew up an agreement to establish a common interchange point halfway between the two townsites. It was also agreed that, in exchange for the privilege of building through Denison, the H. & T. C. would grant the Katy the right to use and occupy the right-of-way claimed by the H. & T. C. Railway Company, or any part thereof, for the purpose of laying a track thereon, adjacent to the track of the H. & T. C. The latter concession, in a word, was gracious permission to do the Central's grading between Red River City, on the banks of that storied stream, and Denison, several miles to the south.

It is getting a little ahead of our story to tell how this queer arrangement worked out, but the tale is worth the telling. For eighteen months the two railroads bullheadedly used their own terminals and steadily ignored each other. Long Katy freights and passenger "flyers" slipped south across the Red River bridge and charged right on through Red River City, picking up steam for the grade ahead, and never paused until they reached the Denison depot. Up from the south rolled the H. & T. C. drags. With warning toots they puffed right through Denison, took the hill and slid into Red River City for the first stop north of Sherman. As a result, switch engines of both companies were kept frantically busy for a year and a half, needlessly switching cars from the respective terminals to the outlandish interchange point that was convenient to neither, until both lines were heartily sick of the arrangement.

For the H. & T. C., it was a losing battle, as Bob Stevens knew perfectly well. The Katy was on the high plain, with the Central "in the hole." When the unpredictable Red River finally took half of Red River City in a flash flood the H. & T. C. gave up the ghost. On September 1, 1874, Bill Hutchins, the vice president of the Central, ratified articles of agreement which provided that "the interchange of passengers and freight between the respective companies shall from and after this date be made at the City of Denison."[6]

John Scullin's Irish tracklayers had the rail truly laid into Denison before Boomer's men had completed the Red River bridge. The depot was nearly up and the place was beginning to take on the semblance of a civilized community before the first train arrived. The Denison Town Company, Robert S. Stevens, President, was living up to specifications by doing a land-office business. It was the Colonel this time, not Judge Parsons, who rewarded the faithful with blocks of Town Company stock, so his friends were not forgotten as was the case at Parsons. John Scullin, the great American tracklayer, was rewarded generously. Chief Engineer Otis B. Gunn and Surveyor George Walker participated. Major George Reynolds and Ben Munson both took big blocks of the valuable stock, and several directors whose names are perpetuated in Denison's street names were given a cut of the melon. Perhaps Ben Munson profited most, and deservedly so. Unlike the others he was here to stay; he had vision and an unbounded faith in the future of Denison and the Lone Star State. He bought, on his own, great tracts of land in and around Denison, brought in the settlers in droves—and prospered accordingly.

For the first ninety days of Denison's existence, the Town Company's lot sales averaged $1,000 a day. Most of Red River City came up the road on rollers. Houses came rolling down the high road from Sherman; shacks rolled in from Preston, from Warren, from Carpen-

---

[6] The struggle with the H.&T.C. for the Red River terminus is reported at length in Katy records.

ter's Bluff. Strangers from the north gawked in amazement to see a city, not a town, rise overnight from the prairie.

With their construction job practically finished and with capital to spare, John Scullin and Bob Stevens started up a bank in Denison, the First National, and put in Scullin's brother-in-law, Ed Perry, as president. Ben Munson, now the big Texas realtor, took the lumber problem in hand and set up saw mills for miles around to meet the demand for building material. Many of the contractors who had followed the end-of-track all the way from Kansas settled down here and looked forward to some degree of permanence.

Hanna and Owens were typical Denison pioneers. They had started out as commissary men to feed their compatriots from the "ould sod," Scullin's Irish Brigade, and as the railhead steadily snaked south, just as steadily the firm grew. By the time the end-of-track reached Denison, Hanna and Owens were doing an enormous business. Not only were their ox-drawn wagons hauling the groceries to the graders, the construction gangs, and the survey outfits that were away out ahead of track, they were also bringing back to the railhead great loads of freight, chiefly buffalo hides, cotton, and produce, to make the back-haul worthwhile. They had their yards laid off and offices set up before the first Katy train arrived. This firm prospered with the great area it served, and, with the advent of A. F. Platter to the organization, and later E. B. Waples and his sons, this great grocery house was to become about as important, as necessary, and as native to the Southwest as the Katy Railroad itself.

Maurice and Graham's Overland Transit Company, which had been organized and financed by Bob Stevens and Katy Director J. R. Barrett of Sedalia to do the heavy freighting from the end-of-track, settled down in Denison. Now equipped with hundreds of great "ships of the prairie," they opened immense wagon yards in the new city, and from the beginning did a tremendous business. Some indication of the volume of freight moved by the lumbering wagons may be gained from an estimate that during the first month of Katy operation into Denison the amount of freight shipped to Denison from St. Louis was between 75 and 85 cars daily, or about 850 tons. Of this amount, 8 per cent was destined for points beyond Denison. It would require 550 wagons to move such a mountain of supplies, each wagon, of course, with a driver. Moreover, for every dozen prairie schooners a wagon master was needed. Since Charlie Maurice paid his bullwhackers $25 a month and his wagon bosses $50, it was easy to compute the Overland's payroll from these figures; the company was putting nearly $20,000 a month into circulation in the "infant wonder" that was Denison.[7]

So it was with others. John Degan, the Katy beef contractor, settled down here and opened a wholesale meat market. Major Walker's best assistant surveyor, young Arthur H. Coffin, who was a son of A. V. Coffin of Burlington, Kansas, a signer of the Katy's original charter, found the end of the rainbow here. He soon became a civic leader and served this city of his own making faithfully for many years. Bredette Murray, a "buffalo chip printer with a shirttail full of type," started up the *Denison News,* a lively frontier journal that has survived to this day, changed only a trifle in name. As the *Denison Herald,* it is a first-class daily of some 10,000 circulation, publisher Fred Conn and editor Claud Easterly being worthy successors of worthy pioneers.

As for empire builder Bob Stevens, already his mind's eye was looking far beyond Denison, beyond Texas even. He was musing over—visualizing—what Judge Parsons had said before he left for Europe:

> The extension [of the Katy] to the City of Mexico is a thing of the uncertain, perhaps remote future. Yet if a way can be found, in a line so direct as that proposed, into the heart of the oldest and in many respects the richest civilization on the continent—it is surely a legitimate project. I have satisfied myself that a line penetrating the country from the north and running from valley to valley, can reach the City of Mexico on a maximum grade of 60 feet to the mile, and pass at the same time through the most productive portions and the wealthiest cities of the Empire.[8]

Maybe, after all, Bob Stevens was just having a dream; aye, but what a dream!

[7] Harlan Lowe, "A Short History of Denison" (unpublished manuscript).
[8] *Chicago Railway Review,* November, 1870.

TWENTY-ONE

First into Texas from the North

On Saturday afternoon, December 21, 1872, Assistant Principal Engineer S. W. Shellenberger, who was in command at the end-of-track at Colbert's Station, entered the shack that served as temporary offices and wearily poured himself into a chair. For a while he sat motionless, idly listening and watching. Through the window he could see Boomer's bridge men scurrying around, packing up, cutting across to the Texas trail where it curved down to the ferry crossing. To a man they were headed for Denison and for the bright-light district there which already was doing a roaring business. They were through, finished; it was the final payoff. Mr. Keepers, Boomer's superintendent, had just turned the bridge over to him, complete and ready for the iron.

The door opened and in walked John Scullin and Dick Yost, the latter in charge of tracklaying for Shellenberger. Taking seats across the table from the weary engineer they waited while he busied himself with some papers. Then abruptly he turned to Yost and asked: "Everything ready?"

"Ready to go," said young Yost with some display of enthusiasm—

Scullin broke in: "I've got a hundred men standing by, ready to go to work. I can put you over the bridge by Monday night if that's what you want."

"There's no hurry," said Shellenberger slowly. "I want to be absolutely sure that everything is just right. We'll schedule the crossing for Tuesday afternoon—that'll give Major Gunn and Colonel Stevens time to get down here if they want to make the first crossing." And so it was arranged.

Tuesday was Christmas eve. The weather was biting cold. The sky was overcast, and flurries of snow presaged a "blue norther" when the heavily loaded construction train, piled high with rails and ties to test the solid strength of the bridge, pulled out of Colbert's station, Texas bound. The extra car on the back end had standing room only for the railroad officials and locally important people who wanted to make the first trip .The work cars ahead were festooned with humanity, railroad men, Indian 'breeds, terminus types—all the flotsam and jetsam of the border that cared to steal a ride to Denison.

All eyes turned to Colbert as the train reached the middle of the stream. There, below and a little to the east, was the Indian's ferry, still crowded, still busy, but doubtless doomed. For many years Colbert's ferry had been bringing in something like a hundred dollars a day, while the working expenses of the ford were not more than twenty dollars weekly. Yet the Indian never batted an eyelash!

The denizens of Red River City (there were no citizens) lined the right-of-way and shouted vulgar taunts at the Katy's motley passenger list as the construction train rolled on past their tent town and sturdily took the "hill" to the new townsite. Denison turned out en masse for its arrival, but since the community was not yet organized the ceremonies attendant upon such an occasion were, although entirely adequate, quite unofficial. Any attempt at dignity or formality was useless. The crowd dissolved into hilarious groups, wildly celebrating all over the tented townsite's God-forsaken acres.

The next day was Christmas. That evening a twenty-five-year-old Irish-American, Pat Tobin, tied down the whistle of locomotive No. 15 and took the first regular train ever to enter Texas from the north screaming over the Red River bridge. The Katy had won another race! First into the Indian Territory, it had crossed the Indian Bridge in the space of thirty months; incredible going for those days.

Although Pat Tobin never knew it, his noisy coming was, in its way, anti-climatic. The more boisterous souls in the community were strangely quiet, the consequence probably of their having celebrated too enthusiastically the evening before. Even the *Denison News* was subdued. The following, from the files of December 26, 1872, is its story of the history-making event:

> The first through train from the north over the M.K.&T. Railway arrived in our city Christmas night at 7 o'clock.
> There were two passenger coaches and one Pullman Palace car with the train, and over 100 passengers.
> Satanta and Big Tree, the celebrated Indian Chiefs, were on the train, in charge of the officers, and remained in Denison

overnight. They are being taken back to the State prison at Huntsville . . .[1]

For a new terminus town, Denison was an extraordinary place. It was a cross between the North and the South. Whereas the typical Texas town (Sherman is a good example) was built around the town square, or plaza, with all manner and class of business establishments intermingling freely, Denison was laid out on northern lines. Instead of the oldfashioned square, here was a broad Main Street, eighty feet wide, running east and west, all the other streets being laid out with due regard to the points of the compass.

The Denison Town Company permitted no questionable enterprises on Main Street. Saloons—such as the Crystal Palace—pool halls and dance houses, had to be reasonably respectable to remain on this fine thoroughfare. Razorback hogs and scrawny cattle might wallow in the mudholes of Main Street but houses of ill repute must stay in the next block south, on Skiddy, if they wanted to keep their licenses. This interesting arrangement accounts for the fact that honest travelers were invariably impressed with the safety and orderliness of the new town, while at the same time Denison was achieving a reputation both among lawmen and outlaws as the toughest town on the border.

The Town Company was able to enforce its extraordinary separation of the sheep from the goats simply by incorporating in its charter a proviso (Section 55) which gave it the power "To license, tax and regulate billiard tables, pen alleys, ball alleys, disorderly houses, tippling shops, barrooms, dramshops, or other places wherein liquors are sold or dispensed, bawdy houses, houses of prostitution or assignation, gambling and gaming houses, lotteries, and all fraudulent devices and practices, and all kinds of indecencies . . ."[2] This most remarkable charter provision made it easy for the city fathers to control and profit greatly from the frailties of the citizenry.

Before the H. & T. C. reached Denison in March, 1873, there were houses still on rollers; their owners kept them that way so they could move away if things did not go right. There were other houses, however, which had been thrown up hurriedly but were intended to stay; there was a post office; there was the Alamo Hotel almost completed; there was a church; and there was a schoolhouse. There

---

[1] Satanta and Big Tree were the powerful war chiefs of the Kiowas, a numerous tribe of wild plains Indians who were then committing depredations in the Indian Territory and constantly raiding into Texas.

[2] Act of Texas Legislature, March 7, 1873.

were dozens of saloons open for business, two dozen gambling places, several dance halls. Over on Woodard, in a tent, Bredette Murray, the wandering printer, was sorting a mess of type and setting up the *Denison Daily News*.

Skiddy Street in new-born Denison was one block south of Main.[3] Actually it was the "rat alley" of that ambitious avenue and most appropriately named, for the modern Skid Row couldn't compare with it. It was really nothing but a ravine with the underbrush cleared away, and lined on both sides with the most depraved collection of tents, shacks, and cotton cloth and board houses that case-hardened railroad construction men had ever seen. Here, crowding each other into the befouled former watercourse, were the tented gambling hells, the hurdy-gurdy joints, lowest class saloons, cockfighting pits, variety houses, and the deadly "dovecotes" that served as houses of prostitution for all races, colors, and creeds. Here on Skiddy, Millie Hipps (another well-chosen name) and her soiled "doves" from the incubators of Mollie Andrews in Sedalia, catered to the higher class trade, presumably from Sherman.

Here Rowdy Joe, Cherokee Jake, and that master of legerdemain, "The Original Jack o' Clubs," held forth as masters of the houses and gaming tables. These cold-eyed men, and dozens like them, were the spawn of the border and dismay of Denison for many years. The frequent and always disturbing presence of their kind in the struggling city during the formative years is easily explained. Men who were "on the dodge" either from the Indian Territory or from the Texas Rangers were within jumping distance of the border here, where law could not cross. An enterprising horse thief, for example, could make away with a span of horses in Denison or Sherman, sell them in A-tok-a, steal an Indian pony at Caddo, sell it in Red River City, and be back in Denison well heeled, his innocence established by sworn proof of his steady gambling at the Sazerac—all within forty-eight hours!

Rowdy Joe was all that his name implied. A fair gun fighter, he rested his reputation on his prowess as a "muscle" man. He loved a brawl, liked more than anything else to beat a disgruntled patron to the draw by a sledge-hammer blow to the jaw, followed by a scientific disabling kick. On one notable occasion, during a difficulty with some of the sporting gents at the Crystal Palace who had started to get hostile, the sheriff intervened. There were hot words between the

---

[3] Named for the fastidious Francis Skiddy, Katy director and president of the Land Grant Railway and Trust Co. It is now Chestnut Street.

lawman and the houseman. Sheriff Vaden "threw down" on Rowdy Joe and quickly the crowd melted back. Looking down the barrel of a "Navy six," Joe showed his hands, palms up. Then he spat on them carefully, rubbed them together, raised them high over his head—and kicked the shooter clean out of the sheriff's hand. The hair-triggered pistol went off, and Billy Campbell got the bullet through the neck.

Cherokee Jake, on the other hand, was a cold killer. When he went too far and beat Policeman Day to the draw, he had to light out for the Territory. The Original Jack o' Clubs, better known as Monte Jack, or "The Original," was the gambler of classic report. When the city fathers visited him in the Nelson House and invited him to leave town, he carefully donned his spotless white gloves, picked up his gold-headed cane, and said nonchalantly: "Well, gentlemen, if I never see you again, remember yourselves in your prayers."

Yes, it was reasonably quiet and decorous on Main Street in early Denison, even if hardly a day passed without someone's reporting "There's another dead man lying on Skiddy." Main Street was quiet except on Sundays, strange to say. On that day the frail daughters of Skid Row donned their finest plumage and paraded through the town. Some of them, still high-spirited, rented luxurious rigs from Farmers' livery stable, across from the Sazerac, and drove their equally high-spirited, matched pairs, hell-for-leather up and down Main Street. Gaily they spattered their betters, and screamed with laughter in the doing of it [4]

Ben Munson's wife, the attractive, blue-eyed former debutante from Sherman, Mary Ella Newton, remembered particularly the way the young Indian hellions, mostly 'breeds, tore in and out of town, on ponies wild as themselves, and made the town impossible for well-bred young ladies. "The Indians, male and female, came down to Denison for their liquor," Mrs. Munson recalled. "Sober on the way in, they were gloriously drunk on the way out, and they streamed past the house all night long."[5]

In January, 1873, Edward King, the ubiquitous reporter, turned his observant eye on Denison. "The Gate City" was then less than four months old; the papers incorporating Denison had not yet been received. King wrote wonderingly:

[4] These incidents were culled from early issues of the *Denison News*.
[5] Mrs. W. B. Munson, Sr., active almost to the end of her life, died in Denison on April 24, 1951, at the age of 99.

It was indeed like magic, the building of Denison. All the lumber for the houses was brought hundreds of miles, there being none suitable in the vicinity; and carloads of timber were changed into rough but commodious business establishments in a twinkling. [Shades of Ben Munson!]

It is exceedingly remarkable, also, that in a community one-half of which is undoubtedly made up of professional ruffians, "terminus" gamblers, and the off-scourings of society, and where there is not yet a regularly organized government, there is not more of terrorism. Every third building in the place is a drinking saloon with gambling appurtenances, filled after nightfall with a depraved, adventurous crowd, whose profanity is appalling, whose aspect is hideous.

Western towns of the middle and late nineteenth century all appear, according to historians and the motion-picture writers, to have had at least one "fearless two-gun sheriff," a rare character who upheld law and order against seemingly insurmountable odds. Such a man in reality was "Red" Hall, first sheriff of Denison. "Red", more properly known as Captain Lee Hall, 25 years old and late of the Texas Rangers, had been impressed by the Town Company to clean up the community. He did a workmanlike job and he did it in a workmanlike way. We return to Edward King:

Red Hall seemed to bear a charmed life. He moved about tranquilly every day in a community where there were doubtless a hundred men who would have delighted to shed his blood; was often called to interfere in broils at all hours of the night; yet his life went on. He had been ambushed and shot at, and threatened times innumerable, yet always had shown a proper scorn of his enemies, which finally ended in forcing them to admire him.[6]

Denison was rough and tough when the railroad came, as was every pioneer town in the Southwest established in that period. Any attempt to convey a softer impression is a reflection upon the courage of the original settlers. Law and order came eventually, as it always has in the history of the country, and it came to Denison more rapidly, perhaps, than to many other pioneer towns.

Building straight north from Sherman, the Houston and Texas Central Railway reached Denison and made junction with the Katy

[6] *Scribner's,* July, 1873, pp. 283–86.

Red (Ranger Captain Lee) Hall, first sheriff of Denison, Texas
—from *Scribner's Magazine*, July, 1873

on Tuesday, March 18, 1873. On that day, too, the famed Alamo House, brilliantly lighted by Chinese lanterns, had its formal opening, and again the whole populace celebrated. For this event, a group of Katy officials and their guests came four hundred miles by special train from Sedalia, Missouri.

Pavilions were constructed around the Alamo House and food was served to the multitude. There were "delicate bits of birds and beasts," which was understandable in a city like Denison, where quail sold for 50 cents a dozen, wild ducks brought 10 cents each, and a plump deer, freshly shot, could be had for $2.00. Champagne was produced and toasts proposed (the multitudes probably had to be content with beer), and Colonel Bob Stevens, when the proper time came, made a rousing speech.

The reason for the presence of the Sedalia delegates soon became apparent. The General Manager lauded the Katy management to the skies, pausing and bowing graciously while the multitude applauded him personally, for its magnificent effort in "spanning the Indian Bridge." Then he promised his hearers, the Sedalians in partic-

ular, that work would be begun immediately on the northern extension towards Chicago.

Ben Colbert, the Chickasaw Indian who owned and operated the
ferry at Red River City, was an honored guest at the celebration. Ben
Munson, who was seated with him, must have wondered what was
passing through the Indian's mind as the latter listened, expression-
less, to Bob Stevens' talk. Ben wondered what the Indian thought of
white men who could wine and dine him while they brazenly ruined
the business that was his livelihood.

Some inkling of Colbert's thoughts may be had from his subsequent actions. With Ben Munson as a silent but very active partner,
he built the largest and best ferryboat on Red River, 72 by 14 feet,
capable of crossing six two-horse teams and wagons. He also built
a sturdy wagon bridge, 557 feet long and 16 feet wide, completing it
by July 1, 1875. This toll bridge was erected by C. Baker and Company, St. Joseph, Missouri, and was said to have cost $40,000.[7]

Legend has it that Ben Colbert had gold buried all over his fertile
head right. Certainly he was a wealthy man, enriched by the profits
of the ferry alone. Moreover, he had eight hundred acres of the finest
land in the Southwest under fence, and owned several other fine
tracts in the Indian Territory. Later, at Colbert's Station, he erected
a steam saw mill, a gristmill and cotton gin, and became one of the
most earnest advocates of the opening of the Indian Territory to
settlement.

Ben Colbert was, in retrospect, a tragic figure. The finest type of
American Indian, he made a startlingly successful bid to survive in
competition with the white man. But it was only a temporary, evane-
scent success. Denison has grown and prospered mightily; now a
thriving community of nearly 20,000 enterprising, forward-looking
citizens. Across the storied Red River, on the other hand, at Colbert's
head right, nothing remains. His bridge is gone, ferry gone, even the
last traces of the deep-gouged Texas Trail are nearly gone. His ornate,
many-roomed home was burned to ashes before the turn of the century, and his private domain is now a pasture.

Nothing remains—nothing, that is, but the broken stones of the
old Colbert burial plot. His last resting place is now located in a
pigsty. In these unromantic surroundings, the historic and romantic
past may be recalled by the venturesome. The tombstone is inscribed:

[7] *Denison Daily News,* August 29, 1875.

First into Texas from the North

COLBERT

B. F. Colbert
Born Dec. 18, 1826
Died March 11, 1893

Ben's expensive headstone is the only one still upright; all the others are down, battered and broken.

On March 7, 1873, Denison was incorporated by act of the Texas Legislature. In the beginning there was some little support for the move to name the new town Red River City. No one knew the Katy vice president then; he was no more than a name. He is but little better known today. George Denison was not a railroad man, not an empire builder. By present-day standards he was a buccaneer, operating on the fringes of legally organized business. He came of good family, of course. Born in 1822, in Colrain (Coleraine), Massachusetts, he was then just fifty years old, big and stoutish, florid, and given to outbursts of choleric temper. He apparently had no close friends, but he had money and power in the early seventies.

George Denison was second youngest of the eleven children of Major David Denison, gentleman farmer, whose wife died "of a lingering away" at the age of forty-five. Although in moderate circumstances, the Denisons were a proud lot. They could trace their ancestry back to Captain George Denison of Stonington, Connecticut, valiant progenitor in the early seventeenth century of a little dynasty which has since given many pioneers, many leaders, to the country. The Denison who gave the Gate City its name first came into prominence during the Civil War. By appointment of President Lincoln he was made controller in the Bureau of Customs, Port of New York.

During the early war period there were strange rumors of merchant vessels that were circumventing the blockade at various ports and doing a tremendously profitable business. It appeared that certain ships loaded with contraband were sailing under two colors. In southern waters they were Confederate ships attempting to run the Union blockade, and all their papers were in order. In northern waters, however, they appeared to be Union ships running the Confederate blockade. The business was fantastically profitable, and in the light of Commodore Vanderbilt's known activities at this time, it might seem that he was the man who, conceivably, was behind such a scheme. Perhaps; but investigation revealed that ships and cargo were registered in the name of a Mr. George Denison, who may not, of course, have been the controller of the customs.

Then George Denison turned up as collector of customs at the Port of New Orleans, and again strange things began to happen. Valuable cargoes of cotton and other materials cleared mysteriously from "hither to yon" and back again, until eventually a suspicious admiral hove in sight and began to make inquiries. Strings were pulled, however; power came from somewhere to stifle the investigation, and war's end made it pointless.[8]

It may be that the Katy vice president who deeded his name to Denison had some knowledge of these things, but he was a man who kept his own counsel. His wife (he had no children) was equally silent. When he died "in a fit" in the old Arlington Hotel in Washington, D. C., on February 15, 1876, the 54-year-old enigma of the Katy Railroad let his past die with him.[9]

[8] U. S. Navy Department. Official Records of the Union and Confederate Navies.

[9] *New York Times,* February 16, 1876.

George Denison, vice president of the Katy Railroad in the seventies, who gave his name to the thriving Red River city of Denison, Texas

The Katy's great bridge across the Missouri River, connecting
Boonville with storied old Franklin. The second bridge to be built
across the great river, it was completed six months before
the famous Eads Bridge at St. Louis

TWENTY TWO

Sedalia Gateway Opened—On to Chicago!

During the year Bob Stevens had chosen to build his line from the Arkansas River to Texas, work on the Northeastern Extension of the road, from Sedalia to Boonville, Fayette, and Moberly had not been entirely neglected. As funds became available, contracts had been let for the grading of sections, the building of masonry and trestle work, and other purposes—all in preparation for the Colonel's final drive when the time was ripe.

Not long after they completed their work at Denison, Scullin's track forces boarded their thirteen-car construction train and headed north to Sedalia. Then, in quiet exultation, Stevens began to lay on with the "rod of terror" which heretofore he had merely waved over Andrew Peirce's head.

The first ten-mile section eastward from Sedalia to Clifton City was completed on April 10, 1873. The track reached Pleasant Green on April 24, and by May 18 the railhead was at Pilot Grove, that grateful grove of hickory trees on the old Osage Trace where early travelers from Kit Carson's town of Old Franklin en route to the Osage Mission generally encamped. Just two weeks later, on May 31, 1873, the end-of-track reached Boonville, on the broad Missouri River opposite Franklin, and was now ready to leap that big and muddy stream.

In the meantime, grading had been completed and track-laying commenced in May on the north side of the river. Here in the "Boon's Lick" country construction was started at both ends at the same time. The ten-mile stretch from Moberly south to Higbee was completed by May 15, and the stretch north from the river through the ruins of historic Franklin, starting point of the Santa Fé Trail, to

Kingsbury, New Franklin, and to Major Estill's was finished at the same time. The two construction crews met at Fayette, the "Little Dixie" headquarters of Central College, on June 20, 1873. Incidentally, a cholera epidemic broke out here and raged throughout the summer. This misfortune was charged to the Katy Railroad, but history records no true cause of the outbreak.

A big celebration to mark the completion of the Northeastern Extension was held in Boonville on July 4. The line was still minus a bridge over the river, of course, but cars were ferried across until the structure was completed. There were the usual ceremonies. Congressman John Cosgrove lauded the Katy, lauded the General Manager, and gave the St. Louis Board of Trade and the Pacific roads something to think about. Bob Stevens announced that work on the Katy's great Missouri River bridge, a million-dollar project, would begin on September 1. The big iron structure was to be one of the wonders of the country, he declared with enthusiasm. It would consist of two fixed spans 258 feet long, three fixed spans of 225 feet, one fixed span of 84 feet, and a gigantic draw span of 363 feet to allow passage up and down the river. The openings of the draw, he said, would be 160 feet in the clear at low water, and would be operated by handsome steam engines.

As usual, the General Manager lived up to his promises. Boomer's bridge gangs started work in September, and by the end of the year the structure was ready for the iron. Big John Scullin's crack track-laying crews completed the approaches, laid on the iron, and the first Katy train crossed over on the completed bridge on January 10, 1874, six months before the great Eads Bridge across the Mississippi at St. Louis was completed.

In 1930, the old Boonville bridge was replaced by an entirely new structure located 65 feet downstream. Plans provided for three 300-foot fixed spans at the north end, a 408-foot vertical lift span over the channel, and a 247-foot fixed span at the south side of the river, all through rivet-connected trusses; also a 60-foot through plate girder over the Missouri Pacific tracks on the south bank. The spans were designed for Cooper's E-70 loading for single track. The American Bridge Company got the contract to build the superstructure.

One wonders what Boomer and Rust, founders of the American Bridge Company who did such fine work for the Katy in construction days, would have thought of the new bridge. The 408-foot lift span was—and may yet be—the longest railroad lift span in the country, and the lifting and automatic leveling mechanisms involved fea-

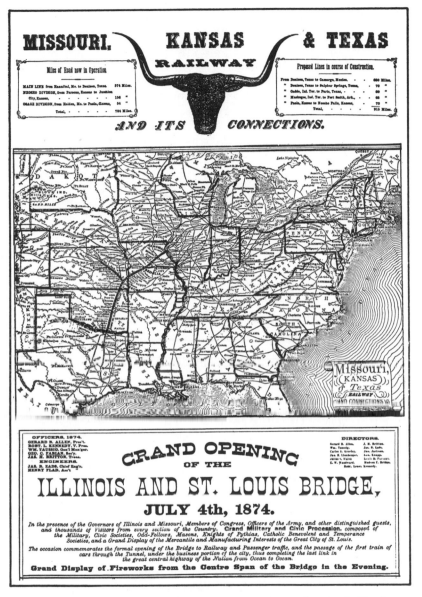

Posters like this flooded the Southwest the moment the Katy's Northeastern Extension from Sedalia to Moberly was completed in late 1873

tures first developed for this bridge. It was opened for operation in January, 1932.

After reaching the Moberly gateway in June, 1873, and making the vital connection with the Toledo, Wabash and Western[1] road, the general manager set his sights up another notch. He purchased from its local "projectors" the Hannibal and Central Missouri road, a seventy-mile short line which had been leased to the Toledo, Wabash and Western. This line was in operation between Moberly, the now thriving home town of General Omar Bradley, and Mark Twain's romantic old town of Hannibal. Colonel Stevens put the road in shape and on August 10, 1873, began operating through service.

It was a proud day for Bob Stevens. The Katy immediately inaugurated the first of many great advertising campaigns. Newspapers and magazines, posters, dodgers, flamboyant time tables, all carried the triumphant news:

The Missouri, Kansas & Texas Railway having completed and opened for business their North-Eastern Extension (The Missouri Division), from Hannibal

to

Sedalia

Have made arrangements to run

PULLMAN'S PALACE SLEEPING CARS

From CHICAGO to

DENISON, TEXAS

via

CHICAGO, BURLINGTON & QUINCY

RAILROAD

WITHOUT CHANGE

Magnanimous in victory, Bob Stevens called into his office his growing traffic staff. There were Traffic Manager H. D. Mirick, James D. Brown, the newly appointed general ticket agent, and Tom Dorwin, who had recently been installed in St. Louis as general passenger agent and given an office in the old Southern Hotel building on Walnut Street. "Gentlemen," he greeted them expansively, "we are now top dog! But let's be careful not to lose any business—or any friends —just to indulge a spirit of revenge. We have been treated shabbily by the A. & P. and the Missouri Pacific but what's past is past. You'll

[1] Formerly the North Missouri; now part of the Wabash Railway.

find they will treat us much better in the future. So—let's have no unnecessary bickering, no recriminations."

Mirick, a privileged friend, said curiously: "What do you want us to do, Bob, kiss and make up—forgive and forget?"

"Not exactly that," Stevens grinned. "But we should start cultivating a careful friendship not only with the Pacific people but also with St. Louis businessmen. There's where we need friends. I want them to know our position, to know that we are for them, not against them. We need their business, they need ours. Let's do what we can to get all the business we can."

Tom Dorwin spoke up. "I'm having complaints in St. Louis about our advertising. The Board of Trade is asking if we intend to by-pass St. Louis—shut them out."

The General Manager considered the question and said, "That's the reason I called you in. We don't want to give the impression that the Katy would do anything that would injure St. Louis trade. All of you, I expect, remember this clipping from the *St. Louis Democrat* . . ." He handed around an article by a special correspondent of the paper, written from Denison and signed "Lone Star," which, after describing the railroad, went on to say:

> St. Louis habitually scoffs at all mention of rivalry on the part of Chicago for trade West or South of St. Louis; but it will not be safe to do so in this case. The M. K. and T. Road has already a branch built from Sedalia Northeast to Moberly, to cross the Missouri River by a bridge, nearly completed, at Boonville. At Moberly connection is made with roads that lead by very direct lines to Chicago.
>
> Let St. Louis take heed. Forewarned is forearmed. If St. Louis does lose the vast and valuable trade of the Empire State of the South—a trade she ought to monopolize, so tremendous is her vantage-ground—it will be the result of the most beastly stupidity and contempt of the first law of nature, which is self-preservation.[2]

All of the General Manager's men were familiar with the *Democrat's* articles—too painfully familiar. They waited expectantly for his next words. Stevens went on with his talk: "I want everyone to know that we still believe St. Louis is our natural outlet—that we feel the great bulk of our traffic should come to us, and go through, the

[2] *St. Louis Democrat*, January 17, 1873.

St. Louis gateway. But—and you can't make this too clear—it must not be routed via Vinita. I will not be short-hauled!"

Then the General Manager turned to James Brown, the new advertising genius of the line, and said: "In all your advertising hereafter don't neglect to feature prominently the fact that through trains, both sleeping cars and day coaches, will continue to run from St. Louis to points on our line as heretofore, via Sedalia. Emphasize *VIA SEDALIA!*"[3]

And so the advertising ran, emphasizing VIA SEDALIA.

One might expect that, in the hectic rush to complete the Northern Extension of the line and checkmate the Missouri Pacific, all else would have been forgotten. On the contrary, nothing was forgotten; if there was a reasonably honest penny to be earned it was earned. Although central Missouri had been more or less settled for some fifty years, in the 1870's it was still a land of opportunity for the projector and the city planner. Between Sedalia and Boonville, for example, a stretch of thirty-four miles, there was hardly a house, much less a settlement. The "trace" was a trace and nothing more. Here was opportunity. Pilot Grove was laid out immediately after the road arrived, on May 30, 1873. Pleasant Green came into being on June 28; Harriston followed on July 10, and Clifton City, belatedly, was platted on September 29.

Nor was central Missouri, even as late as the seventies, over-civilized. Although Boonville was founded in 1817 and Fayette in 1823, and despite the fact that both were thriving cities when the railroad arrived, central Missouri was open country still. Historic old Franklin, starting point of the Santa Fé trail, had been washed down the river in the spring of 1828, but what remained of the city that had published the pioneer newspaper, the *Missouri Intelligencer,* had moved up on the bluffs and was still struggling along courageously when the Katy spanned the broad Missouri there.

Despite these evidences of progress, the section through which Bob Stevens drove his tracks still carried the marks of the frontier. Sedalia, a dozen years old by this time, was slowly settling down, but men still carried side arms for protection, and the end of town patronized by the railroad workers remained nearly as primitive as Denison. Lillie Allen's pleasure palace had come up somewhat in the social scale recently and was featuring her "Nymphs du Paive" as something special, but Mollie Andrews, better known as "Irish Moll," still disdained the fripperies and ran her place high and wide open,

[3] General Manager's Report.

if not handsome.[4] The eastern papers occasionally took notice that central Missouri was still young, still suffering from growing pains. On July 13, 1873, the *New York Sun* gravely reported that Joseph C. Howard, an alleged horse thief, was grabbed by a mob and taken to Franklin, "where the deputy sheriff, in addition to his other functions, conducted a whiskey shop," and was summarily "hanged on a tree about half a mile from town."

Missouri had no reason to look down her nose at Kansas or the Indian Territory, or even Texas!

[4] *Sedalia Bazoo*, issues for 1873.

TWENTY THREE

The Panic of 1873

When President Levi Parsons returned from Europe in August, 1873, he found that Bob Stevens had truly built for him a railroad empire. The main line, from Hannibal, Missouri, to Denison, Texas, was 577 miles long. A branch line from Junction City to Parsons, Kansas (actually the parent line) ran 156 miles, and the "orphan"[1] branch from Holden, Missouri, to Paola, Kansas, added another 54 miles. He had a 787-mile road in good operating condition but he had little else. Regardless of size, the railroad as it stood then was incomplete; it was little more than a bridge across wild, unsettled country.

The Judge was depressed. He had spent nearly a year abroad, in London, Paris, and Amsterdam. He had made an all-out effort to interest the bond holders in putting up the additional millions needed to complete the great railway system he had projected. He was remarkably unsuccessful. To make matters worse—and to help him make up his mind quickly to the course he should pursue—the Judge could find hardly an evidence of life in the heart of America's financial world, Wall Street, New York. He resolved almost at once to liquidate his holdings in the Missouri, Kansas and Texas Railway and transfer them to a safer place. Reading the market's distress signals aright, he knew there wasn't a moment to lose.

On September 1 he called a special meeting of the Katy board of directors. In serious tones he advised the board that it had become necessary to launch a new bond issue "to provide for the payment of the floating debt . . . to erect machine shops, and to completely equip for immediate and future use the various lines of railroad owned and operated by the Company, and also to raise the funds required to meet the payments into the Sinking Fund . . ."

[1] "Orphan"—disconnected from the main line.

The directors nodded their heads wisely and promptly approved the issuance of $10,000,000 of second mortgage bonds. That done, the Judge moved that the executive committee be directed to "deliver to the Land Grant Railway and Trust Company $6,000,000 of the second mortgage bonds of the company on account of the indebtedness of this Company to the Land Grant Railway and Trust Company."[2] This too was done, and in the twinkling of a pen Judge Parsons was out of the railroad business for all practical purposes while remaining one of its chief creditors.

On September 18, 1873, the most important banking house in the United States, Jay Cooke and Company of Philadelphia, closed its doors, bringing about the worst financial panic in the history of the country, with the single and subsequent exception of that of the 1930's. Cooke, the principal fiscal agent of the federal government during the Civil War, had been the financial genius behind James F. Joy in the original three-cornered race to the Indian Territory border which was won by the Katy.

The downfall of Jay Cooke had the effect of a thunderclap. Soon allied brokers and national banks and five thousand commercial houses followed into the abyss of bankruptcy. Railroads failed; leading stocks lost thirty to forty points, or half their value; the exchanges were closed; the stampede, the "greatest" crisis in American history, was on. The Union Trust Company of New York, the Katy mortgage holder, was in difficulties at once, and within sixty days that powerful banking house was declared insolvent.[3]

The Joy system was one of the first to come apart. Then tumbled the Northern Pacific, the Memphis and Little Rock, the Kansas Pacific, the International and Great Northern, the Arkansas Central, the Texas and Pacific, to mention a few only of the most important roads that were thrown into receivership. Andrew Peirce's Atlantic and Pacific (then dominated by General J. C. Frémont), which had taken the radical step of leasing the whole of the Missouri Pacific system in order to secure its entrance to St. Louis and to build up a monopoly of Missouri business, now was forced to disgorge that indigestible property.[4] After 1873 neither James F. Joy nor Andrew Peirce appear in the Katy story, so we leave them both here, though Colonel Bob Stevens at this time, with more feeling, left them, unwept, unhonored, and unsung.

[2] Minutes of directors' meeting.
[3] Matthew Josephson, The Robber Barons, 170.
[4] Robert E. Riegel, The Story of Western Railroads, 135.

Judge Parsons was, if anything, behind rather than ahead of the notorious Jay Gould in sensing the impending market crash. "That consummate master of speculation," as the press habitually described Gould, already was pouncing upon wrecked enterprises. Here was his golden opportunity; the pickings were very rich. As a boy, it was said, the Mephistopheles of Wall Street had dreamed of making a transcontinental railroad. Now one broken railroad after another was quickly taken over by Gould through the Middle West and the Southwest. He acquired a working interest in the Texas and Pacific, which had been chartered in 1871 to run between Galveston and San Diego but was virtually unbuilt. He also purchased an important newspaper, the *New York World.* Then he reached for fragments of defunct railroads, franchises, land grants about to be forfeited. These included the ill-fated Kansas Pacific (which had fought the Katy and closed the Junction City gateway), now fallen into receivership; the Denver Pacific; the Wabash; the Missouri Pacific.[5]

On October 22, Jay Gould surreptitiously entered the Katy. Through his henchman, the crafty moneylender Russell Sage, who held the mortgage covering the Katy's Union Pacific Southern Branch bond issue, Gould had placed on the Board one of his own men, William Bond, president of the Denver Road. Bond was immediately elected second vice president, a very strategic post for Gould's purposes. Bond at once took over the active management of the company and began ousting the Old Guard, firing all those in key positions and replacing them with his own men. The stage was being set for another of Gould's gigantic operations.

On October 31, the intrepid Colonel Bob Stevens, still entrenched in Sedalia as General Manager, was disgusted. Plummetted from the pinnacle of success to the depths of defeat almost overnight, he began to prepare for the worst. All of the General Manager's spare cash was tied up in "on-line" investments, principally in banks at Sedalia, Parsons, and Denison, in various coal mining properties along the route, and in townsite real estate. He had, in fact, just managed to save the First National Bank of Sedalia from bankruptcy by bailing out Cyrus Newkirk, the president, and A. D. Jaynes, the cashier. For collateral, he took their deeds of trust on Broadway Houses and all their real estate.

No sooner was the bank deal completed than the Colonel sat down and dejectedly wrote his wife, Mary, who had been spending the summer with her parents in Attica, N. Y., that:

[5] Josephson, *The Robber Barons,* 194.

News from New York City is bad—bad! All have lost confidence in and seem to be fighting each other. If my investments in banks &c., on line of road were disposed of, would resign tomorrow.

Skiddy, Johnson & Gandy work together; Crawford and Denison are another clique, & the Judge for himself. Crawford & Denison are opposed to me, all the others for me—except Judge & he is for himself.

Crawford has resigned as Treasurer—and all seem to be in "suds." In a short time I shall go to New York and have a full talk, when, unless I can remain as heretofore, having the confidence of all & not be made a bone of contention, shall promptly quit.[6]

On November 24 former Treasurer David Crawford, Jr., resigned from the Katy board and was immediately charged with embezzlement. This probably explains Bob Stevens' remark that the eastern directors "all seem to be in 'suds'!" Crawford had been treasurer both for the railway company and for Judge Parsons' construction company—a little Credit Mobilier scandal all over again. It appears, however, that the thieves' quarrel was quickly hushed up and matters adjusted to the satisfaction of all.

Events now began to pile upon each other in quick succession. On November 25 the Union Trust Company was declared insolvent and its doors were closed. The following day Levi P. Morton and J. Pierpont Morgan were made trustees of the Katy mortgage, and they promptly sent Judge Parsons packing off to Europe to do what he could to pacify the bondholders. That proved to be a tactical error, for it left the Katy ship rudderless at the height of the storm. Russell Sage, working in his quiet, devious way, soon had William Bond on the directorate in Crawford's place, and on December 12 Bond was elected, in the absence of the Judge, Katy president pro tempore. Director Frank Skiddy, president of the Land Grant Railway and Trust Company and Judge Parsons' right-hand man, engineered the maneuver, and it looked suspiciously as though he had sold out to Russell Sage and Jay Gould.

Levi Parsons carried to Europe with him a printed circular designed to soften the bondholders' hearts and forestall drastic action while the battle for control of the Katy proceeded. This interesting document read in part:

[6] Stevens letters, Attica, New York.

The failure of projected financial negotiations early in the year and the cessation of the sales of bonds compelled the Company to put out floating obligations in addition to using the current earnings, and when the long stringency in the money markets of the United States culminated in the panic of September last they were unable to meet or renew these obligations and were therefore compelled to suffer them to be protested.

The Company are now compelled to ask reasonable concessions alike from creditors holding funded obligations for payment of interest warrants and from those holding temporary liabilities for extension of their claims . . .[7]

It might be well at this point to examine the condition of this 787-mile road that had aroused the predatory instincts of Jay Gould. For an unfinished project, it had been doing very nicely—and its prospects, up to the time of the market crash, were little short of magnificent. Here are the figures:

Fiscal Year	Miles	Number of Passengers	Tons of Freight	Revenues Gross	Net
1871–72	390	166,258	143,691	$1,112,859	$ 352,472
1872–73	586	152,148	248,222	2,317,568	940,661
1873–74	787	168,608	305,760	3,533,074	1,645,400

Until the panic began to have its paralyzing effect upon the movement of commodities, the Katy was in a good way to becoming the great granger road of the Southwest. Even during the subsequent depression years its strategic position as the only line tapping Texas from the north helped it weather the storm, at least for a while. Only the blood-sucking policies of the Gould regime prevented the Katy, whose freight and passenger traffic kept climbing steadily, from reaching and far surpassing the revenue records of 1873–74 until the eighties.

First among the Katy's basic commodities came cattle; then came wheat and corn. For the three years of the great depression of the 1870's, with the exception of the terrible grasshopper invasion of Kansas in 1874, the small grains production along the Katy route was bumper. Third in the list of the Katy's staple commodities was cotton, a Texas staple long before the road entered the Lone Star State.

[7] This document is part of the minutes of the executive committee.

Another commodity invaluable to the Katy was coal, cheap coal for its own use and precious car loads for the industrial north and Texas. Mining companies had been organized along the line of road in Missouri and southeastern Kansas. As many as forty carloads of coal a day were taken out of Fort Scott alone, and all through the region veins ranging from two to four feet in thickness were but a few feet below the surface. Additional mines had been opened in the vicinity of McAlester, deep in the Choctaw Indian country, and traffic prospects generally were bright.[8]

In the Indian Territory, however, there was stagnation, deep, depressing, absolute. When the Katy built through the Indian domains several towns were laid off and lots were auctioned at prices ranging from $80 to $200; less than a year later the same lots were selling at from $15 to $60. During the seventies the Indian Territory trade was relatively insignificant. Cattle and hides were about the only exports, and the money received from them was all that came into the country, aside from the small government allotments. Nowhere was there a surplus of grain raised, and cotton was but a dribble.

Several times during the seventies, the Katy directorate debated the question of publicly renouncing all claims to the 3,100,000-acre land grant and urging upon the government the necessity of opening up the Territory to pre-emption and settlement. Engineers retained by the company to examine the property advocated the move as a practical solution of the Katy's traffic problems, but cupidity always overruled good judgment and the road's managers fought for the land grant tooth and nail, dissipating the company's money and its energies year after year in a lost cause.

Throughout the deep depression year of 1874, the road's trustees struggled manfully to effect a reorganization of the property. Committees of bondholders were formed in London, Paris, Amsterdam, and in Boston and New York, ostensibly to devise a mutually satisfactory plan for recapitalization of an inherently sound business. As time went on, however, and the committees drew farther apart in their demands, Levi Morton and J. Pierpont Morgan slowly began to believe that someone was deliberately sabotaging their labors. They suspected William Bond, the president pro tem who had craftily shut out Judge Parsons all year, and they took action at once.

On December 18, they addressed a firm note to the Katy directorate: "The Trustees find it necessary to request of your Board the

[8] Geo. W. Martin (Ed.), *Kansas Historical Collections*, Vol. XI, 107, 111.

prompt election of Levi Parsons, Esq., to the Office of President of your Company with full power to suspend or discharge as he may find reason, any of the officers of the Company. It is evident that as matters are at present working in the Company's Offices, good results cannot be expected. In the interest of the Company and its creditors the Trustees therefore call upon you to make the requested election prompt in accordance with your pledge."[9]

The request of the trustees was "respectfully declined" and the two tycoons in high dudgeon immediately threw the company into bankruptcy. They had reckoned without the hidden hand of Jay Gould, however, and on December 31, 1874, William Bond, the image of his master, coldly informed a startled board of directors that Judge Dillon of the United States Circuit Court had made an order appointing him provisional receiver of the company; that he had accepted the appointment. He thereupon made a demand for the transfer to him of all the property, assets, and effects of the company.

The beginning of the Jay Gould regime marked the end of Levi Parsons' dream of empire. One might have forgiven Gould had he merely usurped the Judge's throne, had he carried through to final reality that great conception of a mid-continent rail highway stretching from Chicago to Mexico City and "the homes of the Aztecs." But Jay Gould had no such idea; his fixation at the moment was another transcontinental route—an all-weather route—built on the shaky foundations of the Missouri Pacific, the Atlantic and Pacific, and Tom Scott's Texas and Pacific. Gould's dream was substantially that of the Missouri Pacific system of today; the Katy was never at any time a part of it. Jay Gould, the purest of mercenary adventurers, acquired the Missouri, Kansas and Texas Lines merely as a great feeder line for his Missouri Pacific system, to be bled unmercifully for the benefit of the system, sucked dry, and cast aside. So the dream of Levi Parsons, which had been brought close to realization by Bob Stevens, faded into the future, and the Judge himself, shunted onto a blind siding, was never again a factor in Katy management.

Levi Parsons mellowed with the years. He had no children, and towards the end of his career devoted himself, as many wealthy men of his period did, to the laying up of treasures not of this world. His charities became many; he endowed the library of his boyhood home town of Kingsboro (now Gloversville), N. Y., and his benefactions were gratefully received by the local parishes and pastors. He settled

[9] Minutes of the board of directors.

a large scholarship endowment upon Union College, Schenectady, N. Y., which, as a mark of its gratitude, conferred upon him the honorary degree of LL.D. in 1881.

When the Judge was actively distributing his largess along the Valley of the Mohawk, several deserving young Chickasaws, Choctaws, Creeks, and Cherokees were the recipients of his bounty. Thus was the fruit of the Judge's labors in the Indian vineyard occasionally plowed back into the soil whence it came. Parsons scholarships still are awarded annually, but in late years the Union College and the Mohawk Valley have practically forgotten the Honorable Levi Parsons and the rich southwestern soil from which his largess came. A great eight-foot oil portrait of Parsons, dusty and neglected, leans forlornly against a stack of library debris in a dingy corner of the attic above the library of Union College, defaced and set aside.

Judge Parsons died in New York on October 23, 1887. He was buried in the small Prospect Hill cemetery at Gloversville. Nowhere in the entire Southwest is there anything to perpetuate his memory, unless, possibly, it be the City of Parsons, "the metropolis of southeastern Kansas."

TWENTY-FOUR

The Dark Years

With the arrival of the receiver there began the departure of the men who built the Katy. Chief Engineer Otis B. Gunn, whose work had drawn the praise of a set of jaundiced railroad commissioners, bowed out early, and a long list of lesser lights found their places taken by appointees of the new regime. Through the dark years of the depression, however, the resourceful Bob Stevens was retained as General Manager, for only he had the know-how to keep the road in operation in the face of calamity. He, in turn, tried to keep Irish John Scullin on the payroll as Superintendent of Track just as long as he could, but the great American tracklayer didn't linger long. There were more roads to be built, down Mexico way.

In the mid-seventies Katy trains headed north with long drags of Texas cattle, with slaughtered beef and mutton, hides, grain, coal, and cotton. Prices tumbled to an all-time low, and the farmer, the cotton-grower, the cattlemen, the coal digger, all these were lucky if the returns were sufficient to keep them operating. In many cases they were not. Those Katy cars should have come back to the Southwest piled high with lumber for the building of houses, with foodstuffs which the Southwest was not producing itself, with goods manufactured in the East which should have been decorating the counters of the little stores in the little towns, the bigger cities; with farm machinery, with boots and shoes, with furniture—with all the hundreds of articles and commodities essential to existence and progress. And most important of all, they should have come back with settlers.

The Katy cars rattled back to their bases over the 56-pound iron rails—empty. Passenger fares in the Territory were cut from 10 cents a mile to 7 cents, but travelers stayed away. Settlers saw the products of their industry hauled off to market and sold for what could be got; and they saw their meager returns eaten up in taxes and transportation costs; then they cursed the railroad.

In the Indian Territory feeling ran particularly high, even though some concessions were made in rates. The Indians hated the railroad anyway and dreaded its "civilizing" influence. Trains were derailed with ever-increasing frequency; railroad installations were sabotaged; and organized bands of 'breeds and bad men roamed the almost empty country terrorizing travelers and settlers alike and discouraging all attempts at orderly development. The following press dispatch, only one of many that appeared from time to time, probably served to heighten the alarm rather than allay the fears of those who contemplated traveling via the Katy:

> There is an organized gang of train wreckers along the line of the M. K. & T. in Kansas and Indian Territory. These miscreants have caused the death of one man and the severe injury of three others. The parties have been arrested. They have confessed their crimes and will get justice at the end of a rope at the hands of Judge Parker's court at Fort Smith.[1]

Even the law-abidin', civilized Indian saw little or nothing wrong with making things difficult for the railroad. Tandy Walker, the smart and well-to-do nephew of a one-time chief of the Choctaws, who had a fine double log cabin overlooking the Katy tracks south of the Canadian, thought it good sport to lie in wait for the morning passenger train and greet it with a fusillade from behind some convenient rock. He measured his success by the number of windows he could shoot out of the train before the shifting monster could pull out of range.[2]

In Missouri and Kansas the settlers were rather more subtle in their opposition to the railroad, which they blamed for all the ills that befell them in the seventies. South of Boonville, the track takes a long grade known to railroaders today as "Lard Hill." Few know the origin of the name. Old-timers, however, delight in telling how an Irish slattern with a shack full of children and no sign of a husband

---

[1] Judge Isaac Parker was the "hanging judge" of the Territory. He believed in the frontier law: "Take 'em out, give 'em a fair trial, and hang 'em."

[2] "He [Tandy Walker] was a Civil War veteran who . . . saw fit now and then while deep in his cups to take pot shots at passing trains." Statement by J. G. Kelly, Westcliffe, Colorado, who was born at Chickie-Chockie (Limestone Gap) I. T. Judge Malcolm Rosser, of Muskogee, and his wife, a native of Stringtown, also tell lurid stories of the early days in the Choctaw country.

was responsible for the name. Legend has it that a Katy train killed the family pig one day. Since the pig was rooting where he had no business to be, and it was an evil-looking razorback anyway, the Katy claim agent assessed the value of the damage at $5.00 and would pay the bereaved Mollie no more. She begged, she pleaded; that pedigreed razorback was worth one hundred dollars! When the claim agent merely laughed, she threatened dire things, and he just laughed the more. But Mollie got even. She rendered the fat, and every morning when she heard the engine whistling for the Boonville crossing, she sent her brood out, armed with cans of lard, to annoint the tracks. Katy trains slithered and skittered around the larded "hill" for weeks until the Irish vixen was handsomely reimbursed for the loss of her pig, the legend concludes—but nothing appears in the records. McCoy, in his colorful report on the cattle trade of the West and Southwest, tells us of disgruntled settlers larding Katy rails in the neighborhood of Ladore as they vented their spleen on the railroad.[3]

It is an interesting fact that the two Katy-created towns at the opposite borders of the Indian Territory were, despite the panic of 1873 and the depression of 1874 and 1875, comparatively prosperous cities, oases in a desert of poverty. These towns owed their comfortable existence to the starving railroad; they had become the chief gateways for new Indian Territory trade just ahead of the national crash, and despite stagnation elsewhere they were reveling in the newly created markets.

Parsons already was a well-settled town of some three thousand by the mid-seventies. Here were the company's biggest machine shops, most commodious roundhouse, greatest classification yards, most extensive facilities. Denison, two years younger, also was developing fast. The railroad had installed at its Texas terminal the Southwest's greatest cotton compress and built vast cattle yards, and the city was beginning to settle down into a more or less law-abiding community.

Quite in the depths of the depression a lady reporter for the *New York Daily Graph,* who had been assigned to find out something about the new and promising project of shipping fresh killed meat in refrigerated railroad cars, arrived in Denison. There, where the idea originated, she met the Katy sponsors and the famous cattle-

---

[3] Joseph G. McCoy, *Historic Sketches of the Cattle Trade of the West and Southwest* (Kansas City, Missouri, 1874).

man Joseph G. McCoy. Much taken with the ponderous and dignified organizer of the first great cattle drives up the Chisholm Trail
who had been squeezed out at Abilene, she wrote:

> Today he [McCoy] is an employe of another new enter-
> prise—"The American and Texas Refrigerator Car Company,"
> a product of this city . . . which carries so safely to New York
> markets the cattle slaughtered here in Denison. The project
> looked impracticable and capitalists were slow to invest in
> anything so audacious, but already three trains of ten cars
> each, containing the dressed carcasses of more than 400 cattle,
> have reached Washington market, where competent judges
> pronounce the beef as sweet and perfect as if just killed.[4]

The deep depression years were marked by almost continuous
bickering in the company's executive ranks, and by sudden organizational upsets which brought to the line a long succession of temporary presidents representing, in turn, the different groups of con-
tending bond and stock holders. On March 1, 1876, the Gould faction finally gained the upper hand and effected a reorganization that
took the road out of receivership. Under the plan, the Union Trust
Company again became trustee of the road's consolidated mortgage.
Levi Morton, August Belmont, J. Pierpont Morgan, and other friends
of Bob Stevens thereupon withdrew their interests in the company,
and overnight the General Manager found himself without a single
friend at court.

Regretfully, the man who had built the Katy took the step he
had been preparing to take for more than a year. Decisive as ever,
he quit the road without a moment's delay and without a backward
glance. The first word that the Colonel's friends had of his action
appeared in the newspapers:

> The announcement, last Saturday, that R. S. Stevens, Esq.,
> late Manager of the Missouri, Kansas & Texas Railway, had
> been appointed Manager of the Hannibal and St. Joseph Rail-
> road, took people quite by surprise . . .
> Mr. Stevens' connection with the Southern Branch of the
> U.P. R.R. (now the M.K.&T.) is well known. When he took
> hold of it there was really nothing except a franchise. The
> road had a big land grant and the counties in the Neosho
> Valley had voted bonds for it and it had a charter. To work

[4] *New York Daily Graph*, datelined February 5, 1874.

it up and get the money to build it with required a peculiar talent. It was said at the time that it "began nowhere and ended nowhere." He succeeded and has built one of the best lines of railroad in the West. Most emphatically he built it, for there was not an hour or minute from the time he took hold of the enterprise till he left it, but what his was the master mind.[5]

Bob Stevens' successor as general manager of the Katy was none other than William Bond, late receiver of the property. No great genius as a railroad operator, Bond's efforts were all toward cutting expenses, saving money, particularly on maintenance. The property could go to ruin, it seemed, provided enough cash money could be squeezed out of it to keep the investors happy. Steadily he cut the prices of Katy land-grant acres and company-purchased lands until much of it was selling for as little as $1.00 an acre. He did so well the task he had set for himself—taking in money—that on June 1, 1877, he was elevated to the presidency.

In little more than a year the full effects of the Bond policy began to show up. As of December 31, 1878, the company's funded debt was, in round figures, $25,000,000; its capital stock, $21,000,000. That represented a capitalization of $59,000 for every mile of the 787-mile railroad. Despite this terrific burden, the company's net earnings were steadily decreasing. Although the country was recovering nicely from the effects of the panic, the railroad certainly was not. Earnings for the four-year period ending with 1878 were reported as follows:

Year	Gross	Expenses	Net Earnings
1875	$2,904,925	$1,680,364	$1,224,561
1876	3,217,278	2,001,278	1,216,000
1877	3,197,322	2,245,110	952,212
1878	2,981,681	2,633,198	348,483

It was obvious even to banker King, the wizened old president of the Union Trust Company, who cared only for dividends, that something drastic had to be done or soon there would be no railroad left to operate. A committee appointed to find a solution for the company's difficulties reported that the amount required to make good the depreciation was about $1,000,000. The survey revealed that the

[5] When Joy's Burlington crashed during the panic, the Hannibal and St. Joe broke loose from the system. It was now fending for itself—at least temporarily.

only way to increase the road's business substantially was to complete the system, as originally planned, by long extensions into Texas; it now lacked feeder lines.

One wonders if members of the committeee knew then that Colonel Bob Stevens, late of the Katy, later of the Hannibal and St. Joe, was again active around Denison, was in business for himself. Surely it could not have been too much of a secret that he and Irish John Scullin were together again, that they were again in association with the man who now owned great chunks of Texas, the red-bearded go-getter, Ben Munson. These three pioneers had taken out franchises, had run surveys, and were busily organizing the construction of the lines that were to become the Katy railroad in Texas.

Colonel Stevens had planned and plotted the Denison and Southeastern Railway, to be built from Denison to Greenville, Mineola, and Palestine, thus making connections with the T. & P. and the I. & G. N. on the way to the Gulf. He was also well along with the preliminary work on the Denison and Pacific Railroad, with which he expected to make a connection with the T. & P. in a southwesterly direction on the way to the Mexican border. If the Katy ever got the idea of carrying his and Levi Parsons' dreams of empire through to reality—as the Colonel knew it eventually must—it would have to deal with Robert S. Stevens, personally. The wily former General Manager was not finished with the Katy yet.

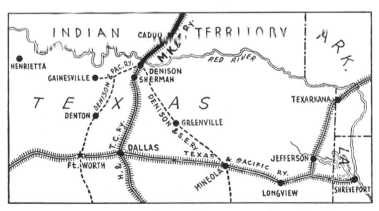

As the Missouri, Kansas & Texas Extension Railway, the Katy was projected deep into Texas in 1878.

TWENTY FIVE

The Rise of Gould's Missouri Pacific

Two years of general prosperity followed the rock-bottom year of 1878, and with prosperity came the railroad highbinders, the market riggers who called themselves speculators, in droves. The story of their manipulations in the late seventies and the eighties has often been told. Our story concerns itself with but one of these, with Jay Gould, the little silken-bearded former map maker who first cast covetous eyes on the road when he learned it was ripe for trusteeship. As has been shown, his first attempts to enter the Katy were surreptitious; the aura of the Erie Railroad mess, that of Boss Tweed and Jim Fiske, still clung to the little man's coattails; and then, as though that were not enough, there was his gamble in gold, the attempted corner which brought about the stock market crash of September 24, 1869, called Black Friday. No, thought most of the Katy's directors, Jay Gould is no character to be running wild among the assets and possibilities of a little railroad just getting back on its feet, preparing to challenge again.

Gould was a man who seemed outwardly to accept "no" for an answer but who in fact rarely did; he had the patience of Job, and if he could not acquire control of the Katy today, why there was always tomorrow and many other tomorrows; he saw it as a feeder for the Gould System; and eventually it became just that, a feeder—to be fed upon and bled almost white before it managed to shake off the coils of the system.

Gould's first pounce on western railroads was the purchase of control of the Union Pacific, built entirely with government loans, none discharged. From then on he went out to buck—and pluck—the great transcontinental line by the purchase of control of western roads that roughly paralleled the route of the U. P. He put in the

Wabash, the Kansas Pacific, the St. Jo and Denver (William Bond, president!), the Denver and Rio Grande, the Denver, South Park and Pacific. He added the T. & P. and the St. Louis, Iron Mountain and Southern. For the heart of his great system he added the Missouri Pacific.[1]

The story of Jay Gould's purchase of the Missouri Pacific is still retailed with relish in St. Louis. Commodore Garrison, who, it will be remembered, had warned Bob Stevens against Andrew Peirce, had assumed the presidency of the Missouri Pacific after the Atlantic and Pacific lost control during the panic. Gould sent word to Garrison that he would give $1,500,000 for control of the line. The Commodore replied that the offer was $500,000 too low. That brought Gould to St. Louis in person. In his quiet, deceptively gentle way, he let President Garrison know that he thought the price too high, but if it was firmly pegged at $2,000,000 he would be compelled to pay it. The Commodore laughed. No, the price wasn't pegged; in fact, it had gone up since the day before; it was now $2,800,000. Gould, it seemed, had met his match; turning on his heel, he stalked out without a word. However, he needed the Missouri Pacific to complete his jigsaw puzzle of railroads, and the following day he called the Commodore.

"I've been thinking about your price, Mr. Garrison," he said silkily. "I think we can still do business . . ."

Commodore Garrison's booming laugh could be heard all over the office: "I've been thinking about it, too, Mr. Gould," he roared. "The price has gone up another million dollars. It will cost you $3,800,000 now." Again the derisive laughter. "Do you want it?"

Soundly taught the dangers of delay, Jay Gould meekly said: "I'll take it."[2]

As the seventies came to a close, Gould's group, which by then had obtained full stock control of the Katy, moved swiftly to avoid threatened foreclosure by the Amsterdam Committee of bondholders. The road had begun to feel the benefit of resurgent national prosperity. Travel and traffic had picked up considerably from the low of 1878, and although heavy expenditures were required to keep the line in operation, the earnings were a token of what might be accomplished with it. This was no time, the Gould gang knew, to let the railroad slip away from them; not when business was reported as follows:

[1] Riegel, *The Story of Western Railroads*, 194.
[2] Walter B. Stevens, *Centennial History of Missouri*, Vol. I, p. 412.

Year	Passengers	Tons of Freight	Revenues Gross	Net
1879	296,652	676,785	$3,344,291	$1,271,540
1880	355,075	889,219	4,161,671	1,545,625

On January 26, 1880, the despoiler of the Katy began to clear the decks for action. Peremptorily he ordered his puppet president, B. P. McDonald, the Fort Scott, Kansas, banker, to call a special meeting of the board of directors in his office at 98 Broadway, New York. Ben McDonald was a straw man who had been put on the Katy board along with H. C. Cross, an Emporia banker, and C. H. Pratt of Humboldt, back in 1875 when the sovereign state of Kansas had passed legislation requiring Kansas corporations to maintain general offices in that state and keep not less than three resident Kansans on their boards. He was useful, as were the other local men, in arranging the transfer of the company's offices from Sedalia to Parsons, in the handling of delicate Kansas land-grant transactions, and for heading up the meaningless meetings of directors and stockholders which rubber-stamped the actions of Gould's henchmen on the Executive Committee.

Gould's coup that bright January afternoon took little more time than it takes to tell it. Surely there must have been a touch of the comic about this grave and serious meeting. One by one the puppet directors popped up and gravely read their resignations. All, that is, except the three Kansas directors, who didn't count. And one by one Jay Gould's hand-picked slate was sworn into office. When the voting was over, Jay Gould was the new president, and these men comprised the board:

Jay Gould	Sidney Dillon	H. C. Cross
G. M. Dodge	C. H. Pratt	William Bond
P. B. McDonald	Edmund D. Barbour	Frank S. Bond
Russell Sage	Geo. I. Forrest	N. L. McCready
	Fred L. Ames	

This railroad wrecking gang, so notorious in the seventies, left such a trail of destruction in its wake that even today, three quarters of a century later, its activities are recalled with a shudder in the financial world. These were the men behind the U. P.'s Credit Mobilier scandal. Frederick L. Ames was the brother of Congressman Oakes Ames of Massachusetts, whose revelations before Congress in 1873 shocked the nation. Oakes Ames, self-confessed corrupter of the country's highest officials, was impeached for his Union Pacific activities "as a warning," it was said, "to corrupt Congressmen against turning state's evidence."[3] General Grenville M. Dodge was the construction engineer who bragged that it was he who built the Union Pacific—at the fantastic cost to the government of nearly $100,000 a mile. Banker Sidney Dillon and the others were Gould's confederates, damned by association.

With the turn of the decade the Katy was firmly in the hands of these men.

On February 16, 1880, the Katy's Osage Division, the 54-mile line from Holden to Paola, was leased to the Missouri Pacific, the consideration being the net earnings. In May the stockholders at their annual meeting gave Gould the green light to go ahead with fantastic plans for completing construction of the road through Texas and "to the city of Mexico." They also authorized the integration of the line with the other roads of Gould's system, if desired, and approved an involved plan, typical of Gould, to reorganize the road's financial structure and about double its capitalization. All that summer the great stock manipulator worked patiently to get the trustees to endorse his ideas, but they were too suspicious of his motives and blocked him at every turn. Although he assured them again and again that "the existing easy money market renders it more than ordinarily practicable to raise the means," even the bait of easy money failed to attract them. The Union Trust Company apparently was interested only in profitable operation of the existing line, not in promoting extensions

On December 1, 1880, Jay Gould finally had his plans for the Katy perfected. He paid the Union Trust Company all arrearages of interest on Katy bonds ($583,072), thus dissolving the trusteeship, and took the company truly into his own purposeful hands. He called in the outstanding bonds, $28,217,000 in all, and retired them with the proceeds of a $45,000,000 General Consolidated Mortgage Bond issue underwritten by the Mercantile Trust Company of New York, leaving him nearly seventeen millions for proposed construction. He also floated another $25,000,000 stock issue, and thereafter the Katy, the helpless feeder line, was a ripe plum upon which his voracious Missouri Pacific system could feed.

But this was only the beginning. That same day Gould leased the entire property to the Missouri Pacific, the rental as usual again being

[3] Josephson, *The Robber Barons*, 164.

the net earnings. From that moment until the road was wrested from him nearly a decade later, the Katy was short-hauled, discriminated against, and abused in every conceivable way; it served merely as a network of branch lines, self-supporting, that fed enormously profitable long-haul traffic to the Mo. Pac. System, while the road itself was slowly dying of malnutrition.

By sunset of December 1, General Grenville M. Dodge had resigned from the Katy board. With Jay Gould he organized the International Railway Improvement Company, chartered to build the Katy through Texas to Mexico City. They had another little Credit Mobilier in the making. General Dodge, however, soon ran head on into Bob Stevens and his group of local projectors, who were determined not only to build the railroads that would kite the value of their land holdings, but also to make the Gould regime pay through the nose for blasting Stevens' dreams. The former General Manager consolidated the Denison and Southeastern, which was building via Whitewright to Greenville, with the Denison and Pacific, creeping slowly southwest, and under the name of the M. K. & T. Extension Railway had finished construction of the 52 miles to Greenville and the 42 miles to Gainesville by the time Grenville Dodge was ready to take over.

On February 17, 1881, William Whitewright, nominal president of the Extension Road, unloaded the property on the International Railway Improvement Company, which in turn sold the 94-mile product of pure speculation to the Katy for $3,760,000. The construction company then started the building, buying and leasing of bits and pieces of railroads to complete the Katy to the Gulf and to Old Mexico. Some of the most useless—and expensive—bits of railroads ever devised were unloaded on the defenseless Katy during this period.

TWENTY SIX

The Katy Enters Fort Worth

When the Texas and Pacific, building north from Fort Worth, reached the Katy extension at Whitesboro, twenty-five miles southwest of Denison, Gould arranged a joint-track agreement between the lines. Under the agreement the Katy received (and still retains) operating rights over the T. & P. between Whitesboro and Fort Worth, a distance of seventy-one miles. On April 1, 1881, Katy trains began operating through from St. Louis to Fort Worth, and the Texas cow town began thumbing its corporate nose at Dallas as never before.

Fort Worth has been described in three histories where one might expect to find authentic information as "a sleepy cow town." Cow town it was, cow town it is, but to refer to Fort Worth as "sleepy" at any time in its existence is so utterly ridiculous that one wonders why Amon Carter, the greatest press agent that a going concern ever had, has let it go unchallenged. The record shows that Fort Worth never slept in the civic sense; if it had it would have been engulfed by Dallas, twenty-six miles away, just as Dallas, had it ever slumbered, would have been engulfed by Fort Worth.

The following account of the courage and perseverance of the people of Fort Worth during the early period is a Texas and Pacific Railroad story rather than a Katy story; but because the Katy still has trackage rights over the T. & P. and still serves Fort Worth the tale may be worth telling.

Building slowly westward, the Texas and Pacific just managed to get into Dallas ahead of the financial crash of 1873. For three weary, shameful, galling years, the frustrated residents of Fort Worth saw herds of cattle driven through Main Street to embark for their first and last railroad journey—at Dallas, two days' drive away.

The people of Fort Worth were in a fix. Previous to the panic, the

Texas legislature had given the T. & P. a land grant along the proposed right-of-way on condition that the road was completed into Fort Worth by January 1, 1875. But that New Year's day dawned on a still very impoverished Tarrant County (Fort Worth, then as now, was the county seat). Nicholas Darnell, who represented the district at Austin, therefore secured the passage of a resolution which extended the time for entrance for another year.

The people of Fort Worth realized they had to do something, and do it quickly. Obviously the T. & P. was not in financial shape to extend the road in the given time. So the people decided to build the extension themselves; things were getting a little better as the year 1875 moved along, but they were improving very slowly. The citizens formed "The Tarrant County Construction Company," promising to pay in some money and to furnish their own labor and such materials, forage, and supplies as they could gather. The road at this time had reached Eagle Ford, about six miles west of Dallas, and was still twenty-five miles short of Fort Worth.

The first session of the Texas legislature under the new state constitution convened on the second Tuesday of January, 1876. Representative Nicholas Darnell of Tarrant County reported that the people of his district were doing all they possibly could to get the road completed into Fort Worth; citizens were working along the track, not only giving their services free but putting money and supplies into the venture. Despite this splendid example of loyalty to their town, Mr. Darnell's request for another year's extension met with determined opposition.

But suddenly things started to ease up a trifle for the T. & P. itself. There was money coming in which might possibly be diverted to bring the road into Fort Worth; in addition, the prize was a splendid one: sixteen rich sections of land per mile. The shadow of Jay Gould begins to appear here, for the railroad company took over from the Tarrant County Construction Company and went into action.

General John C. Brown of Tennessee was operations vice president of the T. & P., and he was on the job day and night. Major D. W. Washburn, the chief engineer, was equally active; and the contractor, Morgan Jones, is said not to have changed his clothes or gone regularly to bed during that period of unexampled activity. The legislature had finished its labors early in July and the Senate had passed a concurrent resolution of adjournment and sent it over to the House. Now the rails of the Texas and Pacific were but ten miles east of Fort Worth.

The Katy Enters Fort Worth

Then commenced the most strenuous parliamentary battle recorded in the railroad history of any state. The friends of the T. & P. refused to adopt the resolution to adjourn. The vote was so close that the absence of a single friend of the company might mean disaster. Representative Darnell was, of course, one of those who voted against adjournment—and Darnell was very sick. He was carried into the hall every day on a cot and voted "no" on the resolution to adjourn sine die and voted "aye" on a motion to adjourn till the following day. This was continued for fifteen days. On the twelfth day of the wrangle, the rails had reached Sycamore Creek, just east of Fort Worth. Here was a long bridge and a still longer trestle. Bridge timbers and ties were converted into a crib upon which the rails were laid. Then the track left the grade and took to the dirt road, which ran nearly parallel to the right of way. Ties were laid on the ground, supported at either end by stones picked up from the right of way, and the rails were spiked to them. The road was as crooked as a ram's horn, but it held up the rails. On July 19, at 11:23 o'clock A.M., the first train ran into Fort Worth.[1]

A few months short of five years later, on April 1, 1881, long Katy trains from Missouri, Kansas, and the Indian Territory also began serving Fort Worth. Then, as now, the Katy found the Texas cow town wide-awake and very much alive.

[1] B. B. Paddock (Ed.), *History of Texas.* See also Reed, *A History of Texas Railroads.*

TWENTY-SEVEN

The Rape of the Katy

Jay Gould's International and Great Northern Railway was, on June 1, 1881, a 622-mile Texas road which tapped the wealthy heart of South Texas. Beginning at Longview and Mineola, its twin lines converged and became one at Troupe, whence it headed due south to Palestine. There the line branched again into two long legs, one continuing south to Houston, the other veering off southwest to San Antonio. The capital stock of the I. & G. N. at that time totalled only $6,715,000 and stock manipulator Gould knew just what to do with railroad properties which had been so grievously undercapitalized.

On June 1, the Katy directors discovered that the I. & G. N. simply must become a part of the "Texas Extension." Flush with the proceeds of recent bond and stock issues, President Gould of the Katy acquired from President Gould of the I. & G. N. the entire capital stock of the latter road. Reluctant at first, the I. & G. N. president was finally persuaded to make the deal on a basis of two shares of Katy stock for one of I. & G. N. With the aid of the International Railway Improvement Company, the I. & G. N. was building south from San Antonio towards the Mexican border at Laredo, and this construction, too, was included in the purchase. Eventually the deal cost the Katy nearly seventeen million dollars, but it was eminently satisfactory to the managers of the I. & G. N.

On June 25, 1881, less than a month after the I. & G. N. formally entered the Katy family, General Dodge's little Credit Mobilier completed the extension of the Katy from Greenville to Mineola, a distance of fifty miles, deeded it to the road for $2,000,000, and the connection with the I. & G. N. was perfected. It would then have been technically correct to say that the Katy had completed its road to Houston and San Antonio, its present southern termini, but there is more to the story—much more!

A short period of genuine if expensive railroad construction began for the Katy after the signing of the "Denton joint-track" agreement with the T. & P. in April, 1881. While Gould was busily negotiating the purchase of the I. & G. N., General Dodge and his construction gangs began laying track approximately along the route surveyed a decade before by Major Otis Gunn's engineers. Starting at Fort Worth, they had "tied in" to the southern end of the T. & P. joint track and had pushed the railhead fifty miles south to Hillsboro, capital of Hill County, by the end of September. This was later to be the thriving junction point for the Katy's Dallas and Fort Worth divisions; now it was the heart of a vast cotton raising section whose "black waxy" land yielded a bale to the acre year after year. Unfortunately, a great part of the traffic that originated on the Katy here was for many years intercepted—and interdicted—at Fort Worth by Gould's T. & P. and routed east instead of north via the Katy.

Continuing south in classic fashion—breeding towns at the end of each ten-mile section, and selling lots like hotcakes—the railroad reached the important city of Waco on January 23, 1882.[1] Here the road crossed the branch line of the H. & T. C. known as the "Waco Tap" (a good traffic provider that is now part of the Katy system) and entered the true South, the land of immense plantations, immense southern dignity, and immense wealth. The track passed through Temple on March 23, and on June 9, 1882, reached Taylor, 260 miles from the Red River border, where it was to remain for several years. There was little reason for Jay Gould to build the Katy beyond Taylor at this time, for the bustling city was on the main line of the I. & G. N. and a new route was thus opened to Austin, to San Antonio, and, soon, to Old Mexico itself. The Katy could now feed the Missouri Pacific system from both ends and the middle.

While all this main line building was going on, Gould was casting around for other opportunities for investment of Katy funds. His eye fell on the bankrupt East Line and Red River Railroad, and he promptly grabbed it up. His "Improvement" company secured the franchise for $100, assumed the debts of the line, which were, in round figures, $800,000, and on November 28, 1881, sold this property to the Missouri, Kansas and Texas Lines for $2,852,000.

[1] All subsidies granted by towns and counties, or the state, were to the construction company, not to the Katy.

This three-foot gauge, "Toonerville trolley" line is not now a part of the Katy, but it played an important part in the company's plans for extension in Texas. Chartered in March, 1871, the dilapidated little road ran from the then important town of Jefferson, Texas, a Caddo Lake "port" at the head of navigation of the Red River, 124 miles west to Greenville on the Katy road. When Gould unloaded this line on the Katy in November, 1881, he ordered it extended on the same gauge still farther west, another 31 miles to McKinney.

The late president of the Cotton Belt Route, Daniel Upthegrove, who was born and reared in Greenville, had some lively recollections of this old Katy line. He wrote:

> When this train reached a speed of fifteen miles per hour the passengers insisted that the company was tempting providence [no doubt it was!] and if by any chance the engineer had to blow the whistle at a Texas longhorn and it was on the upgrade, the engine would stall, as it did not have sufficient boiler pressure to pull the three freight cars and passenger coach up a hill and whistle at the same time.[2]

All the evidence points to the justice of the charges leveled against Gould's administration by Katy bondholders, stockholders, and, later, managers, that his regime was disastrous to the best interests of the company and that in allowing the Missouri Pacific System to parallel its line and intersect the same at points of its best business, thereby subordinating the M. K. & T. and deflecting from it the business in the territory naturally belonging to the Missouri, Kansas and Texas Railway, his actions were "reprehensible."[3]

As has been shown, the Katy now had a continuous line of railway from St. Louis and Hannibal on the north to the Gulf of Mexico, nearly eighteen hundred miles long. The traffic and travel potentialities were enormous. Had the service been operated for the benefit of its owners, it undoubtedly could have carried and eventually freed itself of its great burden of debt. But the nucleus of Jay Gould's system was the Missouri Pacific-Iron Mountain lines, not the Katy. The I. & G. N., although acquired by the Katy, actually was brought into Gould's system as an extension not of the Katy but of the Iron Mountain (linked by another section of Jay's empire, the one-hundred-mile stretch of track running from Texarkana to Longview).

How Gould was able to circumvent the laws of Texas, which

[2] Reed, *A History of Texas Railroads*, 380.
[3] Report to the Stockholders.

specifically prohibited the construction of lines competitive with the Katy, and get away with it, is easily explained. Although he had only a tenuous hold on the Katy (never at any time did he have as much as fifty thousand shares of Katy stock), Gould voted the Katy stock held by the I. & G. N. and used his power to sink the identity of the Katy in that of the Missouri Pacific. The Missouri, Kansas and Texas Lines was almost forgotten by the country in the eighties. The Mo. Pac., which had no financial interest either in the Katy or the I. & G. N. and was operating both properties on a shadowy Katy lease (the consideration for which was the net earnings of the lines, if any) *was the Katy!*

Gould's orders to submerge the identity of the Katy appeared designed with malice aforethought. In that way it became practically impossible, even for expert accountants, to untangle the affairs of the two companies, to say that this or that was wrong, or illegal, or unethical, or unauthorized. Glaring examples of the erasing of the line between "mine and thine" were set in the Katy shops, at Sedalia, at Nevada, at Parsons, and at Denison. Overnight these properties became "Missouri Pacific Shops," and weird stories of the wholesale overhauling of Mo. Pac. equipment, the switching of good equipment for bad—all charged to the Katy—are heard to this day. At Sedalia and Parsons old-time railroaders tell of long lines of newly purchased Katy rolling stock arriving at the shops to be repainted and relettered with Missouri Pacific indicia. Equal numbers of outworn Mo. Pac. cars, the old-timers assert, then were stenciled with the identification markings taken from the new Katy equipment.[4]

From the vantage point of the years it is now transparently evident that Jay Gould had set himself the decade of the eighties to milk the Katy dry and set up his Missouri Pacific "empire." Starting in 1880 with 34,000 shares of Katy stock (Russell Sage had another 16,000), he steadily reduced his holdings year after year. By 1888, when the furious stockholders closed in on him and threw the entire gang out, neither Gould nor Sage, nor any of the wrecking crew, owned a dollar's worth of the Katy. But they were big men on the big and prosperous Missouri Pacific.

[4] See also *History of Vernon County, Missouri.*

TWENTY-EIGHT

The Katy Enters Dallas

On December 15, 1881, nine months after the Katy reached Fort Worth, the company acquired through Gould and General Dodge the property of the Dallas and Wichita Railroad. This was a thirty-nine-mile streak of rust extending from Dallas northwest to Denton, the home of the notorious bank and train robber, Sam Bass. This little line, incorporated in December, 1871, had a history that is worth retelling here.

In 1872 a route had been surveyed northwest from Dallas with the intention of making a connection with the Denver and El Paso narrow-gauge road. Late in November, 1872, John Neely Bryan, the founder of Dallas, broke ground for the construction of the Dallas and Wichita line. The state, as usual, promised sixteen sections of land for each mile of track completed, and Dallas voted a subsidy of $100,000 to aid in the construction of the road. The panic of 1873 disrupted all plans, however, and actual construction was not begun until 1877. The city bonds were issued on February 24 of that year, and in 1878 the track was laid eighteen miles northwest to the county line before funds were exhausted. The terminus was marked by a big stump on Elm Fork, between Trinity Mills and Lewisville, and here the road remained stumped until 1880.

In February, 1880, the road was bought at sale by Jay Gould, ostensibly acting for the T. & P., but acting, as always, only for Jay Gould. In the following July, he reorganized the line under its original charter and extended it the remaining twenty-one miles to a junction with the T. & P.–Katy joint-track at Denton.

On December 15, 1881, the Katy secured this back-door entry to Dallas for $780,000. Payment was made not in stock but in good, sound 6 per cent gold bonds. The Missouri, Kansas and Texas system now had trackage into both Dallas and Fort Worth—and Gould, of course, took a handsome profit out of the Katy's corporate till.

Dallas, now proudly referred to as "Big D," was founded in the fall of 1843 by John Neely Bryan, a young lawyer turned Indian trader, who persuaded the Caddo and Cherokee tribes to withdraw from the land on which he wished to settle. The city was named for George Mifflin Dallas, a fervent advocate of annexation of Texas, who became vice president of the United States in 1845.

When the Katy made its back-door entry into Dallas, the present financial and commercial hub of the Southwest boasted a population of not many more than 10,000, whereas today it approaches half a million. In its earliest days it was little different from other southwestern frontier towns. Wild and wooly in its long, slow beginnings, it was still a lusty, if gawky, youth when the Katy arrived. The first issue of the *Dallas News,* published October 1, 1885, dutifully reported sixty-eight saloons in the thirsty little community, including such famous spots as the Casino, the Q.T. and, of course, the First and Last Chance.[1]

Dallas then was quite a place; still is!

Towards the end of 1882 the Katy was the victim of still another piece of railroad skulduggery. The I. & G. N. needed a branch line to tap the lumber district east of the town of Trinity on its Houston division. On September 28, 1881, therefore, a company was chartered under the name of the Trinity and Sabine Railway to build the short line from Trinity to Corrigan, in Polk County. This development was about 150 miles away, to the east of the Katy route, yet on December 9, 1882, Jay Gould, in a fast sleight-of-hand operation, bought the "tap" for the Missouri Pacific and sold it the same day to the Katy. What Gould gave for the thirty-eight-mile logger line is not of record, but the Katy paid Gould $40,000 a mile. The Missouri Pacific continued building this branch through the eastern pine forests to Colmesneil, and as quickly as construction was completed the Katy bought the additional mileage. The Missouri, Kansas and Texas Railway had no earthly use for this line; it was wholly and solely a Mo. Pac. feeder, and its acquisition by the Katy was merely another step in the systematic looting of that helpless railroad.[2]

Gould rounded out the year 1882 for the Katy with the construction of about ten miles of coal roads in the Indian Territory and the

---

[1] *Dallas Morning News,* Fiftieth Anniversary Edition, October 1, 1935.

[2] In 1921 the Katy sold this "orphan" branch for which it had paid the Missouri Pacific $2,640,000, to R. D. Duff, a Texas lawyer, for $100,000. He eventually sold it for scrap.

building of an eight-mile branch line from Temple to Belton, completed December 16, 1882. Even this little branch was not honestly come by. Although it was purely and simply a Katy tap, the I. & G. N. built it, becoming the beneficiary of a $30,000 bond issue voted by the city of Belton.

Gould's reign over the Katy began officially on January 26, 1880, and ended June 1, 1888. During the first half of these epochal years, a period of genuine economic boom, the Katy expanded greatly under the impetus of millions in new money derived from Gould's great bond and stock issues. This expansion of the Katy, unfortunately, was one of purchase as much as it was of construction. The program laid down was the connecting, by construction, of Texas short lines which had been largely financed by local capital heartened by the return of prosperity and the renewed stream of immigration.

The Katy management had a definite plan of campaign; it was going over its own rails, by purchase, by trades, and by actual construction, into Dallas, Fort Worth, Waco, Austin, San Antonio, Houston, and Galveston. It took twenty years to accomplish all this—there were more bad times mixed with the good, and times when things were spread pretty thin—but the plan was finally completed.

Little has been said about the Indian Territory in the decade since the panic of 1873, chiefly because there was little to be said. Coal mines were opening up in the neighborhood of Atoka, Lehigh, Coalgate, and McAlester, and some little traffic was being created, but contrary to all expectations the Indians still had possession of their patrimony. They retained it despite the determined efforts, chiefly of the railroads, to dispossess them of it. The whole territory stagnated; it remained a wild, uninviting country; beautiful but dangerous; the few towns that had got an uncertain start, such as Vinita, Muskogee, and McAlester, showed little sign of growth or development. For these were not Indian towns, they were settlements of the despised and distrusted white man, and as such were given a wide berth by the better element of the Five Civilized Tribes. The chief patrons of the Katy's Territory towns until well into the eighties were the outcasts of the various tribes. The outlaw, the adventurer, the cowboy, the bull-whacking wagon driver, and the passing immigrant made up the floating population of the little settlements strung out along the Katy. And these people hated and despised the Indians as much as the latter did them.

According to popular account, the chief trade of the Territory in the seventies and eighties seemed to be centered on liquor. Rigidly banned, both by the federal government and the Indian nations, it was the most profitable form of barter, of bribery and corruption, in the Indian country until the Territory was organized. Old way-bills in the Katy files reveal that whiskey was really big business. The following items, listed in a shipment to several consignees in A-tok-a, are a measure of the volume of this traffic:

13	Cases Bitters	1	Case Matches
3	Brl. Whiskey	10	Cases Gin
12	Cases Gin	4	Bxs. Hardware
1	Case Absinthe	1	Brl. Whiskey
1	Keg Axe Heads	3½	Brl. Whiskey
2	Bx. Flasks	½	Brl. Wine
2	Brl. Brandy	2	Kegs Brandy
1	Case Cordial	1	Keg Cordial
1	Bx. Druggs	5	Boxes Bitters
10	Cases Wine	1	Coil Rope
		1	Keg Wine

If these supplies were shipped in purely for medicinal purposes the denizens of the Territory were a sick lot indeed![3]

There was, of course, a leavening of intelligent, farseeing people scattered throughout the Indian country; it would be grossly unfair to hint otherwise. Indications of their presence were frequent in such comment as the following, taken from the files of the *Vindicator*:

Stations must be established and towns and cities must grow up on the line of the railroad. With all of this, the present Indian system, with its inalienability of real estate, and its non-intercourse laws, is absolutely inconsistent. One or the other must give way and it will not be the railroad system. It therefore follows that the treaties by which the territory was assured exclusively and in perpetuity to the Indians and all the laws based upon that idea must be abrogated. It may be hard for the government which has pledged its solemn faith to these people, to find itself compelled to violate that pledge. But even Governments Cannot STAND IN THE WAY OF PROGRESS.[4]

There were churnings in the Indians' domain during the Gould regime, but Jay had no interest in pioneering, in development. Communities which could not buy his stock were not worthy of attention!

[3] Waybilled from St. Louis, November 25, 1872.
[4] *The Vindicator*, New Boggy, Choctaw Nation, I. T., August 24, 1872.

TWENTY-NINE

The Texas Land-Grant Myth

Much has been written about the storied old fifty-mile Galveston, Houston and Henderson Railroad, chartered in February, 1853, and built chiefly to thwart the growing commercial importance of Houston. Far from injuring Houston, this line quickly became a Houston rather than a Galveston road, and great plans were made for new roads to radiate from its Houston terminus to all points of the compass north. By the end of the seventies, the little road was doing a splendid business, measured in traffic volume, but because it remained an independent short line with practically no local business, revenue from the trifling "prorate" it got on long hauls was seldom sufficient to cover its expenses.

On August 1, 1882, the G. H. & H. had its back to the wall; its creditors foreclosed and put the line up for sale, and the railroad birds of prey winged over it. There was still a little unexpended capital in the Katy's till in 1883, enough to get the G. H. & H. anyway, decided Jay Gould. He acted first, told the Katy later. The great stock manipulator called a meeting of the board of directors on December 18, 1883, and with Russell Sage at his elbow smiling secretively and rubbing his thin, dry hands, Gould announced to his colleagues that "Mr. Sage and I have purchased the Galveston, Houston and Henderson road for account of this company." The directors would be glad to know, he explained smoothly, that "we have received for our interest $1,175,000 of their First Mortgage 5% bonds and $1,000,000 of the Capital Stock of the reorganized line."

Needless to say, the awe-struck directors approved the purchase, which encouraged Jay Gould (if he ever needed encouragement in a business like this) to present a bill from the Missouri Pacific for about $123,000 representing balances from the G. H. & H. for freight, etc. This, too, was approved and ordered paid.[1]

The record does not reveal that he advised either the directorate or the stockholders that, coincidentally with the purchase of the G. H. & H., he had leased it, not to the Katy but to the I. & G. N., an unpardonable oversight that was to have serious repercussions in later years. The Katy, of course, was still 165 miles away from Houston at the time, and management interest in the transaction could not have been too great; but the Katy's final destination definitely was Houston, and it does seem that someone—anyone—might have protested. The consequences of Gould's trickery will appear later.

The purchase of the G. H. & H. apparently emptied the Katy coffers, for thereafter construction ceased for several years. Contributing factors possibly were the repeal of the land-grant acts by the Texas legislature in 1882 and the passing of other legislation adverse to railroads. This session inaugurated a move to reduce passenger fares, and there was a definite threat of further legislative action on railroad rates generally.

At the time construction was halted, the Katy owned in its own name 505 miles of trackage in Texas. Actually it possessed more than twice that much. It owned, leased, or operated 1,388 miles south of the Indian border, thus:

OWNED:	*Miles*
Denison to Taylor via Whitesboro, Fort Worth, Waco, and Temple (not including joint track)	185
Whitesboro to Gainesville	15
Denison to Mineola via Greenville	103
Denton to Dallas	37
McKinney to Jefferson via Greenville (3-ft. ga.)	156
Temple to Belton	9
	505

OWNED, OPERATING UNDER LEASE:	
International and Great Northern Railway	762
OWNED AND LEASED TO I. & G. N.:	
Galveston, Houston and Henderson Railroad	50
OPERATED UNDER JOINT-TRACK AGREEMENT:	
Whitesboro to Fort Worth via Denton	71
Total Texas mileage, year 1883	1,388

[1] Minutes of directors' meeting.

The original builders of some of this trackage had received land grants from the state, and as it is the only part of the present Katy System in Texas which did receive what was then considered a great concession and incentive, it might be pertinent to go into the matter of who got what, if anything.

I.C.C. Valuation Docket 828 gives probably the best available record of Texas public lands granted along the Katy route. It states:

> The Katy of Texas reports that its predecessors received 2,565,120 acres of land grants from the United States government through the State of Texas. The Katy further states that land grants had been sold prior to the date of valuation as follows:
>
> For 1,253,120 acres neither the expense of acquisition nor the proceeds from the sale are reported. The certificates for 128,000 acres were sold for $8,200. For the remaining 1,184,-000 acres, expense of acquisition is reported at $8,147.99. Proceeds of sales aggregate $103,785.10.

These figures indicate no great windfall for the purse-poor "projectors" of the Katy's original short lines. Commenting on these sad matters, Texas railroad historian S. G. Reed states:

> I inherited from my father, and still hold as mementoes, five of the certificates issued by the Missouri, Kansas & Texas Extension Railway Company. [This, it will be remembered, was one of Colonel Bob Stevens' projects.] Each of these certificates calls for 640 acres of vacant, unreserved and unappropriated public domain in Texas and were issued by W. C. Walsh, Land Commissioner of Texas, on November 20, 1880. My father bought the five certificates for $25 apiece—which works out at about four cents an acre.[2]

The catch insofar as Mr. Reed's father was concerned lay in the fact that at the time he thought he was buying thirty-two hundred acres of Texas land, sold in good faith by Bob Stevens acting on his grant, there was no vacant, unreserved, or unappropriated public domain in Texas; not only was there no such land but the state continued to issue certificates for several millions of acres long after vacant land had been exhausted. Reed senior just "slept upon his rights" and others got ahead of him. Ben Munson, for example, garnered himself some millions of acres by the simple process of buy-

[2] Reed, *A History of the Texas Railroads*, 381.

Land scrip issued to the Missouri, Kansas & Texas
Extension Railway Company, 1880

lng up these railroad certificates and locating and filing his claims.[3]

It is interesting to note the Katy traffic trend during the years of Gould's presidency of the company, years when he expanded the system to more than twice its former size and spent more millions than had ever been spent before. In 1880, gross revenue was four millions and the net just over a million and half. Here are the figures for the six succeeding years:

Year	Gross Revenue	Net Revenue
1881	$5,360,837	$2,061,296
1882	6,657,227	2,361,724
1883	7,843,511	3,197,008
1884	7,317,251	2,970,004
1885	6,853,656	2,798,554
1886	7,451,644	3,222,890

[3] The Munson biography, *Ten Million Acres*, privately printed.

In 1886, the Katy, still controlled by President Gould and the Missouri Pacific, went back into construction with the proceeds of still another bond issue. During the summer the Gainesville, Henrietta and Western Railway, organized to build an extension of the Whitesboro division, completed the line from Gainesville to Henrietta, a distance of seventy miles. Fifty-two miles of line were built between Greenville and Dallas under the name and charter of the Dallas and Greenville Railway Company. Under the name of the Dallas and Waco Railway Company, the line was further extended from Dallas to Waxahachie in 1889, and to Hillsboro in 1890. This formed a connection with the main line running down from Fort Worth to Waco and Taylor, giving the Katy an alternate route south via either Dallas or Fort Worth. At the extreme south end of the line, the Taylor, Bastrop and Houston Railway laid 87 miles of track in 1887 from Taylor southwest to Boggy Tank (now Pisek), bringing the parent Katy within seventy-five miles of Houston. In the same year, another "orphan branch" was brought into being with the laying of sixteen miles of track between Lockhart and San Marcos. Utterly useless to the Katy then, this "tap" served as a very useful branch for the I. & G. N., with which it connected at San Marcos.

Ben Munson, the early Katy land agent, now the wealthy president of the Denison Cotton Mills, had been dabbling in railroads himself. He incorporated the Denison and Washita Valley Railway Company in 1886; this road soon had six miles of track in Texas, running from Ray to Warner Junction, on the Katy, and some coal roads in the Indian Territory. Ben disposed of his railroad properties to the Katy in 1892.

With few exceptions, the mileage which became part of the Missouri, Kansas and Texas Lines in Texas up to this time was built either by General Dodge's Railway Improvement Company or by the Missouri Pacific as contractor, the Katy paying for the work by issuance of bonds and stock. Interstate Commerce Commission records do not indicate that the Mo. Pac. profited through the construction work at the expense of the Katy. Whether Jay Gould did—and, if he did, how he did—is still a good subject for debate.

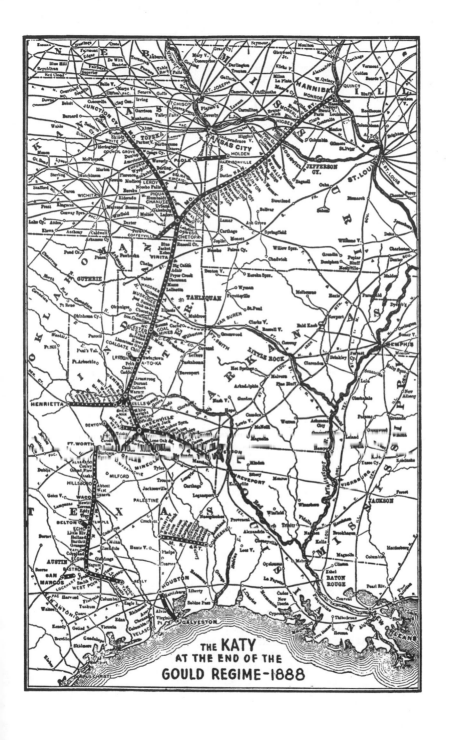

THE **KATY**
AT THE END OF THE
GOULD REGIME—1888

THIRTY

The Passing of Colonel Robert S. Stevens

Despite the all-pervading presence of Jay Gould and his minions in the eighties, there were many men who still kept their faith in the Katy's destiny, although their voices were little heard during the dark years. One of these was the road's first general manager, Colonel Robert S. Stevens. Following his successful venture in building the M. K. & T. extensions out of Denison, Stevens had retired from the field in the face of superior forces. "Retired" describes his decision correctly; he returned to Attica, N. Y., to his old home, wealthy, prepared to enjoy the fruits of his labors. A life-long democrat, Bob Stevens was not permitted to retire for long, however. In a strongly Republican district he was a tower of strength to his political party. Persuaded to use his strength at the urgent call of the party, he was elected to Congress from New York's thirty—first District for the 1882–84 session.

One term was enough for Colonel Bob. "Everyone who works for the nomination of any man," he told his people disgustedly, "thinks he is entitled to wholesome and substantial recognition. Pressure for office is now the bane of American political life." Stevens declined to run for office again; instead he returned to the Southwest, to visit old friends, to look after his investments, spread his benevolence, and, incidentally, to look the railroad situation over.

What Stevens discovered at Parsons put him back in the railroad construction business again. He found that the Katy still was shut out at Kansas City and Junction City. All traffic for the great and growing Missouri River city was still being handled through Fort Scott by the old Border Tier Road, reorganized as the Kansas City, Fort Scott and Gulf,[1] at local rates. Definitely, the Katy needed a line

[1] Now the St. Louis–San Francisco Railroad.

of its own between Parsons and Kansas City. He was amazed also by the tremendous influx of settlers on the Osage Ceded Lands, particularly around Coffeyville, where Captain David L. Payne's Oklahoma "Boomers" were gathering to storm the Indian country.

Promptly the Colonel called on his old friend Judge T. C. Sears, the Katy's general counsel, who was the first to broadcast the announcement that some fourteen million acres of the Indian Territory were already in the public domain and subject to homestead entry, thus causing a premature stampede of Oklahoma Boomers. Their conference resulted in the forming, with Parsons leaders Lee Clark and C. H. Kimball, of a corporation to promote new roads. The Parsons and Pacific Railway Company was the first line organized. It was chartered on December 16, 1885, and the drive for funds was so successful that Parsons put up $40,000, Mound Valley Township subscribed $20,000, Canada Township added another $20,000, and some money was received from Montgomery County.

Bob Stevens got construction started without delay and had the line built from Parsons to Coffeyville and about five miles into the Indian Territory within nine months. The first train left Parsons on September 20, 1886. No sooner was the track well across the Territory line, however, than the venturesome intruder was stopped by Indian injunction. The railhead remained at the tent-shack settlement of Stevens, some thirty-five miles southwest of Parsons, for several years. It is sad to relate that the poisonous little community at the end-of-track, the only settlement ever named for the Katy's pioneer builder, soon was dubbed "Poison" by the scornful settlers of the Ceded Lands. That extraordinary name clung to it and was officially carried in Katy time tables until the settlement finally disappeared.

When work was stopped on the Parsons and Pacific, Bob Stevens organized the Kansas City and Pacific Railway Company, to build from Parsons straight north. Chartered on July 24, 1886, the road started construction at Parsons immediately, and the ninety-five-mile line was completed through Erie, Moran, and Kincaid to Paola, Kansas, by 1887. In aid of this construction, Parsons voted an additional $20,000, and the municipalities in the counties to the north, to be benefitted by the coming of the railroad, extended liberal aid. Colonel Stevens, it appeared, had not lost his winning ways or his silvery tongue. At Paola, connection was made with the Kansas City, Fort Scott and Gulf, and trackage rights were obtained to give the

K. C. & P. through service between Kansas City and Coffeyville.[2] Until Jay Gould's hold on the Katy was broken, it should be reported, Colonel Stevens kept his lines on a strict business footing with the Katy—the good neighbor policy did *not* apply when Gould was concerned!

Because this construction marked the end of Bob Stevens' railroad building career, perhaps it would be as well to round out the intrepid colonel's story. After Jay Gould and his gang disappeared from the Katy, Stevens leased his lines to two old friends, George Eddy, his one-time divisional superintendent, and Harrison C. Cross, president of the First National Bank of Emporia and a Katy director, who had been named co-receivers for the Katy in the foreclosure proceedings that instantly followed the flight of the "birds of prey."

Throughout the reorganization years, the Kansas City and Pacific remained under lease and was operated by the Katy to great mutual advantage. The K. C. & P. was formally consolidated with the Missouri, Kansas and Texas Lines on July 19, 1899.

In Sedalia, in Parsons, and on his trips around the territory, Bob Stevens, now getting old, began complaining of a cold in the hip joints which he was confident could be cured by a good series of baths in salt, vinegar, and other oddments. Finally he returned to Attica and to the sympathetic ministrations of his wife. On Thursday, February 23, 1893, at the age of 68, Stevens died of diabetes in his home, surrounded by a host of friends and relatives. He was survived, besides his wife, by one son, Frederick C. Stevens, president of the West End National Bank of Washington, D. C. A distinguished group of mourners, representing mostly the Katy-served Southwest, attended Bob Stevens' obsequies, and the grief was genuine; The southwest had lost a good friend.

Colonel Stevens left his mark on the Southwest; it is plain on the sturdy "Stevens" buildings that dot the southwestern countryside, in Sedalia, in Parsons, in Denison. His name is perpetuated in stone over libraries and schools; it is still alive in the records of countless business enterprises which he founded or supported; but most of all his memory is preserved in the legendary recollections of the oldest inhabitants of the Southwest.

[2] This trackage rights agreement is still in effect. The Katy uses the Frisco tracks between Paola and Kansas City.

THIRTY-ONE

The End of the Gould Regime

James Stephen Hogg was elected attorney general of Texas in 1886. He won on a platform the main plank of which was to compel railroads operating in Texas to maintain general offices in Texas, to keep their properties in good condition, and to provide adequate service. His announced aim was to abolish control of the state's railroads by "foreign" corporations.

Hogg's principal target was Jay Gould; within six weeks of the date he took office he filed suits against all roads not headquartered in Texas. Gould at this time controlled in Texas the Cotton Belt, the T. & P., the Katy, and, through the latter, both the I. & G. N. and G. II. & H. Like the Katy, all of these lines had been brought to sad condition as regarded equipment, facilities, roadbed, and service through Gould's stock manipulations and his penny-squeezing policies in operation and maintenance.

Hogg brought suit for cancellation of the lease of the Katy and forfeiture of the charter of the I. & G. N. At the same time he filed a suit asking for the appointment of a receiver for a Katy subsidiary, the East Line and Red River Railroad, and forfeiture of its charter. With some justification he charged that it had been allowed to deteriorate to such an extent that "a tramp was afraid to ride its best passenger coach."[1] His main grievance, however, was the fact that it was being operated by the Katy, a foreign corporation. In defense, the Katy claimed that the act passed by the Texas Legislature in 1870, of which mention has already been made, gave it that right. The Supreme Court decided otherwise, and Jay Gould found himself and his sleight-of-hand stock switching deals in a very bad way.

To make matters much worse for Gould, Katy security holders

[1] Reed, *A History of the Texas Railroads*, 383.

now began to show boldly their disapproval of his road-building and buying spree of 1886–87. The consensus was that the line was badly managed, that it was being run at a terrific loss insofar as the Katy was concerned, but greatly to the profit of the Missouri Pacific. In 1888, a commission was appointed which agreed with the views of the security holders; it presented a blistering report at the annual meeting of the stockholders.

Because of the great flotations Gould had made during his eight-year tenure as chief executive of the Katy, stock participation was widespread in 1888, and at the annual meeting held in Parsons in May of that year, bank and investment house representatives from the four corners of the world, loaded down with proxies, were on hand to "throw the scalawags out." Resolutions of censure followed one another thick and fast. All the acts of the Gould directorate were "hereby disclaimed, disapproved and held for naught." It was unanimously agreed at this first meeting for many years whereat the true interests of Missouri, Kansas and Texas stockholders were represented to discharge the management forthwith. The management, incidentally, declined to attend the meeting, refused to turn over the minute books and other necessary records, and pointedly omitted reporting upon the management of the property and disposition of the assets confided to its care.[2]

An entirely new board of directors was elected, mainly composed of representatives of large security-holding groups. That board appointed a reorganization committee to salvage from the wreckage left by Gould all that was worth saving.

Quickly this committee discovered that no relief from the maladministration of the Gould regime was to be had except through the courts. Using the authority delegated to them, they petitioned for a receiver and for the setting aside of the lease with the Missouri Pacific. The court approved, and on June 1, 1888, George Eddy and Harrison C. Cross were appointed co-receivers. At the same time the Missouri Pacific lease of the Katy was terminated. There was a vicious fight between the Missouri Pacific and the Katy over control of the International and Great Northern, but eventually it was awarded to the Mo. Pac. in exchange for a cash settlement.

On February 17, 1890, the Supreme Court of Texas ruled that the Katy, as a foreign corporation, could not retain ownership of the scarecrow East Line and Red River Railroad, and declared the charter of the narrow-gauge line forfeited. The court thereupon appointed

[2] Stockholders' Report.

Early-day railroad construction scene

Early-day railroad construction scene

Steam power of the mid-seventies. Engine No. 54, a "Mason" 4–4–0, built in 1873

Steam power of the mid-seventies. Engine No. 75, a "Baldwin" 4–4–0, built in 1876

a receiver for the property, and Attorney General Hogg, flush with victory in a test case that had far-reaching implications, declared that this was the first time in this country that a railroad charter had been forfeited and a receiver appointed solely upon application of the state.

While this suit involved only the E. L. & R. R., the parent Katy, as already told, had acquired other short lines in Texas, and these provided similar situations in which similar suits could be filed. So steps were taken at once that these pieces of road might be operated legally in Texas. The Twenty-second Legislature met on January 1, 1891. A bill was introduced providing for the organization of a new "Katy of Texas" corporation clothed with authority to purchase all of the parent Katy's Texas properties, and directing the Attorney General to drop the pending suits against all of the company's other subsidiaries. This, by the way, was the first consolidation bill passed by a Texas legislature, except for a few short roads in the earliest days.

The bill was passed with only one negative vote and was approved by the governor on April 16, 1891. All of the little roads which Katy managers, in their devious ways, had secured individual charters for and then constructed with loving and expensive care, now had to be deeded outright to the parent company. Then the parent company had to deed them outright to the new Texas company. The legal transfer of the properties was completed on November 18, 1891.

The only exception at this time to the general transfer was the narrow-gauge East Line and Red River road. This property finally was sold in the forfeiture suit brought by Attorney General Hogg in 1893, and one of the new Katy directors, Henry W. Poor, bought it. He sold it in the same year to the Sherman, Shreveport and Southern Railway.

On December 31, 1891, the M. K. & T. R. R. of Texas, a company incorporated in the State of Texas, with headquarters in Denison, Texas, filed its first report with the Railroad Commission of Texas created in that year. At that time the Katy of Texas was quite a railroad; it extended from Denison to Boggy Tank, within eighty miles of Houston. Its rails reached that spot in the wilderness, identified only by a tank in the brush, via both Fort Worth and Dallas, thence via Hillsboro, Waco, Temple, and Taylor. It also had a line stretching west from Denison through Whitesboro to Gainesville and Henrietta. It owned the Denton–Dallas cutoff, and had branches from Greenville to Mineola, and from Temple to Belton. Finally, it owned two "orphan" branches, Trinity to Colmesneil, and San Marcos to Lock-hart.[3]

During the pendency of the law suits, the parent Katy had done no construction except to build an eleven-mile stub line from Denison to Sherman. This line was built under the charter of the Sherman, Denison and Dallas Railway, incorporated March 20, 1890. The road was built in the same year, but was never extended to Dallas, because the Katy already had two lines from Denison to that city.

After the dust of Gould's explosive departure had settled, the Katy's owners inspected the property. It looked something like a grinning boy with half his teeth missing. The southern terminus of the road was at a water tank in the brush; south of Dallas an interval of sixty-seven miles interrupted the continuity of the line in its most important part, and several short pieces of track served as feeders for a rival line while being entirely separated from the parent Katy.

The outlook wasn't exactly bright for the future.

[3] "Orphans," in railroad language, are short lines which for one reason or another have become separated from the main line.

THIRTY TWO

The Oklahoma District Run of 1889

While the Katy was embroiled in a legal fight which threatened its very existence, the Indian Territory pot boiled over. Because the road was so identified with the extinction of the Indian title to these vast domains—although the territory through which it ran was the last to be opened—and because the effects of the first opening were so far-reaching, some record of that stirring event must be given here.

Back in the seventies, while laying track through the Choctaw country, the Katy had discovered, on its own, a four-foot vein of fine bituminous coal on land occupied by Joshua Pusley, a Choctaw. The road made a lease with Pusley, paying him one-half a cent per bushel of coal mined; the Choctaw Council demanded and received a like royalty. In a few years coal production had reached such volume at McAlester, Krebs, Savanna, and Lehigh that the Katy began building trackage to bring the coal to the main line, whence it was shipped to many points, mainly in Texas. Four thousand white American coal miners gathered at Krebs in the summer of 1888, and in an orderly fashion petitioned Agent Tufts for governmental co-operation, through his office, in establishing themselves under municipal rules and regulations. The miners' petition went to Washington, endorsed by both Agent Tufts and the Katy; it was said to have had considerable effect on the officials in the nation's capital.[1]

Ever since the Katy first entered Indian Territory, it should be remembered, the Five Civilized Tribes had been violently opposed to further railroad building. For almost fifteen years, supported by a majority of the lesser tribes, the Big Five held out successfully against encroachment, even rejecting a proposal for territorial government similar to that of North and South Dakota, Montana, and

[1] Foreman, *A History of Oklahoma*, 228.

Wyoming; the proposal would have made the Indians United States citizens with the same rights and representation in Washington as the other territories. But to the Indians this meant invasion by the railroads and consequent mass invasion by white homeseekers, a surmise which was well-founded. Precarious as was their sovereignty, they preferred to take chances on continuing it rather than submit of their own volition to what their leaders termed vassalage.

In the mid-eighties, however, railroad lawyers and the squatter lobbyists again were working hard in Washington. Captain David L. Payne had revived the lure of free land in the minds of thousands of men itching for adventure, and this Anglo-Saxon–American trait was once again at fever heat. Throughout the nation, folks had concluded that all the free land had been grabbed up, until David Payne started booming. Delegations waited on Congressmen daily; great eastern newspapers were pointing out that the population had grown since the Declaration of Independence from three millions to sixty-three millions, the people needed room; lands from which a few already rich half-blood Indians made money through the toil of white men precariously supported a mere handful of full bloods, all too lazy, they said, to till and cultivate on their own, preferring to hunt, to sleep, and to eat. This land, it was asserted, could support millions of industrious whites.

The Railroad Act of 1886, fostered by the Katy as well as by other roads planning to populate and develop the Indian domain, laid the territory open to further railroad encroachment under the right of eminent domain, and divested the Indian nations of some of the sovereignty they then possessed. It was no longer necessary to ask permission to lay steel in the Territory. At once the Santa Fé extended its line south from Arkansas City, on the southern Kansas border, to Ponca City (the little settlement then called White Eagle) in the Cherokee Outlet. Within a year it had a depot, after a fashion, on the present site of Oklahoma City. It continued building south and reached Purcell, connecting there with the north-building Gulf, Colorado and Santa Fé, in the spring of 1887. The Santa Fé then had a through line all the way from Kansas City to Galveston.

At the same time the Kansas and Arkansas Valley Railway began building west from Fort Smith and up the valley of the Arkansas to Kansas. The Cherokees fought this line bitterly in the courts; they refused permission for ties to be cut along the line of road, and in general made things difficult for the K. & A. V. Eventually, however, the courts decided against the Cherokees, and by 1889 the road had been completed to a crossing of the Katy line at Wagoner's Switch, fifteen miles north of Muskogee, and to Coffeyville on the Kansas border, where it made connection with the Katy extension built by Colonel Stevens. Still other roads, including the Denison and Washita Valley road (which was Ben Munson's pet project), the Kansas City, Fort Scott and Gulf, and the Chicago, Kansas and Nebraska Railway, all received Congressional approval to enter Indian Territory in 1886.

The Atlantic and Pacific, which already had a permit by treaty to cross the Indian Territory, had resumed construction in the winter of 1881. Its line was then extended from Vinita to the Indian villages of Claremore (Osage Chief Clermont's town) and to Tulsa (the Creeks' Tulsey Town), which it reached on August 21, 1882. Andrew Peirce's A. & P. finally was wiped out by mortgage foreclosure in 1897; its assets and its franchise to build to the Canadian River and thence to Albuquerque were sold (in the Station at Vinita where the tracks crossed the Katy) to the St. Louis and San Francisco road.[2]

The Katy, except for lengthening its coal hauling trackage from Lehigh to Coalgate, was having enough to do just staying out of bankruptcy during this flurry of railroad building. It had been well and truly laid through the heart of Indian Territory, and if one portion of Poor Lo's lands was to be opened to white settlement then, assuredly, it would all be opened, and soon.

On June 19, 1888, an international council of the Indians met at Fort Gibson. The principal speaker was Chief Pleasant Porter of the Creeks. The wise old warrior told the assemblage just what was going on, just what was bound to happen; among other things he advised education and speedy adaptation to the ways of the white man. The inevitable, the chief said, could no longer be postponed. The government had made him an offer for the entire western half of the domain of the Creek Nation lying west of the division line established by the Treaty of 1866.

The offer was $2,280,857.10. It was accepted. A similar agreement was arranged with the Seminoles, who received for their land, ceded in the same treaty, the sum of $1,912,942.02. The area was a sort of island surrounded by Indian reservations and included practically the whole of these six present-day Oklahoma counties: Cleveland, Oklahoma, Canadian, Kingfisher, Logan, and Payne.[3]

---

[2] Judge John R. Thomas, historian Grant Foreman's father-in-law, entered the decree of foreclosure.

[3] Foreman, *A History of Oklahoma*, 230.

On March 1, 1889, these coveted, fertile acres were declared public lands and open to white settlement at an appropriate time. On March 23, President Harrison proclaimed that the Oklahoma Lands (not to be confused with the much larger area which surrounded it) would be opened to pre-emption and settlement as of noon on April 22, 1889.

Possibly the most extraordinary race ever witnessed by mankind started from a line on the Kansas border just south of Arkansas City. Restrained on the borders by several companies of soldiers, hordes of impatient settlers, wildly excited, strained at the leash. When the bugles blew at exactly twelve noon, bedlam broke loose. With yells and cheers the land-hungry thousands began the mad race for selections of farm land and town lots, all too few for ten times as many fortune hunters. They piled headlong into the public lands, in wagons, buggies, on horseback, on foot, in every possible manner—and thousands came from the north and south on trains crowded to the cowcatchers.[4]

The soldiers' only trouble was with "Sooners." Since March 1, when the plan to open the Oklahoma lands was announced, they had been busy routing out men who had sneaked into the Neutral Strip with the purpose of getting a head start on the thousands of racers back at the Kansas border. It should be mentioned that all the public lands prepared for entry had already been government surveyed and marked in sections; townsites in what were to be Oklahoma City, Guthrie, Edmond, Norman, El Reno, and Kingfisher, among others, already had been platted. Successful "Sooners," the enterprising few who came bouncing out of the tall grass, crawling from hidden ravines, dropping from leafy trees at the sound of the bugles, had a fifteen-mile start on the rest of the contestants, a good ninety-minute lead on the fastest horse, buckboard, or wagon.

At noon on that great day there was nothing on the site of Oklahoma City but the Santa Fé's little depot, a post office, the land registrar's office, and half a dozen board shanties which had been used by the surveyors. At 2 P.M. the first train pulled in, loaded to the cowcatcher. It would be nice to say that the Santa Fé won the race to the future capital of the state, but a hundred-odd Sooners were well ahead of everyone else. Ten more Santa Fé trains came in that day, each of them carrying an estimated thousand people from the border; some of these would drop off on sight of nice bottom land or attractive townsites; others, who did not like what they

[4] Foreman, *A History of Oklahoma*, 240.

had looked at, would climb aboard on succeeding trains and go on.

Figures on this great race vary considerably; those given for the orthodox starters run from 30,000 to 70,000. But folk came in also from the south as well as the north, though only one race had been staged; the Gulf Line is said to have hauled up 6,000 people on that first day. There can be no estimate as to the number of the Sooners, but unquestionably many of Oklahoma's first families of today, many captains of industry and business, can thank for their riches a not so far distant ancestor who "beat the bugle" on April 22, 1889.

THIRTY-THREE

Recovery on the Katy

Co-receivers George Eddy and H. C. Cross operated the Katy Railroad from 1888 until July 1, 1891, when it was returned to the management in vastly improved condition. The receivers were honest railroad operators, not stock market speculators. A splendid property had been almost wrecked for personal, unscrupulous gain and their duty was to retrieve what they could of it, with the assistance of the reorganization committee, and put it back on its operational feet. There was plenty of freight to be hauled if there were good freight cars to haul it; there were passengers wanting to ride if they were assured of seats to sit in, rain-proof roofs and regular schedules. The road had to be made safe, of course, but even after that there was money to be made for the stockholders if it was not diverted to illegitimate projects.

Eddy and Cross did their job well. In the nearly three years of their stewardship, relieved for the time being of a mountain of interest debt, they purchased almost a complete turnover of rolling stock; they repaired the decrepit trackage and rebuilt or refurbished the depots. New locomotives, passenger cars, freight cars were of greater weight and capacity; where old wooden bridges were replaced they were rebuilt with steel or iron structures capable of maintaining heavier strains and higher rates of speed. In place of the mud surface on which a great portion of the track had rested, there came renewals with stone, gravel, and sand ballast.

When the receivers relinquished control on July 1, 1891, they were succeeded immediately by a board of directors, all of whom had acquiesced in the submission to the courts of a new reorganization plan. They were led by John D. Rockefeller, who never at any time had any love for Jay Gould and was now furious with him for imperilling a sound investment. Henry C. Rouse became president and chairman of the board, and under his management conditions improved rapidly.

On December 1, 1892, the company completed a thirty-six-mile extension westward of its San Marcos–Lockhart orphan branch to a connection with the main line at Smithville, Texas. On April 10, 1893, the Katy finally arrived at Houston by completing an eighty-mile extension of the main line from the railhead at Boggy Tank. At long last the gap which had kept the Katy poor and made other roads rich was closed and the Missouri, Kansas and Texas Railway henceforth would participate in the through traffic. After some legal difficulties with the I. & G. N., a connection was secured with the Galveston, Houston and Henderson Railroad, and the first Katy train into the Island City, the Oleander City, arrived on August 31, 1893.

"The desire of the management," begins the 1893 report to Katy stockholders, "has been to create for the Missouri, Kansas and Texas Company a continuous system of lines reaching from the points where the traffic originates to the great centers of distribution by land and sea." That had now been accomplished, and in the keen competition for business which immediately followed, the Katy was able to secure its proper proportion of the available traffic.

Entry into St. Louis was achieved by the Katy's taking over the operation of the Missouri, Kansas and Eastern Railroad, which was originally financed by a group of St. Louis capitalists, some of whose names appear in towns along the right of way: McKittrick, Case, Gore, Wainwright, Steedman. The bonds were guaranteed by the Katy, which finally acquired ownership in 1896. The M. K. & E., connected with the Katy main line at Franklin, Missouri, and ran 162 miles east along the north bank of the Missouri River to Machens, twenty-six miles from St. Louis, where it connected with the Chicago, Burlington and Quincy Railroad, giving it access to its greatest city. The C. B. & Q. already had a connection with the Katy at Hannibal, affording there the best connection to Chicago.

The new alliance between the Katy and the C. B. & Q. permitted, under lease—and still does—all Katy trains to run into St. Louis. (When the St. Louis Union Depot was completed in 1895 at a cost of $6,500,000, the Katy became a one-sixteenth owner of the station.)

Another notable achievement of the new Katy directorate was the straightening out of the East Line and Red River Railroad mess, referred to in a previous chapter. The parent Katy fathered the road in a manner subrosa, changed its tracks from narrow to standard gauge, and eventually succeeded in bringing it back into the Katy of Texas fold—but it took more than six years to do it.

In spring of 1899 a bill was introduced in the Texas legislature which authorized the Katy of Texas to reacquire this 153 miles of track then operated by the Sherman, Shreveport and Southern, to extend it to the eastern line of Texas and there connect with any railroad extending to Shreveport, and to acquire or lease trackage or running rights over such line. The bill, passed and approved by the governor on May 16, 1899, also provided:

> That the acceptance of the provisions of this act is an agreement on the part of the M. K. and T. of Texas to abide by and submit to the rates, rules and regulations and requirements of the Railroad Commission of Texas until the same are set aside by a court of competent jurisdiction on final hearing and that the act shall not be conclusive of the rights of the State as to any question of law or fact necessary or presumed to have been determined by the Legislature in order to comply with Article X, Sections five and six of the Constitution of the State of Texas.[1]

This was a most unusual provision. Nothing like it appears in any of the other consolidation bills of the Katy in Texas or of any other railroad in the state. It was and still is very effective. It has caused the Katy to refrain from many suits against the Railroad Commission in which it has had cause of action similar to that of other roads which have brought such suits, and it has prevented many suits from being filed by other roads, suits which they were averse to filing unless all lines, including the Katy, joined in. In at least one case this provision of the act has been circumvented by the intervention of the Central Trust Company as a holder of Katy bonds.

Immediately after the passage of the act, the Katy went to work to extend the main line from San Marcos to San Antonio so that, in the last year of the century, it had linked up every major city in Texas as of that period. At the same time work was being hurried on the extension of the Sherman, Shreveport and Southern from Jefferson, Texas, to the state line at Waskom. From there trackage rights were secured in 1900 over the Vicksburg, Shreveport and Pacific to Shreveport. That winter, service was inaugurated to San Antonio and Shreveport, and as the new century dawned the Katy was doing business in four states and one territory, Missouri, Kansas, Texas, Louisiana, and Indian Territory.

[1] S. G. Reed, *History of the Texas Railroads,* 384–85.

THIRTY FOUR

The Cherokee Outlet—the Run of 1893

Perhaps it was just as well, in the not-so-gay nineties, that the new management of the ill-used Katy had its hands full getting the property back in good operating condition. Otherwise the excitement—and the illusion—of the opening of the western Indian Territory lands to preemption and settlement might have set off a new splurge of railroad construction in that raw and undeveloped section. As it was, the company had enough to do completing its road north to Kansas City and St. Louis and south to Houston and San Antonio.

The effectiveness of the new policy is shown in the revenue returns from the improved property after Gould's departure. Whereas in 1888, the last year of Gould's administration, gross revenues were $6,320,954, they had increased in 1891, the end of the receivership, to $0,775,120. Despite greatly increased expenditures for rehabilitation, net revenue for 1891 was up nearly 100 per cent over 1888, and the security holders were understandably happy. This accounts for the fact that Katy managers could watch without envy as other lines built furiously into the western Indian Territory. Snugly and smugly the Katy sat tight, with its end-of-track at Poison, née Stevens, content with the cattle trade of Coffeyville, while other lines consolidated themselves at Tulsa and Oklahoma City.

Oklahoma Territory (now known as Old Oklahoma, to distinguish it from the Indian Territory and from the State of Oklahoma, which did not come into being until 1907) was organized as a separate territory by act of Congress on May 2, 1890. It comprised approximately the western half of the original Indian Territory. In the several years that followed the passage of the "Organic Act," many tribal titles were extinguished west of the domain of the Five Civilized Nations, and the lands thrown open to homesteaders.

In 1892 the Jerome Commission completed negotiations with the powerful Cherokee Nation for the sale of more than six million acres comprising all of the Cherokee Outlet, and this great sweep of wonderfully fertile Indian country also was thrown open to those who could get there "fustest."

For this opening, it was planned to put on a better show than that of 1889. The "run" was set for September 16, 1893. The land was to be "rushed" from both north and south, and preparations were elaborate. The northern line extended along the Kansas border from Caldwell to Arkansas City; this time there were no fifteen miles of neutral lands to be traversed in order to reach the prizes, for the so-called "Strip" was itself part of the prize. The southern line ran from Orlando to Stillwater. Some 30,000 racers started from Arkansas City; from Orlando, 15,000; from Caldwell, 15,000; from Hennessey, 15,000; from Stillwater, 7,000; from Kiowa 10,000; from Hunnewell, 10,000, from unscheduled places, 4,000. The new counties of Oklahoma Territory formed after the rush were Kay, Grant, Alfalfa, Woods, Harper, Woodward, Major, Enid, Noble, Pawnee, and part of Ellis.[1]

A nervous newspaperman from Fort Smith who watched the race of '93 with bulging eyes reported:

> Several men were shot in quarrels over claims. Four men were killed by soldiers for starting on the Strip before the hour of noon arrived. Several were thrown from their horses and either crushed or trampled to death. Among the latter victims were three or four women. Fully 100,000 started in the race, and estimating the families of the married men at one to each certificate bearer, the Cherokee Strip has a population of 200,000.[2]

Oklahoma Territory was finally white man's land, with Guthrie its capital and with a governor appointed by the president of the United States. It had federal courts and municipal courts; it had mayors and marshals and police. But the vast region served by the Katy to the east was still little tenanted Indian country, and the white squatter settlements strung along the narrow ribbon of the Katy Railroad still chafed under the restrictions of the several tribal

[1] George Rainey, *The Cherokee Strip*, 273–74.
[2] *Fort Smith Elevator*, u.d. For a colorful account of the race, see Marquis James, *The Cherokee Strip*, 54–63.

councils. Oklahoma Territory in 1893 was rude and rough, but Indian Territory was ruder and rougher.

East and west, the land was a refuge for bad men and more than a few bad women. Thieves, holdup men, railroad bandits, cheating gamblers and prostitutes abounded everywhere; and yet no little community sprang to village, town, or city which did not have a church almost as quickly as it had a bank. Oklahoma City was a little cattle place; Tulsa was an old Creek Indian settlement with no thoughts whatever concerning oil; Guthrie, though capital of a territory, was still a shack town; Pa-hus-ka was the capital of the Osages —a tribe so poor in land quality that nobody was jealous.

Muskogee was still the headquarters of the Union Indian Agency; it was also the most important city in Katy-traversed Indian Territory, though not the largest. The 1890 census had given it a population of 1,200; Ardmore had 2,100; Krebs, 3,000; Lehigh, 1,600; Caddo, 2,170; McAlester, 3,000. The first white man's court in the Territory had been organized in Muskogee on April 1, 1889, with James M. Shackelford of Indiana as judge. The clerk of the court had authority to issue marriage licenses, for the first time in the town's history, permitting a lot of laggards to catch up with their vows. Thirteen hundred and twenty four such permits to bliss were issued within the first thirty days—about a hundred more folks than were actually in town.

Here the Dawes Commission settled down in 1894. Senator Dawes' toughest job—and, after him, Tams Bixby's job—was to persuade the Five Civilized tribes that the best thing they could possibly do under the circumstances would be to drop tribal government and take up American citizenship. They would have the same status as the white men; equality in all courts, the right to vote at all elections, freedom of press and of speech. In return the Indians would have to forego all title to their lands, ceded by treaty or otherwise, and accept individual land allotments and cash.

The result, through a series of arguments, friendly pow-wows and acrimonious discussions at the commission studies and hearings, was as the government and those men in charge of the movement well knew it would be. Once the five great tribes came in, the rest would be easy—nothing at all. But it took the Dawes Commission, and particularly Tams Bixby, four years to break down the resistance. In 1897 the Chickasaws and Choctaws voted acceptance of the Great White Father's proposition. Then came the Creeks in short order. With three of the great tribes lined up, Congress on June 28, 1898, passed the Curtis Act, originating with Charles Curtis, himself part Kaw Indian and at the time congressman from Kansas. The bill offered by Curtis, who later became U. S. senator and vice president of the United States, transferred all property rights from the Indian councils to the United States. The Cherokees and Seminoles figuratively threw up their hands—and the battle was over.

The Indian sun had set forever.

THIRTY-FIVE

Bandits—the Daltons and Others

The first railroad into the wild Indian Territory, alone and practically boycotted for a generation, suffered as did few others from the long-continued depredations of the lawless. Katy trains were derailed, looted, held up regularly all along the lonely line from the early seventies until well into the present century. Blue Jacket, Pryor's Creek, Wagoner's Switch, Eufaula Bottoms, Limestone Gap, the Stringtown Cut—all these were favorite spots for ambush, where mounted gangs could block the tracks, stick up a train, and light out for the hills. Even a mere listing of all the major robberies on the Katy would be boresome here, but one or two incidents were so typical of the era—and the participants so notorious—that a brief mention of them seems warranted.

The first Katy train robbery of record was committed by a band of Cherokees. It occurred some ten miles north of the new Red River city of Denison in the summer of 1873. The bandits were said to have taken in a total of some two thousand dollars in cash plus a sizeable load of rings and watches. The last grand assault on the Katy's person was that of the notorious outlaw, Al Spencer, which occurred on the morning of August 21, 1923, in the Osage "badlands," near Okesa, Oklahoma.

The most daring, most lethel raid along the Katy line, however, was that of the Dalton gang on two banks at Coffeyville, Kansas, near the end-of-track on the Territory border, on October 5, 1892. This gang of train robbers had been a thorn in the Katy's side for several years, but their activities did not come to national attention until the spotlight of country-wide publicity was turned on them by O. Henry's short story "Holding Up a Train."

"Along in '92," this factual story by the master storyteller began,

Form 706. —Revised.

MISSOURI, KANSAS & TEXAS RAILWAY CO.

Cherokee DIVISION.

SPECIAL AND ACCIDENT REPORT.

For _Passenger_ Train No. _2_ Section _Left Parsons_

For _Parsons_ at _7 ³⁵_ P.M., on _July — 14 —_ 189 _2_

STATEMENT: _Mr. O Herrin ½ R_ _Sir_
this train Arived at Adair Station at
9 ³⁵ Was fagged the train Was Stoped
When three armed Men came on the
Eng ordered us off takings the Engineer
off on the right side of the train and me
on the left side I Was orderd To take the Pick
and Brake the express car door open I Hamered
on the door With the Pick after some Delay
the door Was open from the insid Too of the men
Went in the car every thing they got they Put
in a sack During this time there Was a
Euite a number of slots fired on The east side
of the train When they got in the car they
came out and all started West from The train
there Was 7 or 8 in number this Work that
I did Was done under Heavy threats
of Being Shot if i did not obey there
orders
    train delayed about one Hour

[SIGN HERE.] _Y. Brandenburg_

Engine No. _115_

Glen Enind Engineer _____ Brakeman.

Y Brandenburg Fireman _____ Brakeman.

_____ Baggageman _____ Brakman.

(Give Full Names of Persons.) _Geo Scales_ Conductor.

☞ Note Instructions on other side.

Employee's report of the train robbery at Adair Station
(Cherokee Nation) I. T., July 14, 1892

"the Daltons were cutting out a hot trail for the officers in the Chero-kee Nation. Those were their lucky days, and they got so reckless and sandy, that they used to announce beforehand what job they were going to undertake. Once they gave it out that they were going to hold up the M. K. and T. Flyer on a certain night at the station of Pryor Creek, in Indian Territory.

"That night the railroad company got fifteen deputy marshals in Muscogee and put them on the train. Besides them they had fifty armed men hid in the depot at Pryor Creek. When the Katy Flyer pulled in not a Dalton showed up. The next station was Adair, six miles away. When the train reached there, the deputies were having a good time explaining what they would have done to the Dalton gang if they had turned up, all at once it sounded like an army firing outside. The conductor and the trainmen came running into the car yelling: " 'Train Robbers!'

"Some of those deputies lit out the door, hit the ground, and kept on running. Some of them hid their Winchesters under the seats. Two of them made a fight and both were killed. It took the Daltons just ten minutes to capture the train and whip the escort. In twenty min-utes more they robbed the express car of twenty seven thousand dollars and made a clean get-away."[1]

At 9:42 on the morning of October 5, 1892, the Katy telegraph operator in the Parsons depot listened to his chattering key, idly at first, then tense and alert; his colleague at the Katy depot in Coffey-ville, twenty-nine miles away, was giving him some startling news.

"The Daltons are holding up the London Bank!" ticked the key. "Shooting has started!"

A special train to carry a big posse for the relief of the beleagured citizens of Coffeyville was quickly made up by Division Superin-tendent J. J. Frey; the posse climbed on board and the run was made at the rate of a mile a minute. However, when the Parsons men ar-rived in Coffeyville the bloody battle was over.[2]

The Parsons Special has given a sort of basis to the story that the Katy people were well informed of the raid in advance and took the opportunity to run a profitable excursion to "the shooting." This piece of folklore is also in line with O. Henry's story that the Daltons used to announce their raids ahead of time.

[1] *Complete Works of O. Henry* (Garden City, N. Y., Garden City Publishing Company), 818–19.
[2] Related by W. M. Fenwick, Katy passenger traffic manager, retired.

It was a trifle after 9:30 on that fateful fall morning in 1892 when five heavily armed horsemen trotted along Eighth Street in Coffeyville; these were Bob, Grat, and Emmet Dalton, Bill Powers, noted bad character since early youth, and Dick Broadwell.

Grat Dalton, Powers, and Broadwell proceeded to the Condon Bank while Bob and Emmet Dalton moved toward the First National. Both banks were almost directly opposite each other on Union Street and about half way between Eighth and Ninth streets, between which thoroughfares ran an alley. Charles Gump, a wagon driver, was sitting in his conveyance on the First National side of Union Street when he noticed the two armed men approaching. He recognized the beardless boy, Emmet, at once.

"The Daltons! The Daltons!" he yelled, leaping from his wagon seat and running for the shelter of the nearest store. Bob Dalton shot at Gump from the hip, the bullet passing through the driver's right hand. From then on events moved with lightning-like speed. The battle was on but the two holdups were also on—at one and the same time.

In the Condon bank, Grat Dalton covered Cashier Charles Ball. Broadwell and Powers were at the door to cover the getaway.

"Open the safe!" shouted Grat.

The cashier kept his head. He had unlocked the safe at nine o'clock. He glanced at the bank timepiece. It showed 9:42. There was eighty thousand dollars in that safe.

"Can't open it till nine forty-five," Ball told Grat. "Time lock don't work till then."

"I'll wait," said Grat calmly, the muzzle of his Winchester moving from one employe to the other. He had heard the shot across the street but not Charles Gump's howl of warning to the people of Coffeyville.

At the same time, at the First National, Bob Dalton had tossed a sack at Cashier Tom Ayres.

"Fill it!" he shouted. Ayres started to put in silver dollars.

"With bills!" roared Dalton. Bills, it was; twenty thousand dollars' worth of them.

Outside, armed citizens were moving on both banks. Shots came crashing through the windows.

"Lie down or your friends will hurt you," shouted Bob Dalton to the First National's three customers. They lay down.

Now citizens were shooting at the bank doors. Bob Dalton pushed Cashier Ayres and two other officials ahead of him as a screen. He

made for the door. In a doorway across the street stood a young
clerk, Lucius Baldwin. He had a revolver in his hand. Bob Dalton,
still shooting from the hip, sent a bullet into the youth's heart and
he fell dead. In the doorway of a drugstore stood George Cubine,
fingering a Winchester. Bob Dalton was again quick on the trigger.
He dropped Cubine mortally wounded with a single shot.

Emmet Dalton had hold of the sack with the twenty thousand
dollars.

"Go ahead to the horses," Bob shouted to him as they emerged
from the First National with their screen of employes, "I'll take care
of things here."

But "things" were getting too much for him; as Emmet ran, a
citizen's bullet hit him in the left arm and broke it. He kept going.
Bob's screen of bankers broke and ran from him. Powers and Broadwell were shooting from the door of the Condon bank; Grat Dalton
had decided not to wait for the time clock to function, was joining
his cover-men. Cashier Ayres of the First National, now no longer a
screen, had grabbed a Winchester from another citizen, had backed
into the part shelter of a grocery store; as he turned to begin shooting Bob Dalton fired and hit Ayres under the left eye; the heroic
banker lived to tell the story to his grandchildren.

It was now break-and-run for all five desperadoes; the alley where
their horses were hitched was the objective. Charles Brown, a shoe-
maker, had seized the gun which had fallen from the hand of the
dead George Cubine. As Brown straightened up Bob Dalton sent a
bullet through his breast; he fell, dying. All five bandits managed to
make the alley—still called "Death Alley."

The desperadoes were all wounded. As Emmet Dalton reached
his horse he was shot again, in the hip, but struggled to mount, hanging onto the sack of money.

Armed citizens were now at the eastern end of the alley, shooting but taking cover in between shots. The four bandits still on their
feet, but staggering, were shooting indiscriminately. Emmet Dalton
was still trying desperately to get into his saddle. Around him three
of the five horses were dead or floundering in death agonies.

Two brave men, disdaining cover, entered the alley—Charles
Connolly, the town marshal, and John J. Kloehr, a liveryman, considered one of the best rifle and revolver shots of his day. One of the
staggering bandits, said to have been Grat Dalton, fired, killing Connolly. Kloehr came on, firing; and Grat Dalton fell dead under the
unerring marksmanship of the liveryman. Broadwell, though seri-

ously wounded, reached the other living horse, jumped on its back and galloped thruogh the alley, shooting behind him as he went. He tore along for half a mile west on Eighth Street, then he fell from his horse, dead.

Bob Dalton had dropped to the ground some ten feet from where his brother Emmet had at last succeeded in mounting his horse. The dying bandit waved his hand to his young brother and Emmet backed up, reached down, and tried to pull Bob up onto the saddle; as he leaned over, Kloehr, who had now reloaded, shot him in the back. Emmet fell beside Bob just as the latter must have died. The citizens closed in, and on the call to surrender only Emmet raised his un-wounded right arm. As the clocks struck ten the battle ended—four dead bandits, four dead, brave citizens.[3]

No record of the wild characters who infested Katy territory would be complete without mention of the Starr family. Belle Starr, most glamorous of the gang, not only was a bandit in her own right but she was the leader of most desperate bandits. Strangely, she came of no moronic, underprivileged stock; she was no product of poor environment, as the "gun molls" of today usually are. Belle was the well brought up daughter of Judge John Shirley of Carthage, Missouri. Hot-headed southern sympathizers, the Shirleys had lost everything in the Civil War, which is understandable, for Belle—christened Myra Belle—acted as a spy for Quantrill's guerrillas during the period her brother Edward was a member of that outlaw group.

In 1880, Belle married Sam Starr, the Cherokee Indian outlaw. Married to an Indian, she made claim to Indian land; the application was approved and the Starrs settled on the Canadian River, west of Eufaula and not far from the Katy crossing. Her log house, ambitiously named "Starr Villa," became headquarters for train robbers and outlaws of all types. All sorts of crimes were attributed to her and to what became known as "the Starr Gang;" but, for a part of every year, the beauteous gun woman would make trips east with her two children, staying at the best hotels in St. Louis, Chicago, and New York, buying expensive clothes and spending money lavishly.

In 1882 she and her husband were convicted as horsethieves and sentenced to prison in Detroit; on her release she decided, for the sake of her growing children, to "go straight." But the mysterious and lasting disappearance of her twelve-year-old son broke down her

[3] See *The Journal,* Coffeyville, Kansas, October 5, 1892.

resolve and she turned again in a big way to horse-breeding and horse-stealing. Her husband, Sam, along with other members of the gang, was caught robbing a post office. He escaped and remained at large until advised that if he would surrender his sentence would be a light one. Belle accompanied him when he rode forth to give himself up. En route they stopped at a ranch where a dance was in progress. A quarrel arose, guns were drawn, and Sam Starr was killed.

In 1889, at the age of forty-three, still showing traces of the face and figure which had made her a belle of Civil War days, Belle Starr, too, died by the gun. She was ambushed and killed, reportedly by Edgar Watson, one of her outlaw tenants, on the way home from a trial of one of the Starrs, "for the family vice—horse stealing." Watson knocked her out of the saddle with a charge of turkey shot; as Belle died a legend was born.[4]

Al Spencer, the worst bad man in the Osage Badlands, had no use for gloves. But he had been fingerprinted by the federal government and various police forces more than once, and he knew he had to be careful about leaving marks on any "job."

One day he wandered into McAlester, "taking a chance," and in a drugstore saw a woman buying a rubber finger stall.

"That's what I'll wear on the next job," swore Al—which he did and so met death.

On the morning of August 20, 1923, Joseph Kirby Ellis, chief of the private police of the Missouri, Kansas and Texas Railroad, received an anonymous note. It stated that unnamed train robbers were preparing to hold up the southbound Katy Limited near Bartlesville, Oklahoma. The warning had first been sent to Special Agent Joe Palmer of the Katy at Oklahoma City.

Shortly after midnight on the morning of August 21, the Katy Limited, southbound, pulled up for a flag stop at Okesa. Two passengers got out. One was Charles Carson, a Katy section foreman; the other had boarded the train at Bartlesville, the previous station. As the Limited entered the cut at Okesa, and before it had gathered speed, six masked men swung aboard and ordered the engineer to halt the train. All wore masks made out of women's silk stockings. The Pullman passengers were lined up and divested of their money and valuables. The robbers entered the baggage car and there seized a shipment of $21,000 in Liberty bonds. While the looted train was still at a standstill, the Katy police chief, Ellis, came roaring up on

4 Duncan Aikman, *Calamity Jane and the Lady Wildcats*, 206.

a special train with ten of his own men, all armed to the teeth. A small army of other police officers was soon on the scene, led by United States Marshal Alva McDonald. But the bandits were now well on their way with their booty.

On the floor of the rifled mail car Chief Ellis, poking around, found a single rubber finger stall.

"Why," said one of the railway mail clerks, "those bandits were all wearing those things."

Someone had taken off or dropped one of the stalls—probably Al Spencer, after finding it was doing his trigger finger no good. Anyhow, there it was, and Ellis picked it up. He set about checking all drugstores between Parsons and Bartlesville. In the latter town he found a storekeeper who had sold a boxful to "a farmerish looking fellow." The man who had left the train at Okesa at the same time as did Section Foreman Carson looked like a farmer, and Ellis quickly located the suspect. Under grilling, the farmer soon admitted he had purchased the finger stalls and had ridden the Limited for the sole purpose of having it halted at the flag stop. More than that, he named Al Spencer as the leader of the gang and "put the finger" on his five aides, most of whom were quickly rounded up and placed in jail. Spencer, however, got away.

Some time later, the chief of police at Bartlesville was visited by a cowhand who held out a fistful of Liberty bonds.

"Al Spencer gave me these to cash for him," the cowhand casually told the astonished officer. "I'm to get the money and meet him alongside the school house just this side of Coffeyville."

Quickly the police chief rounded up a posse, surrounded the schoolhouse, found it empty, then set an ambush for the desperado. Spencer walked into the trap carrying a shotgun in the crook of his arm, a revolver dangling at each hip.

"You're covered, Al," shouted Katy Special Agent Jack Adams. As Spencer whirled and raised his shotgun, a dozen shots nearly blew him apart![5]

[5] Recounted by J. K. Ellis, Katy chief special agent, retired.

THIRTY SIX

Progress—and "The Great Train Wreck"

Henrietta, a typical Texas cattle town on the Fort Worth and Denver road one hundred miles west of Denison, was the western terminus of the Katy's Whitesboro division from 1887 until 1894. A lively junction in '94, with extensive cattle yards, Henrietta had every reason to believe it was destined to become the metropolis of the great north central plains—after the cowboys quit shooting up the place. Its hopes were shattered, however, by an ambitious grocer who lived in Wichita Falls, then a little town on the Denver road about eighteen miles farther west. Whereas Henrietta was at the western edge of the famous tangled forest long known as the Cross Timbers, little Wichita Falls was right in the heart of the prairie pasture, and the far-sighted grocer, Jos. A. Kemp, saw unlimited opportunities for his little town if it could only secure another road, one going northeast instead of northwest, in addition to the Denver line.

During the depression years of 1893–94, he bombarded the Katy management with propositions for extending their line to Wichita Falls, but in view of the fact that a line already connected the two points, the company side-stepped the venture as too risky. Katy President Henry C. Rouse assured Joe Kemp, however, that if the latter would organize and build the extension with locally secured funds, the Katy would be happy to lease and operate it.

Kemp, enthusiastic and energetic, saw prosperity on all sides through rail transportation. He tried to sell his idea to Frank Kell, his brother-in-law, who was in the milling business. But because of the depression Kell was cautious and would not take a chance at first. Eager and impatient, Kemp went out and found most of the cash himself. The balance was subscribed by local businessmen. A charter was obtained on July 5, 1894, in the name of the Wichita

Railway Company and by fall the Katy extension was completed from Henrietta to Wichita Falls. The clarity of Kemp's vision is shown by the fact that, within six months of the Katy's arrival, the population of Wichita Falls had jumped from two thousand to five thousand. And the growth has been steady; today Wichita Falls boasts a population nearing the 85,000 mark.

The extension of the line from Franklin, Missouri, eastward to St. Louis, under the charter of the Missouri, Kansas and Eastern Railway, was completed by the Southwestern Construction Company and opened for operation on April 1, 1894. The work on this division took two years to finish, chiefly because of Missouri Pacific opposition. On March 9, 1892, the *St. Louis Republic* reported that Katy workers were organizing "for the purpose of preventing the Gould interests from retarding the building of the M.K.&E."

The St. Louis division was opened for local traffic as far east as St. Charles in July, 1893, but entrance to St. Louis was delayed until the Burlington finished its bridge across the Missouri at Bellefontaine. Construction of the Katy's terminals and connection with the Union Passenger Depot, St. Louis, were completed on March 16, 1895, and through passenger service was inaugurated on that date.

With the St. Louis gateway now wide open, the construction crews moved west again to close the final gap in the company's Missouri system left by the Gould administration. President Rouse had told his board of directors that "our line extending eastwardly from near Kansas City, reaches Holden [on the Missouri Pacific] only thirty-five miles from our main line." Were the interval covered, he pointed out, it would afford a direct and easy route between St. Louis and Kansas City. It would also "exercise a powerful strategic force by affording a means of reprisal for aggression," Rouse said meaningfully. The project was approved and the gap was closed by construction from Holden to Bryson, near Sedalia, in 1895.[1]

As might be expected, the mid-nineties on the Katy were marked and marred by traffic wars and rate wars. The system was growing, feeling its muscles; the trunk was complete; it needed only a few more members—a leg to San Antonio, arms to reach into Old Oklahoma and North Texas—to make it a really powerful transportation system. Naturally it inspired fear in its competitors, chiefly the Gould system, and they fought the growing line tooth and nail. Earnings for 1895, however, were the largest in the history of the company.

[1] Minutes, Board of Directors.

Progress—and the Great Train Wreck

It was at this juncture in the road's affairs that the Katy's first great press agent hit the national spotlight. The road had had "promoters" before but none like the new general passenger agent, William G. Crush. Bill Crush liked to do things in a big way, and when President Rouse told him the road needed some publicity to let the world know it was in business in the great Southwest, stunt-man Crush thought up the idea of the now-famous "Great Train Wreck." He set the date for September 15, 1896, and publicized the stunt in a nation-wide advertising campaign . . .

Picture a long prairie, wooded along its sides, a few miles north of Waco, Texas. All around, the ground slopes slightly towards the center, and shiny tracks, nicely spruced up for the occasion, split this natural amphitheater exactly down the middle. It is cool but not cold, Indian-summer weather. Fifty thousand people are milling about the prairie pasture, some in trees, some on improvised platforms, standing in wagon beds, or seeking vantage points on the higher ground. Suddenly the crowds become tense. Distant train whistles sound long hoots from either end of the long valley, and slowly two resplendent thirty-ton locomotives, one painted red and the other green, with all brasses polished and sparkling in the sun, steam majestically along the track until they are pilot-to-pilot at the arranged point of collision. Photographers swarm around to take pictures; then the trains back away to take their appointed positions at starting points on opposite hills two miles apart.

It takes almost an hour for two hundred deputy sheriffs to herd the boisterous crowds back beyond the safety lines. Finally all is ready; spotlight-seeker Crush, mounted on a spirited charger, has quit galloping up and down the track. Dramatically he gives the high-hand signal to start the superannuated equipment, locomotive No. 999 at one end, No. 1001 at the other. The report of the wreck which the *Waco News-Tribune* carried is a classic:

> There is a mighty roar from the crowd as almost simultaneously there comes in sight, tearing toward each other at the unbelievable rate of ninety miles an hour, two huge red and green locomotives. There is but a single track across the prairie. A crash is inevitable. Closer and closer the locomotives, each followed by a string of box cars and flat cars, rush to the spot where the crowd is holding its breath waiting the crash of the two monsters.
>
> Suddenly there is an ear-splitting roar as the two powerful

behemoths smash and rip and tear into each other, box cars and flat cars climb atop their leaders and disintegrate, the engines rear up like battling lions and then fall slowly back to earth, each telescoping the other.

Up until this moment the show had been a glorious success and Bill Crush was delighted with himself. Scores of tents had been set up on the prairie, including one enormous circus tent that served as a super restaurant. A more durable edifice of wood was erected to serve as a "cooler" for the sure-to-be-present hotheads, pick-pockets, and bad actors in general. A 2,100-foot station platform was built to accommodate the multitude of excursionists who came to watch the iron gladiators. Eight tank cars were equipped with the necessary piping, faucets, and tin cups, to provide for the thirst of the better element in the vast attendance. Those who didn't care for water brought their own brands of thirst quenchers, and they, too, were multitude. Bill Crush had built here a veritable "city for a day."

The newspaper report tells of the fatal denouement:

In a split second after the crash there is another deafening roar—the boilers of the locomotives have burst, tossing thousands of chunks of metal hundreds of feet in the air, to rain down on the helpless spectators.

The crowd surges apart.... Pieces of metal from the sky fell some, but most escape the barrage. A man falls from a mesquite tree, his skull ripped open by a flying chain; another falls from another tree, his leg broken and twisted. A farmer's wife suddenly drops to the ground and a 14-year-old boy behind her screams in pain as one bolt from an engine fells both of them.

A Hewitt man, standing between his wife and another woman, is practically decapitated while neither of the women are touched. A photographer standing on a hastily erected platform suddenly can only see red out of one eye. A farmer's wife, riding along a public road half a mile away, is knocked out by a piece of timber thrown through the air by the mighty explosion.[2]

Bill Crush had truly made a Roman holiday. The unprecedented attraction was a distinct publicity success, but at what a price! While the Katy had advertised the stunt modestly, publicity in newspapers, magazines, and railroad journals ran into amazing lineage. Kenneth

[2] *Waco Tribune-Herald*, Centennial Edition, October 30, 1949.

Foree, the gifted *Dallas News* feature writer, reported that "Crush's dream caught the Gay Nineties' fancy. It spread, until people talked of little else; politics, the chief entertainment at Texas crossroads, went into hibernation until the wreck was over." The publicity was greater, if anything, after the wreck than before it.

More than thirty special trains, loaded to the guards with "low-rate" excursionists, had converged on the scene by the morning of the collision, and until the debacle General Passenger Agent Crush could think of nothing but the success of his brain child.

Before the sun went down on the appalling wreckage of his dream on September 15, 1896, William G. Crush was "fired off the railroad" by a suddenly indignant and mortified management. It is gratifying to report, however, that before the sun was well up the following day President Rouse personally had rescinded the order and put the crestfallen traffic man back on the job.

M. K. & T. advertisement of the nineties,
featuring the "Katy girl"

THIRTY SEVEN

Progress—Oklahoma Becomes a State

It was the turn of the century before the Katy finally reached San Antonio "on the direct run." The line had been shut out at this great traffic gateway by the I. & G. N. ever since that former Katy-owned property had passed into the hands of the Gould interests. On the failure of repeated attempts to make a joint-track agreement with the I. & G. N., Katy President Rouse went ahead and ordered the necessary forty-five miles of new construction from San Marcos to the Alamo City. The work was finished in 1901 and the road now for the first time had access over its own rails to the city which the Katy president described to his directors as the chief emporium of southwest Texas.

In a further move to improve its competitive position in south Texas, in December, 1902, the Katy took out a charter for the Granger, Georgetown, Austin and San Antonio Railway, authorized to build southwest from the main line at Granger to a connection with its new San Antonio division at San Marcos.

Under this charter the Katy acquired the 16-mile partly-finished Georgetown and Granger Railroad and the scarcely-begun Trinity, Cameron and Western which had been surveyed from Georgetown to Austin. Construction was commenced immediately and proceeded in leisurely fashion throughout 1903.

Katy tracks reached Austin, capital of the Lone Star State, in June, 1904. True to its early reputation, the frontier road established its first offices in a converted bawdy house, a well-known and convenient location.

On July 1, 1905, the I. & G. N. (now being squeezed in turn) finally agreed to permit the Katy use of its tracks between Austin and San Marcos. This joint-track agreement, still in effect, saved the Katy thirty miles of parallel construction, and thereafter Katy trains were routed direct to San Antonio through Austin rather than via the longer route through Smithville and San Marcos.

Several bits and pieces of line—and some profitable branches—were added to the system in the early years of the present century. A branch from Walker, on the Sedalia division, to the then very popular health-resort town of Eldorado Springs, Missouri, a distance of fourteen miles, had been completed in 1899. Another branch, from the main line at McBaine to the Missouri university town of Columbia, eight and one-half miles, was finished in 1901.

Great attention was being paid at this time to attracting to the line industries of every description, and the company reported marked success. Industrial trackage was built or acquired to develop properly this new business; a branch line was run from a point on the main line some seven miles south of Parsons to West Mineral, Kansas. This branch was extended in 1902 to Joplin, Mo., the heart of the lead-mining district. In that year, too, a useful branch line, from Moran on the Kansas City division to Iola, Kansas, was acquired, as was a ten-mile stub line from the main track at Egan to Cleburne, Texas.

The turn of the century also brought back to the parent Katy its wayward child, the "Toonerville trolley" line of the old East Line and Red River Railroad, then known as the Sherman, Shreveport and Southern. This road, which of course was continuously operated by the Katy, had been changed from narrow to standard gauge in 1893. It was formally reacquired on May 6, 1901, and held in operation for twenty years. It was finally disposed of during the reorganization of 1921.

Dividend-conscious stockholders learned with some misgiving that all was not peaches and cream in 1902. The management was concerned about conditions in the twin territories, Oklahoma and Indian Territory, where the Katy had done practically no construction for a generation.

Settlers had been flooding into the newly opened country; towns and villages were multiplying amazingly, growing enormously; trade, commerce, industry, were developing fast—and prospects for a merger of the Indian Territory and Old Oklahoma into one great state seemed more imminent every day. This remarkable growth, and the luscious traffic prospects it offered, had so stimulated competitive railroad building west of the Katy's line that other roads were beginning to syphon off much Katy traffic.

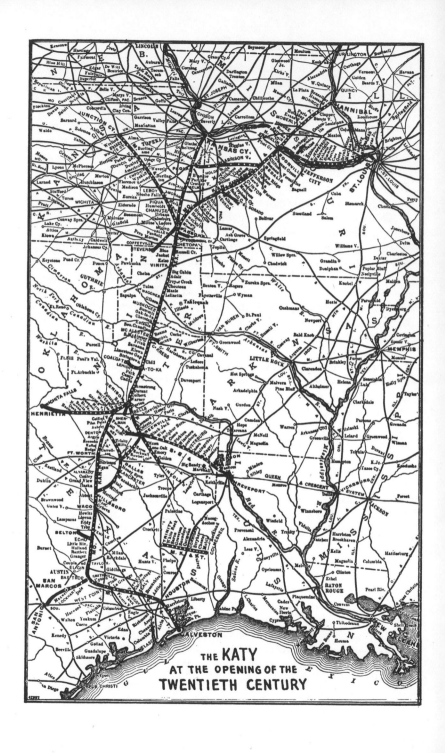

THE **KATY**
AT THE OPENING OF THE
TWENTIETH CENTURY

The management proposed to regain this lost business by extending the near-stagnant Coffeyville branch from Stevens, I. T. (Poison!), down through the Osage Nation to Guthrie and Oklahoma City. Also submitted for approval were plans to construct a connecting line through the fertile Arkansas River Valley, from Muskogee west through Tulsa to the projected Oklahoma City line at Osage. A further extension of the road from Oklahoma City southeast to a junction with the main line near Atoka also received approval at this time.

Surveying parties were out and construction crews were being assembled before the stockholders had got home from the meeting. The work was handled in the usual way, under a separate charter issued in the name of the Missouri, Kansas and Oklahoma Railroad, which passed the property over to the Katy immediately upon completion. This was a favorite device, as will have been noted, all during the construction period. It had many merits. The chief advantage in building under a separate charter lay in the simplicity of financing the work. This could be arranged without disturbing the underlying securities of all the other portions of the parent line. There were other advantages, into which, perhaps, it might not be politic to inquire too closely.

Building south from Stevens on the Kansas border, the track reached Dewey, on the Santa Fé, on October 17, 1902. Trackage rights were secured over that line between Dewey and Bartlesville (four miles) and mixed train service was inaugurated on that date. Regular passenger service between Parsons and Bartlesville began on Sunday, January 18, 1903.

On the Tulsa division, the railhead crept west from Wybark, reaching Porter, sixteen miles out from Muskogee, on December 26, 1902. It passed Coweta on March 4, 1903, Broken Arrow on April 13, and reached the ambitious community of Tulsa—so soon to be great—during the first week of May. Tulsa was then celebrating its twenty-first birthday, its coming of age, and was beginning to feel the first faint stirrings of destiny. It had a Commercial Club and a twenty-eight-piece band. And it had oil! Six producing wells had been brought in at Red Fork, only four miles away, and Guffey and Gailey's Well No. 1 was drilling in the Osage Nation, just two miles from Tulsa.

Not a sign of the times so much as a portent of the future was Tulsa's brand-new bath house, an extraordinary innovation in the Territory. It had just been located at a spot now occupied by First and Cheyenne, and the amazement of the *Tulsa Democrat's* perhaps overly sensitive reporter shows in every line of his story:

> The place is fitted up in a manner calculated to make the foulest clean in the shortest possible time and with a minimum expenditure of energy on the part of the bather. The place is fitted with hot, cold, tub, shower, or steam baths and most excellently carpeted dressing rooms. It is also fitted for the accommodation of ladies who can visit any time except Saturdays.
>
> The value of such a place, easily accessible to all, cannot be over-estimated by our people, and it is receiving the liberal patronage so richly deserved.

Continuing on west from Tulsa, the track reached Osage, the planned junction point of the Oklahoma City line, on August 19, 1903, and rested there awaiting the locomotive from Oklahoma City.

Oklahoma City in 1903 was by far the biggest city in the two territories. Growing at an incredible rate, its population then was thirty thousand, an increase of twenty thousand in three years. For the edification of visitors and citizens alike, the city was bannered with great signs that read:

MORE SCHOOLS—FEWER JAILS
SINGLE STATEHOOD ON TERMS OF EQUALITY
ONE GREAT STATE OF THE TWO TERRITORIES!

Except possibly for the jails, Oklahoma City was to have its wishes granted very soon.

The Katy broke ground in Oklahoma City in March, 1903. Building northward to meet the line coming down from Kansas, the track reached Witcher on April 14, Arcadia on May 18, Luther on June 25, Fallis on July 23, and Agra, fifty-five miles to the north, on August 23. Service was inaugurated between Oklahoma City and Agra on September 2, 1903. Taking note of the event in a restrained way, as befitted a great city with some dignity to maintain, *The Daily Oklahoman*, now one of the country's great newspapers, apologetically reported:

> The advent of the "Katy" into the city as a competitor for railway business marks another epoch in the progress of Oklahoma City, being the fourth trunk line. While the rejoicing may not be so demonstrative, it is fully as great as when the

The famous planned train wreck at Crush, Texas. The locomotives measure each other for the battle.

Excursionists who had come hundreds of miles to witness the planned collision

End of the era of steam. Locomotive No. 906, a "Mikado" 2–8–2, built by Lima, 1923.

Locomotive No. 201, a three-unit diesel-electric built by Electro-Motive Division of General Motors at La Grange, Illinois, and delivered in 1947. For all practical purposes, the Katy is now completely dieselized.

third line came—the Frisco—since which time the city has made wonderful strides.[1]

The railhead reached Cushing by mid-November, Yale by Christmas, and stopped at a point ten miles south of the Arkansas River, awaiting the southbound crews, on January 12, 1904.

With grading and tracklaying crews to spare after the completion of the Tulsa division in August, S. B. Fisher, now chief engineer, moved rapidly to close the gaps north and south of the Arkansas River. Gangs working north from Osage reached Hominy on September 17, Wynona by the end of October, and Pershing by mid-November. They were then transferred below the Arkansas to work on the southern approaches to the bridge over that wide stream. Other construction gangs at the north end also resumed work that fall south of Bartlesville. They reached Okesa (scene of the Al Spencer train robbery) on January 12, 1904. Nelagony was reached on January 25, and the lines were linked at Pershing on February 10. By this time the Arkansas bridge had been completed, the approaches finished, and the line connected through. As of that date the construction of the Osage, Tulsa, and Oklahoma divisions was complete. The lines were formally incorporated into the Katy system on June 30, 1904.

The 120-mile link between Oklahoma City and the main line near Atoka was under construction at the same time as were the lines mentioned above. On March 1, 1903, ground was broken at Coalgate, tip of the fourteen-mile branch from the main line at Atoka, and by the end of September the track had reached Centrahoma. The line was carried through Stonewall by mid-October and reached Ada on November 30. Regular train service was established between Coalgate and Ada on December 10. The end-of-track reached Shawnee, eighty-two miles out, on February 9, 1904, and arrived in Oklahoma City on March 25. A twenty-three-mile branch line from the Territorial capital at Guthrie to the Oklahoma City line at Fallis also was completed and opened for operation on February 10 of that year. These lines later were disposed of and no longer are a part of the Katy system.

In 1904 another great sweep of immigration hit what was to be the eastern part of Oklahoma but which was still Indian Territory. The towns and cities along the Katy right-of-way doubled, trebled, in size and population. Muskogee had jumped to ten thousand, Mc-

[1] *The Daily Oklahoman*, September 3, 1903.

Alester to six thousand. Titles were passing to owners of town lots; allotment of Indian lands had chopped up the great farms of the rich Indians of the previous decade. The Indian country was still not a territory as was its neighbor to the west, Old Oklahoma. The bill creating the state of Oklahoma was not enacted into law until June 16, 1906.

The Oklahoma Constitutional Convention met first in the city hall of Guthrie, November 20, 1906, adjourned and reassembled July 10, 1907, to adjourn finally six days later. The presiding officer was William H. "Alfalfa Bill" Murray, later governor of the state. September 17, was set as the date for a popular vote on ratification of the constitution and the nomination of state and county officers. On the morning of November 16, 1907, President Theodore Roosevelt signed the proclamation joining Old Oklahoma and the Indian Territory into one as the state of Oklahoma.

The Indians' "Trail of Tears" had ended in dissolution.

THIRTY EIGHT

Land-Grant Race—Winner Disqualified

When the Katy won the exciting race into the Indian Territory back in June of 1870, its managers thought, with good reason, that they had secured a prize worth millions of dollars. Hadn't President U. S. Grant, in effect, formally awarded the road 3,110,400 acres of the "beautiful Indian Territory" in his directive of July 20, 1870![1] Bonds had been sold, millions in stock issued, largely on the strength of the luscious land grant. Now, in 1907, however, there was no Indian Territory; there was only the sovereign state of Oklahoma . . .

The Act of Congress dated July 25 and 26, 1866, which brought about the mad construction race to the Territory line specifically provided that the railroad "first reaching in completion the southern boundary of the state of Kansas shall be authorized, upon obtaining the written approval of the president of the United States, to construct and operate its line to, at, or near Preston [Denison] in the state of Texas with grants of land according to the provisions of this Act."

Much was promised in this act. The winner of the race was to receive "every alternate section of land, or parts thereof, designated by odd numbers, to the extent of ten sections per mile on each side of said road." Title to the promised land was to come to the company "whenever the Indian right shall be extinguished," provided that the lands became a part of the public lands of the United States. Unfortunately for the Katy, in 1914 the U. S. Supreme Court finally ruled that the Indian domain "never for a moment has become a part of the public domain."

Long before a final ruling was had upon the Katy's claim, these disputed acres had become incredibly valuable, and that fact alone

[1] See page 76 above.

was enough to guarantee powerful opposition from all sides. Muskogee, McAlester, Durant—to name only the major communities— had sprung from settlements to cities on land actually promised the Katy.

While this litigation was on its way through the courts, the road had fared badly elsewhere with its land grants. In addition to the Indian Territory grant, it will be remembered, the Katy had been awarded something like one million acres in southeastern Kansas. Of this, the government gave 270,970 acres back to the Indians because they were located in the Osage Reservation. Another 128,938 acres were lost because of conflicting limits with other roads, preemptions of claims, and for others reasons.[2]

Out of the Kansas grants, the Katy sold 660,450 acres for a net profit of only $1,120,266, not a substantial sum of money with which to build a 250-mile railroad through wild Indian country. At the regular construction price of forty thousand dollars a mile, in fact, it represented only twenty-eight miles of road in southern Kansas.

The acreage in Kansas which the Katy received was hardly the benevolent gift it seemed to be. Under the statutes awarding the grants, the Katy was to remain forever a "free" land-grant railroad; that is, it was to haul government shipments without charge. In the course of the years the government more than got its money back in the movement of "non-revenue" military supplies.

For upwards of forty years the Katy's claim for the tremendous Indian Territory land grant was fought viciously in the courts. When the Court of Claims eventually ruled against the line, the company's legal staff, headed by the brilliant lawyer, Joe M. Bryson, took its case to the United States Supreme Court. Here, too, it lost. In October, 1914, Justice Oliver Wendell Holmes delivered the majority opinion which said, in effect, that the government would return the land to the Indians and have done with it.

"Taken literally," the eminent jurist wrote in his opinion, "the grant or covenant of the United States was subject to two conditions precedent. 'Whenever the Indian title shall be extinguished' means when and not until that occurs, and contemplates it as something that may or may not come to pass . . . [It] attaches the further condition that if the Indian title is extinguished . . . the lands become a part of the public domain."[3] Justice Holmes reasoned that since the

[2] See page 78 above.
[3] Missouri, Kansas and Texas Railway Company *vs.* United States, 235 U. S. 37 (1914).

Indians still held land, and since the land had not become public domain, it remained theirs and not the property of the Katy. Thus, the Katy lost land and improvements worth, at real-estate values in 1914, some six billion dollars—the "prize" that was to have been the railroad's for winning the land-grant race. What they are worth today is beyond computation, considering the oil and other mineral developments that have occurred since 1900.

There is a final, slightly more cheerful paragraph to the story of the Katy's land grants. On October 1, 1946, the Boren Land Grant Bill, passed the previous year, became law with President Truman's signature. The act forever removes any governmental claims for lower freight rates from railroads because of free land—which it started passing out with an award of 2,593,133 acres to the Illinois Central back in 1855.

Now the Katy hauls government freight at its regular rates, but even so, it will be a long time getting back those lost billions that way.

THIRTY-NINE

The Katy Attains Full Growth

When Oklahoma was admitted into the Union in 1907, the Katy's managers optimistically looked forward to a vast increase in population almost overnight. The road's expensive construction program in the Territory during 1903 and 1904 through a near-wilderness had added nearly four hundred miles to the system, and a great influx of new settlers, greatly increased agricultural and industrial activity all along the new right-of-way, would be required to support the extensions. As ill-luck would have it, the panic of 1907 and the nation-wide depression that lasted well into the following year effectively put a damper on all hopes.

The new Katy territory built up with maddening slowness and it was not until 1910 that the road felt sufficiently strong to undertake the acquisition of additional feeder lines for its main system. Its first move then was to acquire the historic Hetty Green road, the Texas Central.[1] This highly productive granger line ran from Ross, a point about thirteen miles west of Waco on the "Waco Tap," northwest for some 270 miles into the heart of the western plains, north and west of Abilene, Texas.

The traffic of Hetty Green's little gold mine was composed principally of cotton, grain, and other agricultural products, lumber, coal, flour, and livestock; the cotton movement alone averaged 125,-000 bales a year. Until the Katy bought the Texas Central, practically all of this traffic moved over the Houston and Texas Central Railroad, via Ross, which is understandable since the H. & T. C. built

---

[1] Hetty Green, "the witch of Wall Street," was a fabulous character whose "financial wizardry, coupled with her masochistic stinginess," enabled her to leave a fortune of $100,000,000 when she died in 1916.—*Life Magazine,* February 19, 1951.

the line originally and operated it for a decade as its Northwest Extension.

When that road got into difficulties in the eighties, a committee of the security holders acquired the property. This long feeder line, incorporated back in 1879, was reorganized in December, 1892, as the Texas Central Railroad Company. In 1900 the road, which then terminated at Albany, was extended to Stamford. A thirteen-mile link from Ross to a Katy connection at Waco was completed in 1905, and during 1906 and 1907 the road was further extended from Stamford to Rotan, its present terminus. To complete the property, a forty-one mile branch was built from DeLeon to Cross Plains in 1911.

In June, 1910, the parent Katy secured control of the Texas Central by purchase of the entire capital stock and took over the operation of the property. On May 1, 1914, the line was leased to the Katy for ninety-nine years.

The last important feeder lines to be acquired came into the company's hands in July, 1911. These were the Wichita Falls and Northwestern Railway and the Wichita Falls and Southern Railway, part of whose line, from Henrietta to Wichita Falls (*see* Chapter Thirty-six), had been operated under contract by the Katy since 1894.

The tremendous increase in population and business, the great surge of prosperity, that followed the arrival of the Katy at Wichita Falls in the nineties, had made Joe Kemp's brother-in-law, Frank Kell, a wealthy miller, see the benefits of rail transportation. He began looking across the Red River border into Oklahoma, which was being rapidly peopled, and he visualized the grain fields there growing larger year by year. In 1906 Frank Kell took over a half interest in the Henrietta-Wichita Falls extension on condition his brother-in-law would go into a venture to build a road across the Texas-Oklahoma line into the new grain territory. They planned to join Wichita Falls to Frederick, Oklahoma. First, they obtained a charter in Texas for the Wichita Falls and Northwestern Railway of Texas. In 1906, under that charter they built north seventeen miles to the Red River.

The Kemp and Kell road reached Frederick, Oklahoma, thirty-two miles north of the border, in November, 1907. Working in close connection with the Katy, for which they were now a feeder line, they decided to extend their Oklahoma line northward from Frederick, to reach still farther into the new grain and cotton sections that formerly were the buffalo ranges of the Indian country. The end-of-track reached Altus, another twenty-six miles farther north, in 1909.

It got to Elk City, sixty miles, in 1910; Leedey, thirty-six miles more, in 1911; and reached Woodward and Forgan, 133 miles, in 1912. This long extension into the early buffalo country, a total of 305 miles from Wichita Falls, was made under an Oklahoma charter issued in the name of the Wichita Falls and Northwestern Railway Company. Because of state rulings regarding railroads, they had to organize still another company, the Wichita Falls and Wellington Railway Company of Texas, in order to build a fifty-seven-mile branch west from Altus, Oklahoma, to Wellington, Texas.

These Kemp and Kell railroads, which had come under control of the Katy in July, 1911, were leased to the company on May 1, 1914, for ninety-nine years. But the two men who, by their initiative and belief in the all-round productive qualities of the iron horse, had transformed Wichita Falls from a dawdling village into a thriving, progressive city, had still another railroad. This was the Wichita Falls and Southern Railway Company, incorporated in June, 1907, to run 125 miles southwest from Wichita Falls to Cisco, made famous —or notorious—by the two-gun "kid" of that name. This line had a double commercial purpose: to haul coal from newly developed fields at aptly named Newcastle, and to tap the grain fields for the benefit of Kell's flour mills. The Wichita Falls and Southern was leased to the Katy Lines along with the others on May 1, 1914.

Several other branch lines, wholly owned but operated under special contract arrangements, were absorbed into the system during this last expansion period. These included the Dallas, Cleburne and Southwestern Railway, a ten-mile "tap" built in 1903 and leased May 1, 1914, which branched from the main line at Egan, twenty miles south of Fort Worth and ran to Cleburne on the G. C. & S. F. Another was the Denison, Bonham and New Orleans Railway. The Katy sponsored the building of this branch in 1901 from a point on the main line six miles south of Denison (called Bonham Junction) through Ravenna to Bonham on the T. & P.

The Beaumont and Great Northern Railroad, a forty-eight-mile lumber road serving the same general area as the Katy's orphaned Trinity division, was purchased in 1912 and brought under lease on May 1, 1914. This branch extended from Weldon to Livingston, Texas, and intersected the orphan division at Trinity. To complete his expansion, optimistic President Charles E. Schaff secured a 50 per cent interest in the Houston and Brazos Valley Railroad in the expectation that Freeport would become a great seaport rivalling Houston and Galveston. Naïvely he told his security holders in connection with the unfortunate purchase of the two latter roads that the full benefits from his speculative acquisitions "will not be derived until connections with the main line have been built." Connections, of course, never were built; it would have meant many hundreds of miles of additional highly competitive trackage.

FORTY

Two World Wars

During the years of the second expansion of the Katy system, interest charges on the crushing pyramid of mortgages grew to frightening proportions, yet cash dividends were religiously paid all during the period. The end was inevitable. As of June 30, 1915, the mileage owned and operated totalled 3,865 as compared with 3,253 miles now in the permanent system; scarcely a fourth was profitable main-line trackage.

On May 1, 1915, just when America was beginning to come under the strain of vastly accelerated production incident to the war in Europe, a fat portfolio of short-term notes totalling $19,000,000 matured and conditions did not at the time permit of a refunding operation. Immediately a committee was organized to readjust the company's financial position. The measure of its success may be gauged from the fact that on September 26, 1915, President Charles E. Schaff was appointed receiver for the property. Again the line was to go "through the wringer"—and it was facing America's entry into World War I.

Long before America went to war in 1917 the railroads of the country, and particularly of the West, now overexpanded, over-capitalized, and overregulated, were creaking and groaning under the tremendous added burden of modern war traffic. With the entry of the United States into the conflict, the burden upon an unprepared railroad transportation industry was doubled and redoubled. Terminals became congested, traffic backed up for miles at coastal points, and before railroad managers could bring order out of chaos, President Woodrow Wilson, by proclamation of December 26, 1917, brought the railroads of the country under federal control. The order was effective on January 1, 1918, but for six months government

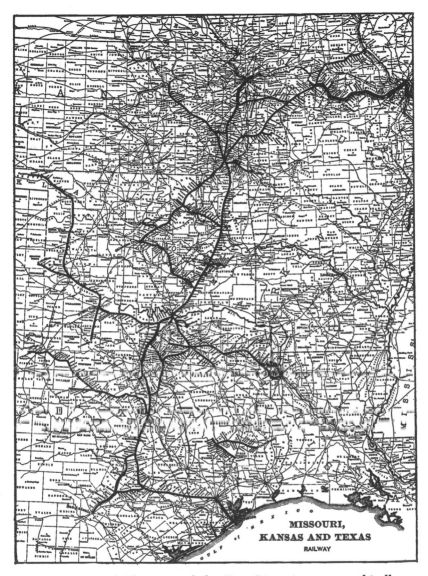

Over-expansion! This map of the Katy Lines in 1915 graphically points up the looseness of the over-built system and foretells the bankruptcy and receivership which befell the road in that year.

authority was exercised through the receiver insofar as the Katy was concerned. On July 1, 1918, however, federal managers, none of whom had had any previous connection with these properties, moved in, and thereafter Receiver-President Schaff was to mourn that he "had no voice or authority in the actual operations of the Missouri, Kansas and Texas Lines." Federal control was terminated on February 29, 1920, and Receiver Schaff then got his road back.

The achievements of the country's railroads during two world wars—under federal control during World War I and under private enterprise during World War II—have been compared so often that it is necessary here merely to remind the reader that government operation was attended by a distinct lack of success. This history, then, will be as reticent in this respect as Receiver Schaff, who glumly reported when he got his railroad back that the properties at the termination of federal control were "not returned in as good repair and as completely equipped as they were on January 1, 1918, when taken over by the Government." This was masterly understatement.

The Katy reorganization committee, using a surgeon's technique, got busy as quickly as the property was freed of government red tape, and on July 6, 1922, the Missouri-Kansas-Texas Railroad Company (note the hyphens) came into being. Under the new corporation, the old system was completely reorganized effective April 1, 1923. The following lines were sloughed off at this time:

	Miles
The Denison, Bonham and New Orleans Railroad	24
Sherman, Shreveport and Southern (East Line & R.R.)	182
Wichita Falls and Southern Railway	125
Dallas, Cleburne and Southwestern Railway	10
Trinity & Sabine Railway (Trinity Division)	67
Beaumont and Great Northern Railway	48
Houston and Brazos Valley Railway	20
Total miles	476

On August 1, 1923, the old Hannibal and Central Missouri, one of the first links in the original system, was leased to the Wabash Railway. This was the seventy-mile stretch of track which ran between Moberly and Hannibal, Missouri, the self-same line that Bob Stevens had held as "a rod of terror" over the heads of the Missouri Pacific managers in 1872. This line had long since lost its usefulness to the Katy, for the St. Louis gateway was now directly served by Katy tracks and the Hannibal gateway was closed. The road was sold out-right to the Wabash on December 15, 1944.

The Shawnee division, running 120 miles southeast from Oklahoma City to Coalgate, was also left out of the reorganized system. This road leased the branch line from Coalgate to Atoka in 1924 and thereafter operated the lines independently as the Oklahoma City–Ada–Atoka Railway.

After the reorganization, President Schaff was retained as chief executive. C. N. ("Charlie") Whitehead, long the corporate secretary of the company, who had served as Schaff's assistant all through the hectic period, was made executive vice president, and W. M. Whitenton and Columbus Haile were operating and traffic vice presidents, respectively. On May 1, 1926, Charles E. Schaff retired and the well-liked Charlie Whitehead succeeded him. Whitehead died unexpectedly that December and Columbus Haile, a traffic man all his business life, quite as unexpectedly succeeded to the presidency. Haile, then well up in years, did a four-year term and resigned in October, 1930. He had the distinction, after forty-six years of service with the Katy, of being a member of "the official family" all that time—he had begun his service in Sedalia back in 1884 as the Katy's Traffic Agent. He was one of the few traffic managers ever to achieve a railroad presidency, and his reputation as "the perfect gentleman" was nation-wide. President-Retired Columbus Haile, the only man ever to hold that title on the Katy, died on November 14, 1931.

The depression of 1929 is still too touchy a subject to bear more than passing mention here. Columbus Haile had stepped down before its paralyzing effects were generally felt, and M. H. "Mike" Cahill, late of the Baltimore and Ohio and the Seaboard Air Line came to preside over the sadly depressed Katy. Cahill's career on the road was short but by no means sweet. Reversing the trend of a decade, his first important move was the purchase in 1931 of the Beaver, Meade and Englewood Railroad. This was a 105-mile extension westward from Forgan, Oklahoma, of the Wichita Falls and Northwestern Railway, the Katy's "Northwestern District."

Privately built by local farmers, the B. M. & E. line ran west through Hooker to Keyes, and it boasted a seven-mile branch to Beaver. This prolific granger road controlled the movement of the immense wheat crops raised in those lonely western counties of the Oklahoma Panhandle, long known as "No Man's Land." The competition for this traffic, chiefly between the Rock Island and the Katy, was faintly reminiscent of the range wars of the eighties. President

Cahill put an end to the rivalry by the simple, if expensive, expedient of buying the line outright. This valuable "feeder" is now a part of the Katy system.

Big and impressive, accustomed to success and impatient of failure, the majestic Cahill fought the effects of national depression, of complete business stagnation, of a badly dislocated economy, with no more success than did his contemporaries. Revenues tumbled, traffic dwindled to a trickle, and the railroad suffered severely from malnutrition, despite the loyal efforts of officers and employes to keep the road active and solvent. President Cahill's term of office was something less than four years, painfully depressing years. When he stepped out in April, 1934, operating revenues were little more than half what they were when he assumed leadership in 1930.

Matthew S. Sloan, the super-efficient president of the Edison Electric Company of Brooklyn, New York, who succeeded Cahill, found the Katy in dangerous financial straits. By this time it was obvious that drastic measures would be required merely to ward off bankruptcy. Perhaps that is why the Katy's directorate created some kind of precedent by electing as chief executive a man who had never had a moment's experience in actual railroad operation. Sloan learned his railroading well, however, and steered the company safely through eleven trying years until his untimely death on June 14, 1945. His end came suddenly, in the midst of a clash with his own stockholders.

Matt Sloan is remembered as a hard driver, efficient but merciless with himself and with others. His methods were effective; he succeeded in keeping the Katy solvent during a period when bigger and stronger roads went to the wall. However, within a period of ninety days during the spring of 1945, the Katy lost its three top executives. They died of afflictions rooted in tension, killed by the high pressure of modern business life. The stricken Katy lost George T. Atkins, executive vice president; Frank W. Grace, operating vice president; and Matthew Sloan himself—all victims of the high-geared business tempo. The triple tragedy drew comments from all quarters.

The end of World War II, fortunately, ushered in a new era on the Katy.

FORTY ONE

The Katy Today

In the year that saw the victorious conclusion of World War II, executives of a new type, of a new generation, came to the Missouri–Kansas–Texas Railroad. Definitely, the day of the railroad king, the ruthless empire builder, had come to an unwept end on this pioneer western road. After that year the representatives of great eastern banking and investment houses were seen no more, and new financial giants from the railroad's own Southwest appeared on the scene. The new directorate included such figures as Kay Kimbell of Fort Worth, who had fashioned single-handedly a great Southwestern milling empire; James A. Elkins, chairman of the board of the City National Bank of Houston; and William J. Morris, chairman of the board of the Continental Supply Company of Dallas.

The man who effected this decisive change in the Katy directorate was the newly elected Katy board chairman, Raymond J. Morfa. Able assistant to Robert E. Young, board chairman of the Chesapeake and Ohio Railway, Morfa took over on the Katy in October, 1945.

Dozens of nameless jobs preceded Raymond Morfa's rise to power in the fiercely competitive railroad industry. On the verge of success, however, came World War I, and patriotism flamed brighter than ambition. Private Morfa was happy to serve his country, and Lieutenant Morfa was just as happy to end that flaming episode in his career and return to the wooing of lady success.

Chairman Morfa's first official act when he went to the Katy in 1945 was to elevate to the presidency of the line a railroad executive as youthful as himself. From the company's own ranks he chose Donald V. Fraser, only 49 years old, who then had the distinction of becoming the youngest railroad president in the country.

The Katy Railroad and the Last Frontier

A native St. Louisan of Scottish-Irish ancestry, President Fraser had served the Katy Railroad practically all of his business life. True to his birthright, Fraser had early gravitated to engineering and purchasing, but shortly after he joined the road in 1916 his shrewd mathematical mind was quickly recognized as being much more valuable in the executive ranks than in these relatively restricted fields.

Throughout his long career with the road, Fraser filled many executive positions. As executive assistant to Chairman-President Matthew S. Sloan during the latter's tenure, he was directly responsible for the operation of the road, and after Sloan's death in 1945 carried on as sole contact with the board of directors until the arrival of Chairman Morfa.

The accession to power of Morfa and Fraser was unquestionably timely. They took over the throttle on a line where the slogan was STEAM, only STEAM! Great locomotive shops teeming with mechanics; dozens of smoke-belching roundhouses alive with hostlers and repair crews; serried ranks of water tanks with their long black snouts spouting endless gallons into the gasping mouths of ever-thirsty tenders—that was railroading! Necessary economies were effected by the curtailment of operations; reduction of maintenance expense was achieved by reduction of maintenance, all in the guise of thriftiness. Change, modernization, was long overdue.

Along the line the change came almost overnight. When the word went out that steam would no longer be king on the Katy, the entire railroad mocked in disbelief. Here was heresy! Dozens of young operating department executives and engineers who hadn't dared to reveal their dreams could scarcely believe their ears. The greying titans of the back shops, the all-powerful moguls of the era of steam, were struck dumb with amazement. But the word was out and action followed fast. Long, sleek Diesels, freighted with the Morfa-Fraser concept of modern railroading, slid into Katy terminals, bringing visual proof of vast changes in the making and the solid promise of a new prosperity.

Although the Katy during the war years had made considerable progress in overcoming the effects of the long depression, the road was still hungry for "capital improvement" when the present management took over in 1945. No new or modern power, and only a limited amount of equipment, had been acquired since 1924, and particularly during the war years the line had been starved for machinery, production tools, and other modern facilities.

The Katy Today

Katy Board Chairman Morfa immediately set about strengthening the financial position of the company. He began buying up the road's own bonds, reviving a program started in 1942, and, chiefly in this way, has reduced the road's fixed interest charges something like 50 per cent. With this helpful contribution to the line's net income, the management then instituted a vast modernization and general improvement program that has made the Katy in the few short years since 1945 one of the most modern, up-to-date railroads in the nation.

On the Katy today, astonishing savings in operation and maintenance are reported as the result of the change-over from steam to Diesel power. The road is now, for all practical purposes, completely dieselized, a logical step in view of the fact that it traverses the heart of the country's southwestern oil fields. Physically, the Katy is a greatly rejuvenated railroad; its standard weight of rail is now a solid 115 pounds to the yard; its equipment ownership, boosted by several years of car building and buying, is reaching a satisfactory level. Moreover, the line is fast being equipped with automatic block signals, radio communications, and other modern contributions to safety, speed, and economy.

The Katy management is now busy with recapitalization plans that would free its securities from a mountain of back debt, which could so easily have been sloughed off by voluntary bankruptcy during the depression years. But the Katy is keeping faith with its stockholders; and they in turn are betting their investments that Chairman Morfa and President Fraser will solve their remaining financial problems. The solution, it is indicated, lies in so redesigning the property for efficient, economical operation that it will be able to support comfortably, "out of current earnings," its present capital structure, and at the same time reduce steadily its past obligations to investors. The current operations of the road give promise that the end will be accomplished in the not-too-distant future.

Credit the war—credit the fabulous growth of the great Southwest—credit the energy and vision of Katy managers. Regardless of the reasons, today it is easy to re-echo the words of a Katy president who looked the railroad over some eighty years ago and found it good: "The Katy's future never looked brighter!"

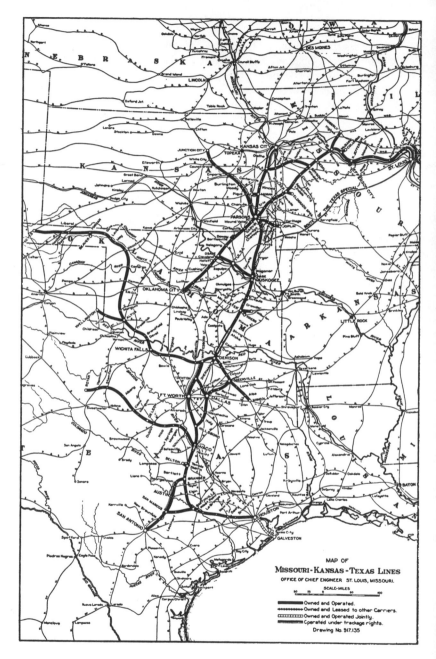

The Katy 1952

Bibliography

This informal history of the Missouri-Kansas-Texas Railroad System was written mainly from the original company records. Because it makes no pretense of being a definitive work, a rather freer use has been made of direct narrative than would otherwise be permissible. It should be understood, however, that factual accuracy has been maintained throughout. The several reconstructions of meetings, of certain episodes, of important conversations, which occur early in the book are by no means fictional. In the main, quoted conversations and eye-witness descriptions are taken directly or paraphrased from a great volume of company correspondence, reports, minute books, and contemporary newspaper accounts, unless otherwise documented.

To the officials of the Katy Railroad must go much of the credit for the successful completion of this work. All needed records were instantly made available, and department heads enthusiastically co-operated by researching their records and uncovering long forgotten data essential to the telling of the Katy story. Particularly do I owe a debt of gratitude to Chief Engineer Kenneth Hanger and Principal Assistant Engineer J. M. Shafer, whose assistance in uncovering the original construction records and in checking and rechecking the manuscript has been invaluable.

The close-knit family spirit which exists among employes of the Katy was never better exemplified than in the way all ranks, from Corporate Secretary N. A. Phillips down to the lowliest section laborer, volunteered their aid for this historical undertaking. Men like Roadmaster Roy Wagner, who helped locate the site of old Ladore (in a cornfield on the historic Neosho division), or Jim Couch, who plodded with me over the old Texas Trail around Gibson Station, showed an interest in the project far beyond the call of duty. Agent O. H. Pennal, of Denison, too, is due my appreciation for his efforts in locating the romantic Colbert's Ferry crossing of the Red River near Denison and finding the neglected grave of the Chickasaw ferryman.

Others who contributed substantially to the work included Mrs. Elliott Yost Simpson, of Sedalia; Mrs. Alice Bryant and Miss Eloise Munson, of Denison; Mr. Luther Cortelyou, president of the First National Bank of Parsons, and his assistant, Dale Wells; Mary Ann Rheam, researcher extraordinary, of Oklahoma City; and Frances Rosser Brown, Muskogee historian. For continued guidance and encouragement, I am deeply indebted to Grant and Carolyn Thomas Foreman, whose place in Oklahoma's history has long been secure.

The greatest single contribution to this work was made by Mr. Frederick C. Stevens, of Attica, N. Y. Grandson of the Katy's first general manager, Mr. Stevens has in his possession a mine of information about early Kansas and the Indian Territory. Hundreds of letters, letter books, scrapbooks, and souvenirs collected by General Manager Robert S. Stevens aided materially in recreating the Katy of the seventies and in bringing to life for a brief moment the men who built the West. To Mr. Stevens, as to the unnamed hundreds of others who unselfishly contributed to the completion of this history, the author would say a grateful word of thanks.

SOURCE MATERIALS

1. COMPANY RECORDS:

Annual reports to the stockholders; minute books, boards of directors and executive committees; General Manager's Letter Book No. 6; valuation dockets; engineers' reports; charters and muniments of title, contracts, and mortgages; *M-K-T Employes' Magazine; The Coming Country—Southwest* (monthly magazine), 1904-13; old time tables and working time cards; historical files in public relations department, M-K-T Railroad.

2. NEWSPAPERS AND MAGAZINES:

Chicago Railway Review, 1870.
The Journal, Coffeyville, Kansas, 1892.
The Dallas Morning News (fiftieth anniversary edition), 1935.
Denison Herald, Denison, Texas (seventy-fifth anniversary edition),
    1945.

Bibliography

The Denison Daily News, Denison, Texas, 1872-77.
The Elwood Free Press, Elwood, Kansas, 1860.
Emporia News, Emporia, Kansas, 1869.
The Monitor, Fort Scott, Kansas, 1871.
Fort Smith Elevator, Fort Smith, Arkansas, 1893.
Life Magazine, New York, 1951.
The McAlester News-Capital, McAlester, Oklahoma, 1948-49.
Missouri Democrat, St. Louis, Missouri, 1870.
Missouri Republican, St. Louis, Missouri, 1871.
Muskogee Times-Democrat, Muskogee, Oklahoma, 1930.
Daily Graph, New York, 1874.
The Sun, New York, 1873.
The Tribune, New York, 1870.
The Daily Oklahoman, Oklahoma City, Oklahoma Territory, 1903.
Osage Mission Journal, Osage Mission, Kansas, 1870-71.
Ottawa Journal, Ottawa, Kansas, 1870.
Parsons Sun, Parsons, Kansas, 1872.
St. Louis Democrat, St. Louis, Missouri, 1873.
St. Louis Republic, St. Louis, Missouri, 1892.
Daily Bazoo, Sedalia, Missouri, 1873.
Southern Kansas Advance, Chetopa, Kansas, 1870-71.
Scribner's Monthly, Illustrated Magazine (Edward King, "The Great
    South"), Vol. VI, No. 3, 1873.
St. Paul Journal, St. Paul, Kansas, 1947.
The Commonwealth, Topeka, Kansas, 1870.
Topeka Mail & Breeze, Topeka, Kansas, 1902.
Tulsa Democrat, Tulsa (Creek Nation), Indian Territory, 1903.
The Vindicator, New Boggy and A-tok-a (Choctaw Nation), Indian
    Territory, 1872.
Waco Tribune-Herald, Waco, Texas (centennial edition), 1949.

3. BOOKS

Aikman, Duncan. *Calamity Jane and The Lady Wildcats*. New York,
    Henry Holt and Company, 1927.
Barker, Eugene C. *History of Texas*. Dallas, The Southwest Press,
    1929.
Beadle, J. H. *The Undeveloped West; or Five Years in the Territories*.
    Philadelphia, National Publishing House, 1873.
Benedict, John D. *History of Muskogee and Northeastern Oklahoma*.
    3 vols. Chicago, S. J. Clarke Publishing Company, 1922.

Biographical and Historical Memoirs of Kansas. Chicago, Goodspeed Publishing Company, 1890.

Case, Nelson. *History of Labette County, Kansas.* Topeka, Crane and Company, 1893.

Chronicles of Oklahoma. Publications of the Oklahoma Historical Society, Oklahoma City, Oklahoma.

Curry, Mrs. Belle. *Parsons, Kansas—1869 to 1895.* Parsons, Bell Bookcraft Shop.

Debo, Angie. *Tulsa: from Creek Town to Oil Capital.* Norman, University of Oklahoma Press, 1943.

Demuth, I. D. MacD(onald.). *History of Pettis County, Missouri,* Sedalia, Missouri, 1882.

The Denison Guide. American Guide Series. Federal Writers' Project, Works Progress Administration. Denison, F. W. Miller Printing Company, 1939.

Douglass, Clarence B. *Tams Bixby.* Muskogee, privately printed.

Duffus, R. L. *The Santa Fé Trail.* New York: Longmans, Green and Company, 1930.

Foreman, Carolyn Thomas, *Oklahoma Imprints, 1835-1907: A History of Printing in Oklahoma Before Statehood.* Norman, University of Oklahoma Press, 1936.

Foreman, Grant. *The Last Trek of the Indians.* Chicago, University of Chicago Press, 1946.

———. *Muskogee and Eastern Oklahoma.* Muskogee, Chamber of Commerce.

———. *A History of Oklahoma.* Norman, University of Oklahoma Press, 1942.

———. *Fort Gibson, A Brief History.* Norman, University of Oklahoma Press, 1943.

———. *Down the Texas Road.* Norman, University of Oklahoma Press, 1936.

Goodlander, C. W. *Early Days of Fort Scott: Memoirs and Recollections.* Fort Scott: Monitor Printing Company, 1900.

Graves, W. W. *History of Neosho County.* St. Paul, Kansas, Journal Press, 1949.

———. *Annals of Osage Mission.* St. Paul, Kansas, 1934.

Harrington, Fred Harvey. *Hanging Judge.* (Judge Isaac Charles Parker.) Caldwell, Idaho, The Caxton Printers, Limited, 1951.

The Complete Works of O. Henry, "Holding up a Train." Garden City, N. Y., Garden City Publishing Company, Inc., 1937.

Bibliography

History of Henry County, Missouri. St. Joseph, Missouri, National History Company, 1883.

History of Vernon County, Missouri. St. Louis, Brown and Company, 1887.

Impson, Hiram. *McAlester Golden Anniversary Celebration Book.* McAlester, Oklahoma, 1949.

James, Marquis. *The Cherokee Strip.* New York, The Viking Press, 1945.

———. *The Raven: A Biography of Sam Houston.* New York, The Cornwall Press, Inc., 1929.

Joseph, Don. *Ten Million Acres.* (The biography of William Benjamin Munson.) Privately printed.

Josephson, Matthew. *The Robber Barons: The Great American Capitalists, 1861-1901.* New York, Harcourt Brace and Company, 1934.

Kansas Historical Collections, Vol. XI. Topeka, State Printing Office, 1910.

Kendrick, J. W. *Report: Missouri, Kansas & Texas Railway System.* Chicago, 1917.

Langston, Mrs. George. *History of Eastland County, Texas.* Dallas, A. D. Aldridge and Company, 1904.

Lopata, Edwin L. *Local Aid to Railroads in Missouri.* New York, Parnassus Press, 1937.

Lowe, Harlan. "A Short History of Denison, 1873-1900." (Unpublished thesis.) Denison, Texas, 1950.

Malone, Dumas (ed.). *Dictionary of American Biography.* New York, Charles Scribner's Sons, 1906.

Mathews, John Joseph. *Wah'Kon-Tah: The Osage and the White Man's Road.* Norman, University of Oklahoma Press, 1932.

McCoy, Joseph G. *Cattle Trade of the West and Southwest: Historic Sketches.* Kansas City, Ramsey, Millett and Hudson, 1874.

McDermott, John Francis (ed.) *The Western Journals of Washington Irving.* Norman, University of Oklahoma Press, 1944.

Nuttall, Thomas. *A Journey of Travels into the Arkansa Territory, During the Year 1819.* Philadelphia, Thomas H. Palmer, 1821.

Nye, Lieutenant Colonel W. S. *Carbine and Lance: The Story of Old Fort Sill.* Norman, University of Oklahoma Press, 1937.

O'Beirne, H. F. and E. S. *The Indian Territory. Its Chiefs, Legislators and Leading Men.* St. Louis, 1892.

Paddock, Captain B. B. (ed.) *History of Texas.* Chicago and New York, The Lewis Publishing Company, 1922.

Poor, Henry V. *Manual of the Railroads of the United States.* New York: Annual.

Puckett, J. L. and Ellen. *History of Oklahoma and Indian Territory and Homeseekers' Guide.* Vinita, Oklahoma, Chieftain Publishing Company, 1906.

Rainey, George. *The Cherokee Strip.* Guthrie, Okla., Co-operative Publishing Company, 1933.

Ray, Bright. *Legends of the Red River Valley.* San Antonio, The Naylor Company, 1941.

Reed, S. G. *A History of the Texas Railroads.* Houston, The St. Clair Publishing Company, 1941.

Report of the Commissioner of Education For the Year 1872. Washington, Government Printing Office, 1873.

Report of the Committee of the Missouri-Kansas & Texas Ry. Co. to Investigate The Financial and Physical Condition of That Company and Its Relations to the Missouri Pacific Railway Co. New York, Benjamin H. Tyrrel, 1888.

Riegel, Robert Edgar. *The Story of the Western Railroads.* New York, The Macmillan Company, 1926.

Ross, Mrs. William P. *The Life and Times of Hon. Wm. P. Ross of the Cherokee Nation.* Fort Smith, Weldon and Williams, 1893.

Scharf, J. Thomas. *History of St. Louis City and County.* 2 vols. Philadelphia, Louis H. Everts and Company, 1883.

Shuck, Oscar T. *History of the Bench and Bar of California,* Los Angeles, The Commercial Printing House, 1901.

Stevens, Walter B. *Centennial History of Missouri.* 5 vols. St. Louis and Chicago, The S. J. Clarke Publishing Company, 1921.

Texas Almanac and State Industrial Guide. Dallas, A. H. Belo Corporation, annual and biennial.

Townshend, S. Nugent. *Our Indian Summer in the Far West.* London, 1880.

Traveler's Official Guide of the Railways and Steam Navigation Lines in the U. S. and Canada. New York, National Railway Publishing Company, monthly.

Tuttle, Charles R. *Centennial History of Kansas.* Madison, Wisconsin, Inter-State Book Company, 1876.

U. S. Supreme Court Reports. (Land grant cases.) Missouri, Kansas & Texas Railway *vs.* U. S.
Kansas land grant: 92 U. S. 760.
Indian Territory grant: 235 U. S. 37, 39.

Bibliography

Wardell, M. L. *A Political History of the Cherokee Nation.* Norman, University of Oklahoma Press, 1938.

Wilder, Daniel W. *The Annals of Kansas.* Topeka, Geo. W. Martin, Kansas Publishing House, 1875.

Wilson, John Grant, and Fiske, John (eds.). *Appleton's Cyclopaedia of American Biography.* New York, D. Appleton and Company, 1888.

Wood, Sylvan R. *Locomotives of the Katy.* Boston, Baker Library, Harvard Business School, 1944.

Wright, Muriel H. *A Guide to the Indian Tribes of Oklahoma.* Norman, University of Oklahoma Press, 1951.

Index

Index

Beach, A. F., and Company: 18, 23
Beadle, J. H.: 17n., 54n., 89n., 122n., 145n., 163n.
Beaumont and Great Northern Railroad: 280; disposed of, 284
Beaver, Meade and Englewood Railroad: 285
Belmont, August: 23, 25, 26, 211
Belton, Texas: 228
Bender Mounds mystery: 120–22
Benedict, John D.: 104n., 130n., 155n.
Big Cabin, Cherokee Nation, Indian Territory: 102, 104, 126, 128
Big Tree, Kiowa Indian chief: 184, 185n.
Big Turkey Creek: 50, 54, 57
Bixby, Tams: 253; chairman, Dawes Commission, 170–72
Blue Jacket, Cherokee Nation, Indian Territory: 103, 255
Blunt, General James G.: 153, 167
Boag Luxy: 161
Boggy Depot: 152, 164, 168, 170
Boggy rivers: North Boggy, 169; Middle Boggy, 170; South Boggy, 170; Clear Boggy, 170
Boggy Tank (Pisek, Texas): 23, 249
Boliver Point, Eastern Texas and Red River Company: 81
Bondholders' committees: 205, 215, 240
Bond, Major Frank S.: 124, 132, 179, 216
Bond, William: 200f., 205, 215f.; appointed receiver, 216; elected president, 212
Bonds, railroad: 17, 40, 79ff., 130; none sold in Indian Territory, 151; Parsons and Pacific Railway, 237
Bonham, Texas: 167, 280
Bonham Junction, Texas: 280
Boomer, L. T.: president, American Bridge Company, which see
Boomers, Oklahoma: 237
Boon's Lick: 193; Trail, 4
Boonville, Missouri: 36–37, 94, 106, 150f., 193f., 197f.; Lard Hill, 209–10
Border Tier Railroad: 27f., 33, 35f., 58f., 65, 100, 102, 106, 236
Boudinot, Elias (Buck Watie): 104
Boudinot, Elias Cornelius: 7, 44, 57ff., 72, 101n., 103, 126–27; founder of Vinita, 104–105

Bowes, L. A.: 55f.
Bridge, Hudson E.: 119
Bridges, construction of: 50n., 54, 57, 65, 84, 117, 140, 152, 155, 179, 183, 194
Broken Arrow, Oklahoma: 271
Brown, A. O.: 93, 110
Brown, Captain: 93, 119
Brown, James D.: 196, 198
Brown, General John C.: 220
Bryan, John Neely: 226
Bryson, Missouri: 264
Bryson, Joseph M.: 276
Buffalo, last of the: 7, 17, 166
Burlington, Kansas: 20, 29, 43, 50
Burlington Railroad: Chicago, Burlington and Quincy Railroad, which see
Burney, Chickasaw chief: 161
Butterfield Stage Line: 165
Buzzard's Roost, Indian Territory: 161

Cabin Creek: Cherokee Nation, Indian Territory: 102, 104; battle of, 126–30
Caddo, Indian Territory: 172f.
Caddo Lake, Texas: 224, 253
Cahill, M. H.: 285f.
Caldwell, Kansas: 252
Caldwell, Senator: 138
Calhoun, Missouri: 248
California Road: 161, 164
Canada Township, Kansas: 237
Canadian County, Oklahoma: 245
Canadian River: twin forks, 152; track reaches North Fork, 155; bridge collapse, 155; bridge opening, 156
Caney, Indian Territory: 172
Canville's Trading Post, treaty of: 13, 14n.
Capitalization: 13, 99, 212, 217, 289; of International and Great Northern Railway, 222; of East Line and Red River Railroad, 223–24
Carney, Fention and Company: 96
Carpenter's Bluff, Texas: 180
Carter, Amon: 219
Cary, Abraham: 95
Case, Missouri: 249
Case, Nelson: 91n.
Cattle taxes: 99, 116, 155
Cattle trade: 17, 41n., 63f., 98–99, 102, 113f., 117, 119, 131, 138, 148f.,

Index

Index

303

Index

Index

Mound Valley, Kansas: township bonds, 237
Muddy Creek, Missouri: 39
Munroe, Missouri: 107
Munson, William Benjamin: 167ff., 173, 175, 178, 180f., 187, 213, 232–33; biography, *Ten Million Acres*, 169n.; Munson Realty Company, 177n.; partner of B. F. Colbert, 190; organizes Denison and Washita Valley Railway Company, 234
Murray, Bredette: 182, 186
Murray, Governor William H. (Alfalfa Bill): 274
Muskogee, Creek Nation, Indian Territory: 116, 144–47, 154–55, 228, 253, 257, 271, 273; naming of, 144; United States Courts inaugurated, 253
Muskogee Phoenix and *Times-Democrat*: 172

Nelagony, Oklahoma: 273
Neosho County, Kansas: 51
Neosho Division: 43
Neosho Falls, Kansas: 50, 53, 88
Neosho (Grand) River: 10, 12, 16, 50, 53, 85, 86, 105, 115, 134
Neosho Valley and Holden Railway: 38, 52, 130; chartered, 54; first train reaches Paola, 130
Nevada, Missouri: 79ff., 83, 225
Newcastle, Texas: 280
New Chicago (Chanute), Kansas: 54, 57, 114
New Franklin, Missouri: 36, 194
Newkirk, Judge Cyrus: 42, 202
Newton, Kansas: 98
Newton, Mary Ella: 187
New York Central Railroad: 19
New York City: 200, 203, 211
New York Daily Graph: 210–11
New York Sun: 199
New York Times: 192n.
New York World: 202
Nivens' Ferry, Indian Territory: 142
Noble County, Oklahoma Territory: 252
Norman, Oklahoma Territory: 246
North Fork Town, Indian Territory: 155
North Missouri Railroad (Wabash): 4, 36, 106, 114, 150f., 196n.

Northeastern Extension, Tebo and Neosho Railway: 106f., 193–98
Northern Kansas Railroad Company: 15
Northern Pacific Railway: 91, 201
Northway, locating engineer: 164
Northwestern District: 285
Norton, Rolla (Director): 27
Nuttall, Thomas: 117n.

O'Beirne, H. F. and E. S.: 104n.
Ohio and Mississippi Railroad: 108n.
Okesa, Oklahoma: 255, 273; Al Spencer train robbery, 261–62
Oklahoma, state of: origin of name, 16n.; reaches statehood, 274
Oklahoma-Ada-Atoka Railway: 285
Oklahoma City, Oklahoma Territory: 244, 246, 253, 271ff.; first Katy train entry of, 272
Oklahoma County, Oklahoma: 245
Oklahoma Territory: organized, 251
Oklahoman, The Daily: 272–73
Oktaha (Honey Springs) Indian Territory: 143, 152f.
Oktarharsars Harjo, Creek chief: 153
Old Sands, 153
Olney, L. F.: 94
Omaha, Nebraska: 7
Opening of Indian Territory and Unassigned Lands, "run" of 1889, 246–47; "run" of 1893, 251–54
Original Jack o' Clubs, The: 186f.
Orlando, Oklahoma Territory: 252
Orphan branches: 200, 234, 242, 280; Trinity and Sabine Railway, 227; San Marcos Branch extended to main line of Smithville, 249
Osage Division: 37, 200, 217
Osage, Fort: 4
Osage Indian Nation: 24, 63, 271f.; ceded lands, 9, 51, 53, 110, 120, 237; chiefs, 13, 245; Canville treaty, 13, 14n.; buffalo hunters, 25; removal from Kansas, 77; vigilantes, 120ff.; population in 1872, 159; national capital, 253
Osage Mission: 35, 56, 70, 86, 120, 193
Osage Mission Journal: 25, 56n., 86n.
Osage Trace: 4, 193
Oswego, Kansas: 100
Ottawa, Kansas: 28, 37
Overland Mail: 153